H A N D B O O K   O F
DATA MANAGEMENT

1995-96 YEARBOOK

Barbara von Halle and David Kull, *Editors*

AUERBACH
Boston and New York

Printed in the United States of America
Warren, Gorham & Lamont
31 St. James Ave.
Boston MA 02116 USA

Contributors

Rocco W. Belmonte
Senior Manager, Nolan, Norton & Co., Los Angeles CA

Michael Jesse Chonoles
Consultant, Advanced Concepts Center, Martin Marietta, King of Prussia PA

Sasa M. Dekleva
Assistant Professor of Management Information Systems, DePaul University, Chicago IL

Richard T. Dué
President, Thomsen Dué & Associates Ltd., Edmonton, Alberta, Canada

Fikri T. Dweiri
PhD candidate, Industrial and Manufacturing Systems, University of Texas, Arlington TX

Elizabeth N. Fong
Computer Systems Laboratory, National Institute of Standards and Technology, Gathersburg MD

Philip Friedlander
Assistant Director, Professional and Organizational Development, Ernst & Young, St. Petersburg FL

Frederick Gallegos
Adjunct Professor, Computer Information Systems Department, California State Polytechnic University, Pomona CA

Hal H. Green
Consultant, Setpoint, Inc., Houston TX

Fritz H. Grupe
Associate Professor of Computer Information Systems, University of Nevada, Reno NV

Kathryn A. Harvill
Computer Systems Laboratory, National Institute of Standards and Technology, Gathersburg MD

Hsiang-Hsi Huang
PhD candidate, Industrial and Manufacturing Systems, University of Texas, Arlington TX

Contributors

William H. Inmon
Senior Principal, American Management Systems, Arlington VA

Mark M. Klein
Managing Director of Management Consulting Services, Gateway Management
Consulting, New York NY

Michael P. Kushner
Senior Software Engineer, Walklett Burns Ltd., Great Valley PA

Jennifer Little
Manager, Data Administration Programs, AmerInd, Inc., Alexandria VA

Daniel Manson
Associate Professor, Computer Information Systems Department, California State
Polytechnic University, Pomona CA

Max H. Miranda
President, Effective Information Technologies & Applications, Inc., Calgary,
Alberta, Canada

Martin E. Modell
Technical Director, Unisys Corp. Facilities Management Contract with NASA,
Hampton VA

Richard J. Murray
Partner-in-Charge, Nolan, Norton & Co., Los Angeles CA

Madhavan K. Nayar
President, Unitech Systems, Inc., Naperville IL

Jonathan B. Novak
Advisor, Integrated Systems Solutions Corp., Atlanta GA

M. Mehdi Owrang
Associate Professor of Computer Science, American University, Washington DC

Steven D. Rabin
Director, Development Technologies, American Software, Atlanta GA

Ronald G. Ross
Editor and Publisher, Data Base Newsletter, Boston MA

Michael Scofield
Data Administrator, Hunt-Wesson Foods, Inc., Fullerton CA

Charles L. Sheppard
Computer Systems Laboratory, National Institute of Standards and Technology,
Gathersburg MD

Robert L. Slone
Business Information Systems Analyst, E.I. du Pont de Nemours & Co.,
Charlotte SC

Il-Yeol Song

Assistant Professor, College of Information Studies, Drexel University, Philadelphia PA

Daniel L. Spar

Technical Manager, Logic Works Inc., Vienna VA

Israel Spiegler

Faculty, Leon Recanati Graduate School of Business Administration, Tel Aviv University, Tel Aviv, Israel

Naomi A. Tellerman

Supervisor, Systems Development, Calgary Oil and Gas, Calgary, Alberta, Canada

David C. Wallace

Assistant Professor, Illinois State University, Normal IL

Kyu-Young Whang

Associate Professor of Computer Science, Korea Advanced Institute of Science and Technology, Daejon, South Korea

Robert D. Wilson

Associate Professor, Information and Decision Sciences, California State University, San Bernadino CA

Contents

Contents

Introduction

Over the past five years the information systems community has been inundated with buzzwords describing various management priorities. Some of the more prominent topics include reengineering, reverse-engineering, downsizing, rightsizing, object-orientation, information engineering, enterprisewide modeling, repository planning, data warehousing, and client/server processing.

Many of these "new" techniques are hailed as the solution to the widespread problems of most IS departments: huge maintenance backlogs, lack of data access and integrity, and applications that are inconsistent with corporate needs and policies. Of course, each new approach has its complement of tools and consulting experts and is promoted heavily.

There still exists a great deal of curiosity as to the true intention and benefits of any given paradigm of information management. There are many benefits to be realized in the proper application of any of the "new" approaches, and it is highly unlikely that IS departments will reach their potential without continuous evolution. However, to maximize the likelihood of success, costs and benefits must be understood from both a business and a technological perspective. The technically correct way may not be the most cost-effective route unless certain thresholds are addressed, such as transaction volume and short- versus long-term time-frame issues.

To manage the growing complexity of the information technology field, a variety of architectural frameworks have been developed with great success. John Zachman's *Framework for Information Systems Architecture* was a giant step in the right direction. Many organizations now use Zachman's framework to classify the scope of their information systems projects. In a simplified sense, part of Zachman's framework clarifies the separation of data and process, as well as the different perspectives of owners, designers, and builders.

The ANSI SPARC Three-Schema Architecture has also provided an invaluable service. It clearly distinguishes between the businessperson's external view of data (and information), the conceptual (technology-independent) view of data, and the internal physical view (technology-dependent). Many modelers have struggled to produce one deliverable for all three target audiences. This architecture explains the different schemas needed for each.

TWO-FOLD EDUCATION

One of the most valuable roles the data administration function can play is in the area of education. All levels of the organization, from business managers to data processors, need to know more about information technology issues. All corporations improve with the benefit of strong internal educational leadership. The challenge data administrators face is to comprehensively understand both the organizational and technological impact of different approaches to information management. Many of the new management methods have considerable organizationwide impact and must be reviewed from short- and long-term business and technology perspectives.

Each year, business and technology options become more diverse. From a business perspective, options include outsourcing and purchasing complete information systems that support organizational functions (such as accounts payable), developing applications in-house, or a combination of the two approaches. In addition, each year information management becomes a greater percentage of the work performed by every organizational division.

DATA: THE COMMON THREAD

A strong common thread links all of the "hot topic" management subjects and improves the quality of each deliverable. That thread is data administration. In fact, the data administration component is the foundation for success in reengineering, client/server processing, and other such efforts, for a wide variety of reasons.

Each approach can benefit from the concepts of standardization, reuse, and rigor. Most of these efforts leverage the relative stability of data and therefore require a logical data model as a core deliverable.

Even apparently diverse topics such as business process reengineering (BPR) and data warehousing heavily overlap with and depend on the data administration function. Whereas BPR addresses effective and efficient process design, it is best accomplished through the construction of process models that are integrated with data models of the organization. Many business rules are reflected in a nonambiguous, viewpoint-independent fashion in the data model relationships. This in turn provides a validation point for the heavily viewpoint-dependent process models.

In contrast, data warehousing has to address issues concerning granularity and partitioning of physical data bases. This is best accomplished through an understanding of both the logical data model foundation and the business processes that call on the data. Then, effective decisions can be made concerning the level of granularity and partitioning to be employed.

So even two apparently unrelated disciplines have the considerable overlap of their core: the data and process models of the business areas addressed by the deliverable. And, of course, the personnel who often contribute the most to the construction of quality information models are the data administrators.

METHODOLOGIES, TECHNIQUES, AND TOOLS

This handbook supplement expands on the strategie.
issues that were introduced in the original *Handbook o*
The seven sections of the supplement each address a major o.
challenge, ranging from the political to the technological. This br.
topics reflects the wide scope of the data administration function.

The first two sections address the highest-level issues concerning organizational mind-set and the political ramifications. Although the business climate has improved in most organizations, many of the challenges data administrators face are political, as so few managers truly understand the impact of the data management function.

The next section addresses the organizational integration of the information management topics. Sections IV and V evolve the IT concepts from modeling methodologies to specific modeling techniques. Section VI covers physical data base design issues while the final section addresses some of the more leading-edge concepts today.

Data administrators have a very broad and critical mission to accomplish, and it spans the disciplines of both information technology and business management. The traditional data administration roles of education, standardization, conceptual modeling, and repository planning all require an understanding of the business as well as information technology.

Data administrators must wrestle with the decision of how to cost-effectively employ and require conformance to standardization in many areas.

This handbook aims to share ideas that are both theoretically correct and practical. The contributing authors have all experienced the challenges of data administration and have broken new ground along the way. I hope that you find their experience useful.

Daniel L. Spar
Logic Works, Inc.
Vienna VA

Section I
Toward a Data Orientation

To elevate the value of data as information and information as a corporate asset—that is the purpose of data management. This section of the handbook is dedicated to describing ways to establish an appropriate environment that fosters data management principles.

Corporations must manage the right data for the right reasons, rather than merely better identify application-driven data requirements. The objectives of "Enterprise Data Management," or EDM, are discussed in Chapter I-1. The chapter examines EDM's major components, which include but are not limited to the data warehouse.

"The Evolution of a Unified View of Data," Chapter I-2, describes the relatively brief history of data base development and the search for a unified model that bridges how designers and users look at data. Two solutions—binary data bases and one of the newer developments on the evolutionary scale, neural data bases—are explained.

Business process reengineering is, of course, a subject that is much broader than data management. Yet if a business undertakes such an effort and it fails, then efforts to introduce data management principles, integrating data models and process models, are also likely to falter. Chapter I-3 outlines the "Most Fatal Reengineering Mistakes" IS professionals should learn to recognize so they can gauge the success of their data management efforts.

The cornerstone of business process reengineering and automated operations objectives is, of course, quality information. Before anything else, the business wants to be sure that the information it uses is accurate. Chapter I-4, "Achieving Information Integrity," includes a small quiz for readers who want to determine their information integrity IQ.

I-1
Enterprise Data Management

JONATHAN B. NOVAK

The information environment today is characterized by application systems that develop and deliver data to specific groups. The data delivery is often achieved in a redundant and costly way because organizational and application barriers limit information transfer. More damaging to the objectives of the enterprise is the limited access and often erroneous or, at best, inconsistent views of what the data represents.

To provide high-quality, consistent data, the enterprise must treat it as a corporate resource rather than the traditional application-specific domain. Application-specific data bases were typically created to be independent from other applications, although often with similar elements. This situation is prominent because of the approach that addresses data requirements within the scope of a given application or process, with no concern or attention to requirements outside that scope for the same, similar, or related data.

To eliminate this tendency and to manage cross-process requirements, data must be addressed at the enterprise level. Resulting improvements in quality make it possible to manage by fact, because all functions and applications use a single logical image of data from the enterprise master copy of information rather than variations generated specifically by and for individual systems.

The core concept of this chapter is to support an architecture, methodology, and set of services to deliver timely, consistent, and quality data elements from a single logical source to all applications, end users, and clients. It is complementary but not limited to developing data information warehouse architectures. The objectives of enterprise data management (EDM) include providing an enterprisewide data image developed from optimum data sources that populate an enterprise data information warehouse and are delivered to authorized end users and knowledge workers.

ENTERPRISE DATA MANAGEMENT PRINCIPLES

The appropriate corporate data environment requires the following enterprise data management principles to be established:

- *Data is a corporate asset.* Within this conceptual framework, data is treated as a corporate resource to be managed as an enterprise critical asset.
- *Data is organized by the business.* Data is organized into categories—subject data areas—and has specific functions and individuals that are accountable for its quality, value, and enterprise satisfaction.
- *Data is separated from the application.* Data development is separated from the traditional method of aligning with an application. Data is developed independently of applications that focus on its presentation or process for the end user.
- *Data is shared.* Data is shared and reused by all lines of business facilitated by an enterprise-managed data warehouse, architecture, and methodology.
- *Data has a single definition and source.* All information of interest or critical to the enterprise has a single data definition and source and can evolve as driven by business to meet specific requirements.
- *Data evolves.* The components of the enterprise warehouse and associated architecture should be developed in an evolutionary manner as needed to deliver information processes in support of business requirements.

ENTERPRISE DATA SCOPE

To determine and organize the enterprise data to be supported by the enterprise data management, the key resources, entities, and functions required by the business must first be identified. This step lays the foundation of the relationships between the data areas and critical processes. Accordingly, the corporation can be assured that it is managing the right data for the right reasons rather than merely better identifying application-driven data requirements.

Subject data areas are enterprise resources and external tangible and intangible entities that are of interest or value to the business from a corporate perspective. Data area groupings are composed of related information and subgroupings identified with the enterprise (e.g., sales, financial, and product).

Functions are groupings of activities that support the mission of the enterprise. An organization is a grouping of corporate resources that are assigned to perform one or more functions of the enterprise and are not synonymous (e.g., marketing, finance, manufacturing, and human resources). Organizational structures are dynamic, whereas functions generally remain static.

Much attention has been given to the requirements and processes of identifying and developing data relationships. Publications by IBM regarding information systems planning and the information warehouse; by John Zachman regarding the data architecture framework; by William Inmon regarding the data warehouse and structures; and by James Martin regarding information engineering all establish approaches to identify and establish critical aspects of managing information (see Exhibit I-1-1).

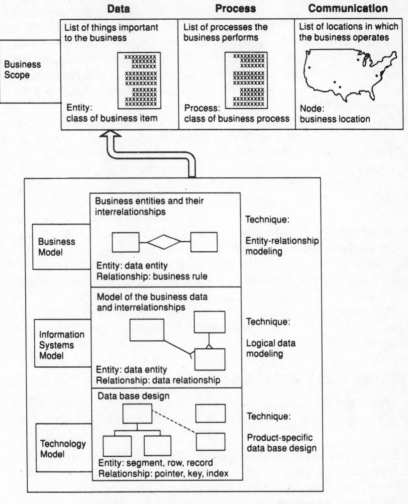

Exhibit I-1-1. Zachman Data Architecture Framework

It is the intention of this chapter to emphasize the need for the top layer of data areas to be identified by the business. Subsequent and parallel efforts can take place as supported by the corporation to understand and take advantage of information systems development approaches. Regardless of the time and resources applied to later efforts, the first step is critical if data is to be managed as a corporate resource and managed by the enterprise.

The major layers for the data aspect and the identification of business owners of that data include:

- *Enterprise data scope.* This is a broad view of the information required by the enterprise. This information is modeled from a subject data area or view level, and their relationships with enterprise functions are mapped.
- *Business data information.* This is data modeled for a particular segment or function of the enterprise—a model of business entities that represent facts about people, places, things, events, and concepts for a specific business segment.
- *Business system design information.* This is a detailed data analysis to support a business system or a business segment of a particular area without regard to the particular target computing environment.
- *Technology design information.* This is data derived from business system design information identified and tailored to the physical target computing environment and data base management system.
- *Data base design information.* This is data required to define physical data structures for the storage of data elements in a data store based on the technology design information.
- *Data ownership.* This is business accountability for the management of data as a vital corporate asset. The data owner is responsible for creating the logical model for the data, ensuring that the business views of the creating and using processes are supported, certifying the optimal source, and educating end users as to the data's business meaning. Data owners are supported by the information systems service providers.

ENTERPRISE DATA MANAGEMENT COMPONENTS

To manage the many and complex aspects of providing a total solution to data management and data warehousing, the following EDM components are identified:

- *Enterprise warehouse.* This provides a logical data store to contain enterprise managed data.
- *Enterprise data warehouse.* This provides a physical data store to contain the master data elements.
- *Client data warehouse.* This provides a downstream physical data store to contain distributed data.
- *Business information directory.* This provides a managed repository to contain metadata.
- *Optimum source.* This identifies the primary source to propagate quality operational data.
- *Extract.* This provides data enhancement and copy management for the data warehouse.
- *Distribution.* This provides seamless consistent data delivery to applications and end users.
- *Access.* This provides transparent user-initiated access, regardless of platforms.

- *Control.* This provides and maintains the rules that govern enterprise data.
- *Manager.* This individual provides the functions that monitor and direct EDM processes.
- *EDM execution.* This step provides the tools and utilities that execute EDM processes.

ENTERPRISE WAREHOUSE—THE DATA

In a logical sense, the enterprise warehouse component is a single master repository of enterprise data and metadata that produces the physical data structures required to store the subsequent informational data of the corporation. Physical implementation may warrant multiple data elements and fields; however, each replication is a clone of the logical master copy.

A single image of a data element is contained in a logical data store, which is the conceptual enterprise warehouse. The corporation has only one logical data element and its associated metadata for any given item. Actual physical data elements of the data are unlikely to be stored in one unique data base. The physical layers of the enterprise warehouse are managed within the enterprise data warehouse or downstream client data warehouses (see Exhibit I-1-2).

The enterprise data warehouse is the primary repository for the physical master data element. It is the first occurrence of physically depositing the master copy of an element or field in an enterprise managed data store.

The client data warehouse contains the subsets of these data elements stored in downstream physical locations to accommodate proximity and platforms. The elements contained therein are identical to the master logical image and are extracted from the enterprise data warehouse. In some instances, individual departmental-specific data elements not needed by other areas are stored in client data warehouses, and supersets are rolled into the enterprise data warehouse as required by the enterprise.

The enterprise warehouse is a logical view of data from a corporate perspective. It is not oriented toward the needs of the individual application, in the physical sense, but is modeled at a higher level to provide the consistent foundation for the data and relationships that different user constituents and applications have in common. It can eliminate the replication of like data parts and the subsequent errors caused by the inconsistencies inherent in different definitions, schedules, and use.

For business and performance reasons, it may be appropriate to produce redundant physical copies of data elements and data bases or files. These replications are managed within EDM to ensure consistency and quality of all enterprise data. Data is thus developed only once and duplicated only where justified, necessary, and controlled.

Duplicate physical enterprise data transported to data bases located on

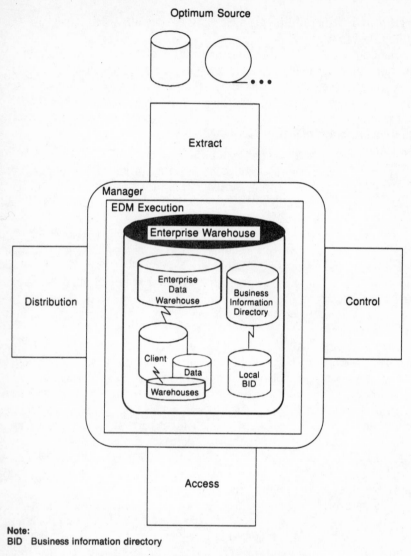

Optimum Source

Extract

Manager

EDM Execution

Enterprise Warehouse

Enterprise Data Warehouse

Business Information Directory

Client

Data

Warehouses

Local BID

Distribution

Control

Access

Note:
BID Business information directory

Exhibit I-1-2. Enterprise Data Warehouse

other platforms (e.g., minicomputers, LANs, and personal workstations) are also client data warehouses of the enterprise data warehouse. Client data warehouses can be downstream of other client data warehouses in a distributed hierarchy. All client data warehouse copies are controlled and provide the single logical data image throughout the corporation to ensure consistency, integrity, and quality for the physical data and metadata. All copies have been justified for replication.

Data not managed by the enterprise is logically stored separately, and by definition these elements are used by only one application. Management of any application-specific data is the responsibility of the application even if physically it may be stored as an extension within a client data warehouse. If any element is later needed by another application, that element, again by definition, becomes of interest to the enterprise. Accordingly, those identified data elements must then be managed by the enterprise data management process.

Metadata is managed in a like manner within the enterprise warehouse with the primary physical identifier stored in the master business information directory. Downstream copies of the metadata are managed by the enterprise and, like their data counterpart, are mirror images of their master copy. The downstream metadata may be stored as needed in a locally based business information directory.

DATA STATES

The following are enterprise warehouse data element states (see Exhibit I-1-3):

- *Mirror image data.* This is data that has been identified and selected from the optimum source, unchanged in content, and stored in the enterprise warehouse.
- *Consolidated data.* This is data that has been identified from more than one source, consolidated into a single data attribute, and stored in the enterprise warehouse.
- *Derived data.* This is data that has been identified from one or more sources and formulated into a single attribute (e.g., a summation) and stored in the enterprise warehouse.
- *Historical data.* This is data that has been identified as point-in-time data (e.g., month-end, quarterly, or year-end accumulative) and stored in the enterprise warehouse. The key differentiator of historical data is the maintenance of additional data elements from current data elements to service historical trends and analysis information.
- *Developed data.* This is data for which content is not available from outside the enterprise warehouse, but developed and originated (i.e., value is added) and stored in the enterprise warehouse. In this case, the enterprise data warehouse data element becomes the optimum source.
- *Metadata.* This is data about the data that is stored in the enterprise warehouse. It is not the actual content of an element or field, but the information defining the attributes and descriptions, including business meaning, of the physical data.

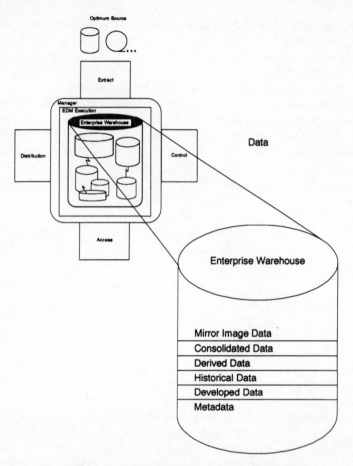

Exhibit I-1-3. Enterprise Warehouse Element States

BUSINESS INFORMATION DIRECTORY—THE METADATA

The associated metadata for each element is contained in the business information directory. The business information directory component provides the
user with a single source or catalog of information about the data in the
enterprise warehouse. The purpose of the directory is to provide a diversified
set of users with the required information about the data that is available to
them and how it is related to other information. This relationship further
provides a link between the business and information systems development
and its terms.

The business information directory contains the necessary information
for its users to navigate in business terms to what information or data is

available to them. That information includes definitions, owners, locations, current status, and what method is used to access it. The information in the directory is accessible at different levels (or views) depending on the user's orientation. For example, an IS developer may wish to access data at the table or data base level, whereas a knowledge worker or data owner may wish to access information at the function, process, or application level.

The business information directory identifies data from the business perspective through data models, catalogs, directories, and dictionaries. The processes to build and maintain the directory objects must ensure consistent data definitions, names and attributes from such original sources as the enterprise data model, data dictionaries, DBMS catalogs and tables, and data owners.

Metadata Contents

The following are some examples of the business information directory metadata contents (see Exhibit I-1-4):

- *Name*. This is the business name of a data element or field. Only one official name exists for any element. The identical business name is to be used by all applications and processes that have the need and are authorized to have access to any given data element.
- *Definition*. This is the definition and description of a data element or field. Only one definition is linked to an element, although there may be layers of descriptors as needed by different users of any given element, including information systems professionals.
- *Source*. This is the operational system that serves as the optimum source for a data element or field. Only one operational source exists for any given element (at least at any possible row or record level).
- *Aliases*. These are the alternative names assigned to accommodate current investment in traditional systems. Aliases identify other names that a data element or field may also be known by in previously developed systems. New development efforts should use the official name.
- *Characteristics*. These are the physical characteristics and attributes of an element or field.
- *Locations*. These are the physical locations in which an element is stored within the enterprise warehouse, including client data warehouses. The physical location from where the data is obtained is also identified.
- *Models*. These are the enterprise, business, systems, and process model information and relationships.
- *Applications or processes*. These are the key applications and processes that are identified with an element.

OPTIMUM SOURCE—THE OPERATIONAL INPUT

The optimum source component addresses the identification, input, and management of data from key operational systems and data bases. Data in the

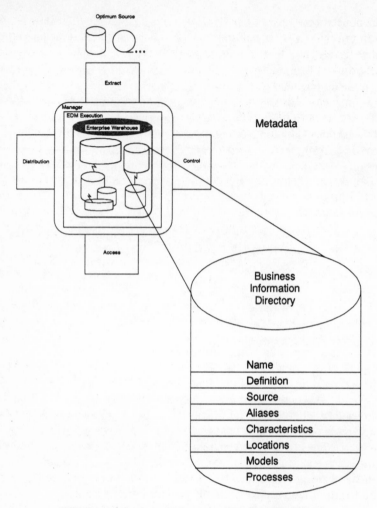

Exhibit I-1-4. Business Information Directory Metadata

enterprise warehouse is grouped into logical subject data areas from a business point of view. Primary functions and applications are similarly grouped as major sourcing (i.e., creating) and reading of those data groups.

The optimum source is identified in support of projects being developed that use common shared data. Support is provided by information system organizations to develop an enterprise data model. Business owners are identified for each of the subject data areas and for the automated processes (e.g., operational systems applications) that support the business functions.

These efforts provide information to start the population of the repository or warehouses with the enterprise data required. It is the identification of the most appropriate operational systems and applications that are implemented or under development. This information is used to establish the process management and control information that is used to populate the enterprise warehouse and the business information directory.

As business changes are made, they are driven through the optimum source processes to determine data changes and expansions required, assess effects, and direct the appropriate changes in the enterprise warehouse. The business data owners are responsible for this process, for resolving any conflicts that result from data definitions and requirements, and for ensuring that the implementation of enterprise data management meets their business needs.

The optimum source data and its operational process must be managed because by the nature of the extracting copy management processes, the operational data can affect propagation of the enterprise warehouse. It is this process that feeds the enterprise warehouse in an assortment of ways. These transport activities can occur at any point within the life cycle of delivering data from the optimum source to any location managed within the enterprise data concept.

The following processes, shown in Exhibit I-1-5, are not limited to optimum sourcing and can recur any time the data is extracted or distributed within the enterprise data management process:

- *Refresh versus net change.* The refresh process entails all the data within a data base or file being replaced on a periodic basis; with net change only those elements that had changes are affected (i.e., how much).
- *Drip versus batch.* In the drip process, data movement occurs continuously on a recurring basis as warranted by modifications, in batch mode, data is bulk-processed at end of completed operational processing (i.e., when).
- *Pull versus push.* Data can be pulled from operational sources as initiated by EDM, or data elements or fields can be pushed down from the operational systems when changes are noted (i.e., who initiates).
- *Element field versus rows and records.* Either only those data elements or fields required by EDM are provided by the operational systems, or completed rows or records are shipped transmitted to enterprise data sites with responsibility for segment selection remaining with those sites (i.e., what).

EXTRACT—DATA COPY MANAGEMENT

The extract component of EDM provides data enhancement and copy management from optimum sources to the enterprise data warehouses. System-initiated processes gather and transport source data, provide preparatory function to meet enterprisewide data requirements and structure, enhance as

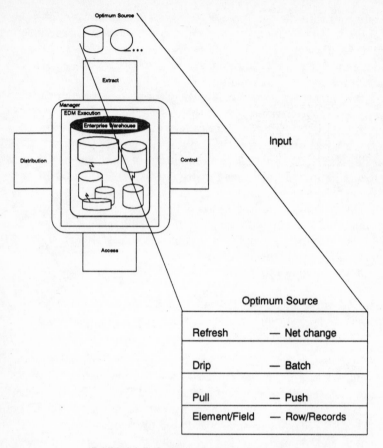

Exhibit I-1-5. Optimum Sourcing Processes

specified by data owners for informational specifications and decision support analysis, ensure update continuity, and store the finished element or field in the enterprise data warehouse.

A significant aspect of this component is to provide data extraction, transformation, enhancement, and storage into the master data store only once for all users. Because all applications and end users subsequently receive their data from a managed corporate data resource repository as defined by the enterprise, the traditional practice of each application developing and preparing its own data is eliminated.

The key functions provided by the extract component, shown in Exhibit I-1-6, include:

- *Copy management.* This function transports data from optimal operational sources.

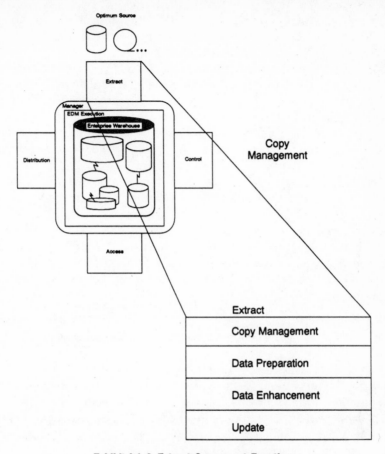

Exhibit I-1-6. Extract Component Functions

- *Data preparation.* This function transforms the data to meet enterprise-managed requirements.
- *Data enhancement.* This function develops data from an operational perspective to an informational and decision support perspective (e.g., point-in-time or summation).
- *Update.* This function ensures synchronization and consistency of data modifications that are authorized and initiated downstream from the warehouses.

DISTRIBUTION—DATA DELIVERY

The distribution component of EDM addresses system-initiated, process-driven delivery of data from the enterprise data warehouse to the subset client data warehouses, applications, and systems. Distribution provides transport processes to ensure consistent, seamless, and transparent data availability by applications regardless of location and movement.

Data delivery activity comprises all aspects of keeping the data accessible regardless of the location. It permits the movement of data and data bases separated from the applications and users so that data base configuration, performance, product, and technical advances are transparent to the development of the enterprise's information presentation and transaction systems.

Distribution establishes the bridges and hooks by which the applications address obtaining data from the data warehouse. This approach eliminates the need for each application to develop its own access procedures and, more important, permits managed control and synchronization of all enterprise data to ensure delivery of a single logical data image. In addition, all movement, modifications, and updates to a data element by an authorized application are reflected in a timely manner to all users of that element regardless of function, application, platform, or location.

As shown in Exhibit I-1-7, the key functions provided by the distribution component include:

- *Distribution.* This refers to all managed client data warehouses, including intermediary nodes, client servers, WANs, LANs, and personal workstations.
- *Connectivity.* This refers to elements and rows because data is created separately from the application. Links and connectors are provided to applications for data availability.
- *Synchronization.* This applies to all copies of data elements to ensure timely and consistent data images, regardless of which managed data repository is accessed.
- *Transparency.* This refers to client data warehouse location or subsequent movement.

ACCESS—USER ACQUISITION

The access component of EDM provides seamless connectivity and access to warehouse client data by applications and ad hoc programs regardless of platform. It enables knowledge workers to initiate acquisition of data from a familiar interface and transparently locate and connect to the data requested by that end user. Although the extract and distribution components of EDM address the automated system initiated delivery of data from sources to warehouses and subsequent applications, the access component addresses end-user initiated data retrieval from the user's terminal or personal workstation to structured and unstructured enterprisewide data.

The function is to establish an upstream accessibility from the final user

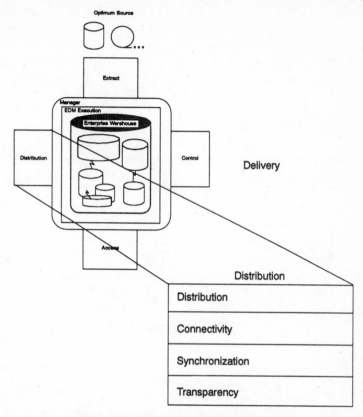

Exhibit I-1-7. Distribution Component Functions

system or tool to the enterprise warehouse over multiple operating systems, hardware, and interfaces without the end user's needing to know or care where or on what type of system the data resides. By information contained in the business information directory, the access component locates specific data elements and provides the user with either its image or the actual data itself as previously established. Because critical navigational information is available for all data within the enterprise warehouse, the system is able to obtain any and all elements requested by the end user without prior data requirements being defined.

As shown in Exhibit I-1-8, the key functions provided by the access component include:

- *User interface.* This provides user-initiated data request interface either directly or by an application that interacts with the end user.

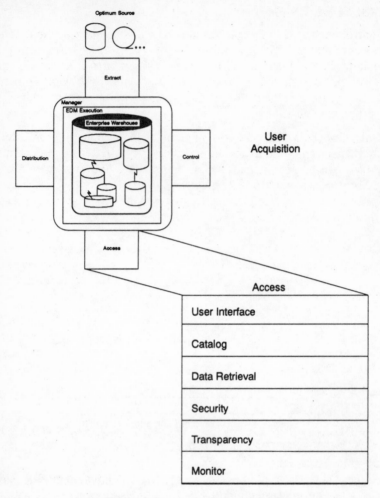

Exhibit I-1-8. Access Component Functions

- *Catalog.* This presents the contents of the business information directory to the user.
- *Data retrieval.* This retrieves data from any source known to the business information directory.
- *Security.* This ensures security through user identification and authentication.
- *Transparency.* This provides consistent navigation regardless of data location or platform.
- *Monitoring.* This monitors user access to data.

CONTROL—THE RULES

The control component of EDM contains the rules to manage the data store and access to that data. The control component contains the rules to propagate data among the warehouses and to ensure that the data is accessible only to those who are authorized to view, modify, or obtain that data. Four major subcomponents are defined within control: data control, process control, user control, and standards.

Data Control. The data control component contains the rules that are used to manage the data in the enterprise warehouse. This component uses enterprise data model and data owner information and applies to both the enterprise warehouse and the business information directory data contents.

The data models contain information that allows the mapping of the data selected from the optimal operational sources to the enterprise warehouse data structures. This mapping is to both the logical and physical views of the data and includes optimum source, enterprise data warehouse, and client data warehouse locations. Through the use of these models and the processes that build the enterprise warehouse, data redundancy can be controlled and the integrity of the data maintained.

Process Control. The process control component contains the rules that are used to manage the data processes that propagate and deliver the data in the enterprise warehouse. This component incorporates data process models and application owner information and applies to both the enterprise warehouse and the business information directory.

The process models are used to identify the flow of data from the operational systems into the enterprise warehouse. They can identify the processes that are required to perform a task, the sequence in which the tasks are executed, the status of tasks, the scheduling information to be used, and execution initiation for the tasks.

Additional information that is available from the process models pertains to the priority of processing in the event multiple sources of information are available, to the indications of the data's current state, and to the identification of information that can be shared, or reused, by other processes.

User Control. User control is composed of security and registration functions and any associated profiles. Additional security is required to control access at the specific data element level. This control is usually managed at the application level today and is typically controlled by a job, data set, or terminal log-on classification with authorization codes for access.

A registration function is the primarily administrative task of identifying people, data sets, or jobs to the system. This function includes the initial entry into the system; the revalidation process to control current status; and the deletion of the access when it is no longer valid.

Profiles to identify a wide variety of user information are developed for proper routing of information and capturing user customization information. These profiles are user controlled and are used by applications and tools to pick up defaults or other variable information at the time of execution. These profiles exist at the system, application, and user level.

Standards. Standards to manage and introduce consistency for data naming, definitions, attributes, and contents must be developed. Establishing a standardized common base for enterprise data ensures that the user can consistently access data elements and extract information regardless of the application or location of the data. The data owner of each category controls the description and contents of data from the business perspective.

Technical standards must be developed consistent with industry direction and tool capabilities to manage data. A variety of tools are used to maintain the data linked to their respective models. These tools are primarily industry standards in information engineering (e.g., AD/Cycle and CASE products). These tools must be defined and installed on development workbenches and within the business organizations where necessary.

Control Types

The control component can be broken down into six subsets or groups of control information (listed in Exhibit I-1-9) that are used to manage the data and related components and ensure compliance with EDM direction and architecture:

- *Security.* This information identifies authorization levels to access data.
- *Standards.* This information establishes conformity.
- *Policies and rules.* This information establishes governing factors.
- *Procedures.* This information identifies enforcement steps to ensure compliance.
- *Guidelines.* This information identifies recommendations.
- *Processes.* This information identifies process control parameters.

MANAGER—PROCESSES

The manager component addresses authorizing and monitoring the processes necessary to manage and implement the enterprise data concept. The manager services the requirements enterprise data management and ensures appropriate actions are executed and exceptions are noted.

The manager uses the rules contained in the control component to determine when and how the processes are to be initiated to identify, source, maintain, access, or distribute the data contained in the data warehouses. As required, movement of data to subsequent data bases is supervised by the manager and delivered by the distribution component. Actual system processing is accomplished by the execution component as directed by the manager.

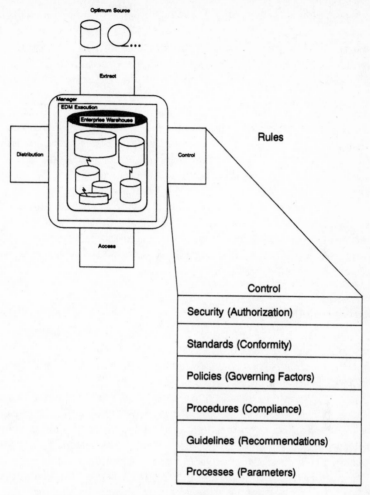

Exhibit I-1-9. Control Information Types

Enterprise warehouse manager activity comprises all aspects of keeping the data up to date, available, and usable. It includes the validation and enhancement of operational data, the processing of complete file replacements as well as net change files, and finally, the processing of end user-generated information.

This activity applies to individual files and across files where multiple data stores are available. In addition, the removal of obsolete data and reorganization of the data bases are addressed.

The manager ensures both data and referential integrity in the repository through the application of controls, management of process execution, and monitoring of data delivery to keep all enterprise data elements accessible regardless of the location. Providing overall availability of the data to the end user includes preparing for unexpected outages. Procedures for backup and recovery as well as for the business interruption (i.e., disaster) planning are addressed.

Modifications to EDM are driven by the needs of the business as organizations and business processes change and are reflected within the EDM architecture. The information systems department assesses these changes, identifies the effects, determines the implementation approach, and communicates the changes and plans to those affected by modifications.

The key functions are to manage data coming into the enterprise warehouse and its development and storage and to provide access and delivery of data to the client (see Exhibit I-1-10). To ensure the provision of necessary data services, the management component must: establish objectives, authorize activities, assign priorities, allocate resources, monitor components, address exceptions, and ensure enactment.

EXECUTION—PRODUCTS

The execution component comprises the actual products, tools, utilities, hooks, and processes that are executed to provide services for EDM. It addresses the actual performing of all the processes necessary to manage the enterprise data and related EDM components.

These utilities and interfaces must have consistently updated and available data elements to provide a single logical image to all applications and users. The central processing of data requirements eliminates the redundant development and processing that would be necessary if all applications and users produced and managed their own data activities, as in a traditional environment.

These supporting products and utilities must be developed and designed to evolve with the current priorities and technical solutions available. Data and data services can be modified and enhanced in a modular manner such that, as new technologies and products emerge, segments can be swapped in and out as warranted by the business.

Products and tools provide the following execution services for enterprise data management: process execution, data identification, data sourcing, data extraction, data storage, data transport, data acquisition, data control, and data services management.

ENTERPRISE DATA MANAGEMENT BENEFITS

The benefits of EDM are both tangible and intangible. The quality of data distributed by the enterprise data management is consistently accurate, timely, and synchronized. Access to this data is transparent to the end user and

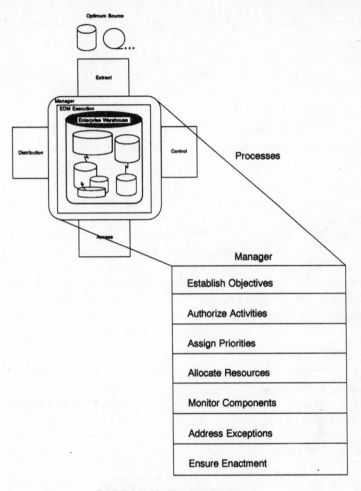

Exhibit I-1-10. Manager Processes

applications. The iterative methodology and data reuse approach fosters quicker deliverables by a reduction in the development cycle through the recurring use of the single logical data resources and processes.

Among the intangible benefits of EDM is that it provides a common source of information to be used by the corporation in processing its operations and making business decisions. The synergism attained by having all functions access and retain information in a common data store improves decision-making processes and allows the system to be more responsive to the needs of the business.

Enterprise data management reduces:

- *Code and data redundancy.* This is managed at the data level, eliminating application re-creation of like elements and fields.
- *The effect of input data.* This is controlled from operational data sources with single update for all data stores and subsequent use functions.
- *Processing requirements.* This is needed only once because not all applications and users repeat data development and extract processes.

Conversely, enterprise data management provides:

- *Consistency of data names and definitions.* It ensures that a common element is available for all applications and end users.
- *Enhanced data integrity and currency.* This ensures consistency in accessing a single data element or field.
- *More timely data delivery.* This ensures the downloading of this common element is provided as part of EDM to the application or end user.
- *Improved quality of information available to the business.* This ensures consistency in meaning, updates, delivery, and contents of data.
- *Improved quality and performance in accessing business.* This ensures consistency in access, catalog, and extract of data to end users.

CONCLUSION

The information most organizations need to control, manage, and run their business already exists. The data is now effectively being used in day-to-day operations. Many corporations recognize that they must look beyond today's systems to use data assets in new ways to:

- Improve productivity of knowledge workers.
- Recognize patterns, spot trends, and improve competitive analysis.
- Integrate diverse activities of the enterprise.
- Understand customer and corporate needs.
- Provide better service.

To accomplish these results first requires managing the data as an enterprise-corporate resource. This EDM involves more than the collection and storing of data parts in a master warehouse. In addition to meeting the business requirements of specific departments and applications, it must also include the numerous components to manage a complete systems integration solution for the needs of the company as a whole entity—both operational and informational.

To help visualize a foundation for achieving an integrated, enterprise-driven information resource, corporate IS departments should develop an infrastructure that can evolve with the current business priorities and technical solutions available. To ensure effective evolution requires a disciplined and strategic architecture.

I-2

The Evolution of a Unified View of Data

ISRAEL SPIEGLER

D ata bases are at the heart of any information system, and yet they cannot always support the varied managerial demands imposed on them. One reason may be the gap between the views of designers and users. A record-oriented design, viewing the data base as a collection of separate entities, may not easily support a content-oriented data base viewed as a collection of attributes. Mapping techniques are usually employed to bridge the gap between those two views of data. The search for a unified view, which may be able to handle both types of operations, covers areas from physical storage schemas, to binary data base, and to neural data base techniques. This chapter discusses and evaluates the three techniques.

HISTORY OF DEVELOPMENT

The history of data base development and the various models devised for data depict a continual thrust toward the end user. The classical data models—hierarchical, network, and relational—are examples of ideas that attempt to render more general approaches to data, making the user less dependent on any specific design or conception of the data base designer. Such models add power, flexibility, and of course ease of use.

Data bases are aimed to provide data independence (i.e., the separation between data and programs processing them). Most data base management systems (DBMSs) have achieved a certain degree of data independence by separating the logical and physical structures of data, sparing users from having to know how and where data is stored in the data base. Although separating the logical structure from the physical implementation improves the independence of data, users may still be locked into a specific data base design that reflects the perception of the designer. Such design supports only certain forms of use and may even impose them. Even users of relational data bases, in which the logical and physical structures are claimed to be the same, are dependent on the foresight of the designer when attempting to perform unconventional operations on their data.

This chapter discusses several approaches that offer a unified approach to data to support different, and sometimes conflicting, user operations. In particular, it presents the ideas of a binary data base and a neural data base. The binary data base is a large matrix that intersects all desired data values on one axis with all entities on the other. Entries in the matrix are, therefore, the binary 1 or 0 bits. This seemingly simple form may free users from a specific design, obviate the need for mapping techniques to perform complex accesses to data, and yield a higher level of data independence.

In the designing of a data base, real-world entities are mapped into symbolic ones. Therefore a record, representing a real entity, is normally distinguished by a unique identifier—the primary key. This design is prescribed by storage constraints, which require an unambiguous address for each data record; the address is used in subsequent data access and retrieval. As a result of this storage-oriented development of data bases, the primary key has become a sole means of record access.

Although the structure of data bases tends to imitate reality, their use, however, determined by the conceptual perception of users, is quite different. From the user's point of view, the storage-oriented structure is relevant only if it can support diverse accesses to the data base. Users may view a person's record as a collection of attributes (e.g., job, income, education, and family), and may want content-oriented access to the data through those attributes and not through the primary key.

The idea of a neural data base is another approach that attempts to break away from the storage-oriented view of data that requires a specific address for each data item. It views data as routes through a network of nodes—each of which acts as a processor. Storage is performed by configuring the system into a set of arcs that represents the data, and retrieval is therefore the process of bringing back the system to such a configuration. The potential application of such a view is an associative ability with which partial or incomplete input data may still yield the same configuration of arcs.

To support the gap between the structure- and content-oriented views and operations on data, some intermediary scheme is usually employed. Conventional solutions take the form of mapping techniques, whereby a data base is first constructed around a primary key and secondary indexing is added to support managerial operations. Some have proposed that records be stored according to secondary attributes, which are likely to appear in user queries. This is problematic because it is difficult to determine, at data base design time, which attributes should be the basis of storage. Selecting any given set of attributes for storage may, again, lock the user into a specific data base design.

Few have sought a unified solution in the form of a model that can encompass both structure and content operations on data. Two possible solutions, a binary data base and a neural data base, seem to be schemes that can bridge the desired gap.

VIEWS OF DATA

In storing and processing data, it is common to define at least three views: the physical, the logical, and the conceptual:

- *Physical view.* This is the internal view of data, or the machine's view—the way data is actually stored on the storage media.
- *Logical view.* This is the external view of data, usually that of the designer or the user of the data base. It is the way data is supposedly seen by the user.
- *Conceptual view.* This is the way in which the real system is described or modeled to design a data base that best represents it.

These three views can also be conceived as the mapping of domains in an information system environment. They reflect mapping between storage, data, information, and reality. Such mapping is depicted in Exhibit I-2-1.

As seen in the exhibit, the mapping between storage and data is the physical view of the data. Implementation of such mapping includes various file organization techniques (e.g., indexed, list, inverted, and many others). The mapping between the data and information levels is the logical view. This is where the classical models of hierarchy, network, and relational structures are found. Finally, the mapping between reality and data levels is the conceptual

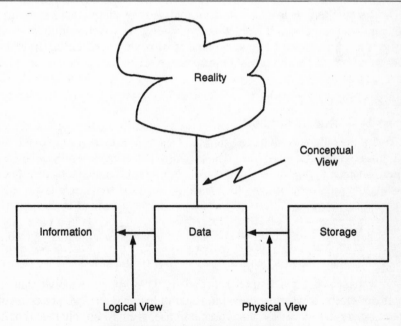

Exhibit I-2-1. Views on Data as Mappings

view. Such techniques as entity-relationship diagrams, data flow diagrams (DFDs), and semantic models are used for such mapping.

Operations about data also assume certain views of the data base. It can be distinguished by two types of operations: structure-oriented and content-oriented. Structure-oriented operations view the data base as a collection of separate entities, or records, the access to which is through the primary key. Content-oriented operations, on the other hand, view the data base as a collection of attributes, the access to which is through secondary keys.

The proliferation of data bases among end users increased the importance of content-oriented operations in relation to the structure-oriented operations. The primary key, which in conventional use is the input data supplied by the user, becomes the desired output data of content-seeking queries. The request: "Find all students with a GPA greater than 90" does not depend on the student's ID-number; the key (ID-number) is indeed the desired output of that query.

The two operation types tend to pull in opposite directions in the design and implementation of data bases. The problem then is to provide for data base access through attributes other than the primary key—namely, secondary keys. An immediate and straightforward method to facilitate such access is either to perform a sequential search of the entire data base or to sort the data according to query conditions. Both are unrealistic in a dynamic information system environment. Other solutions and methods developed to solve this problem may be categorized into three groups: access by a secondary attributes, access by combined attributes, and storage by attribute combinations.

Although this article makes no attempt to survey all the techniques developed for these categories, it highlights some milestones in conventional storage methods as steps toward a more unified view of data that can support both types of operations without mapping schemes.

CONVENTIONAL METHODS
Access by Secondary Attributes

Accessing data by secondary attributes is the basis for mapping techniques to support managerial operations. The idea is to link records that have common attribute values so that subsequent transactions access only the records linked. Two main methods, or design strategies, have been developed: the inverted and multilist methods.

The Inverted Method. In the inverted method, a list of all records that have a certain attribute value is kept for retrieval. Therefore, in addition to the original data records organized according to the primary key, the data base contains:

- A directory, in which each value K_i has a pointer P_i to the beginning of a list of records having that value and a field L_i specifying the length of that list.

- A list file, one list for each K_i value, holding pointers $R_i, \ldots, R_{Li}$ to records that have the value K_i as an attribute.

Access and retrieval are performed through the directory. Certain queries (e.g., counting or checking the existence of entities with a given value) can be answered at the directory level without having to access the data base. Boolean operations can also be performed on the directory before the data base is searched. Update operations, however, are more cumbersome because in addition to changes in data, all related lists must also be updated and new directory entries added for values that were not initially in the directory.

The Multilist Method. The multilist method keeps a list of records having a common K_i value in a manner similar to that of the inverted method. The list, however, is maintained within the records, each record being chained to the next record on the list. Here, the directory points only to the first record in a list rather than holding the entire list of records that contain a specific attribute value.

Although the inverted method is more efficient in retrieval, both methods require redundant storage. The inverted method needs additional space for storing the list file, which can be quite large. Data records in the multilist method must contain extra fields for pointers, which take up storage space. The inverted and multilist methods are the foundations of secondary indexing.

Access by Combined Attributes

Retrieval through combined attributes is another way to facilitate content-oriented operations. The methods suggest that several common attributes be combined and stored together for subsequent search of the data base. For example, if a university file is inverted by department and year of studies, then by this method the inversion is performed on the combination "department and year" according to which, for example, all "management freshmen" and "physics sophomores" are placed as a value in the directory.

One proposed compound indexing scheme uses this method as an inverted file. A different approach, called a double chained tree (DCT), portrays attribute combinations as tree structures. Still another structure, named multiple attribute tree (MAT), comes close in performance to the inverted method. Some researchers claim that the picture presented by MAT is too optimistic. They found a breaking point between the standard inverted method by single attributes and the MAT method. The decision on which method to use is particular to each application.

Storage by Attribute Combinations

A natural development of the preceding methods is the following idea: if one is interested in groups of records having common attributes, why not store them together in the first place? The idea was indeed proposed as superimposed coding, whereby records added to a file are stored in locations relative to the existing ones (i.e., all records that yield the same code through a union operation performed on common attributes are stored in the same location). An extension of the MAT method uses the idea of ordering records in a tree structure according to frequency of use and not by primary key. This may lead to improvements in retrieval as search arguments are directly related to the tree structure.

One scheme designed to solve the storage problem is combinatorial hashing. Another storage method, multidimensional directory (MDD), is characterized by records that are distributed in an N-dimensional space (N being the number of attributes for retrieval).

Extensive work has been done to enable access to data designed with a structure-oriented view to also support content operations. All approaches employ elaborate mapping techniques to enable the user to perform such activities. Few have sought a unified solution that can support both operation types without requiring the use of secondary indexing methods.

THE BINARY DATA BASE

The binary data base imposes a unified scheme on data (i.e., one that can support different types of operations). It views the data base as a large matrix that intersects all data values with all the entities concerned. Entries in the matrix are, therefore, the binary values of 1 or 0, which indicate that an entity has or lacks the corresponding data value. This model is not proposed as a user view of data but rather as a structure capable of supporting different user views and operations without intermediary mapping techniques.

This model can be thought of as a binary inversion of all attribute values of the data base. Despite some advantages in storage and retrieval, this method is hardly dealt with in the literature, primarily because of memory constraints. The idea of bit maps is sometimes suggested, but not as a way to store data.

The inverted method can be extended for data attributes of a binary nature (i.e., the record either contains or lacks a given value). Examples of attributes in this category are sex, citizenship, military service, or passing a test. In such cases, a binary bit for each attribute can be stored; the values 1 and 0 respectively indicate that a record has or lacks the value.

A simple calculation illustrates the merit of a binary method, at least for storage considerations: Let the number of records in the file be N and the percentage of records having a giving attribute value be P. Then, the directory for each attribute value in the standard inverted method will take:

$$N \times P \times B$$

bits of storage, where B bits are required for the storage of any given value. The binary method, on the other hand, requires only N bits—one for each record. Therefore, the breakeven point between the two methods is at

$$N = N \times P \times B$$

showing an advantage to the binary approach at

$$P > 1/B$$

In practical terms, storing data in a binary form becomes more efficient if P (the appearance frequency of an attribute value) is greater than B (the recriprocal of key length in bits). With a typical key representation of 32 bits, the binary method reaches a storage advantage at $P > = 0.03$. This means that even if such attributes as first name, city, major of studies, military rank, or color of items, let alone sex ($P = 0.50$) or marital status ($P = 0.25$), are stored in binary form, the binary method may yield better storage results.

Another direction in binary representation is superimposed coding. According to this method, an **OR** operation among all attributes of a given record can represent, in a way, the essence of that record. An example illustrates this method: baking products are made of various ingredients. These are represented in a binary matrix, where 1 indicates the using of ingredient j in product i. Each ingredient is assigned an 8-bit random code. The matrix is shown in Exhibit I-2-2.

Each product can be represented as the union of ingredient codes making up that product. The products are now represented as follows:

Product	Representation
1	11001101 = (codes 1 U 4 U 6 U 9)
2	11101100
3	11001100
4	11011111
5	11011010
6	11101110
7	10010111
8	10000111

This representation facilitates the handling of such queries as: Which products can be made from ingredients 1, 5, and 8? Taking the union of the respective ingredient codes the answer is:

$$(1000010000 \text{ U } 000100010 \text{ U } 0100010000) = 11011010$$

which qualifies product 5 as the one that can be produced from those ingredients.

The weakness of the method lies in an information loss that results from performing a union on attributes. This can cause the retrieval of records that do not qualify under the original conditions. Knuth calculated the dimensions of the problem where each ingredient is represented by a 32-bit code with only three bits on (three 1's), and each product is made from six ingredients or less. The probability of an invalid record qualifying in a query with one

PRODUCT i \ INGREDIENT j	1	2	3	4	5	6	7	8	9	10
1	1	0	0	1	0	1	0	0	1	0
2	1	0	1	1	0	0	0	1	0	0
3	1	1	0	1	0	0	0	0	1	0
4	0	1	0	0	1	1	0	1	0	0
5	1	0	0	0	1	0	0	1	0	0
6	1	1	0	1	0	0	1	0	0	1
7	0	1	0	0	1	1	0	0	0	0
8	0	1	0	0	0	1	0	0	0	1

Ingredient	Code
1	10001000
2	10000100
3	00100100
4	01000000
5	00010010
6	10000001
7	01100000
8	01001000
9	00001100
10	00000010

Exhibit I-2-2. Product-Ingredient Binary Matrix

ingredient is 0.08; in a three-ingredient query (or more), the probability is under 0.01. Although this probability is small, the method is not foolproof.

The binary view that associates attributes and records as a two-dimensional matrix is found in data compression. Compressing a binary matrix by adding rows and columns is a two dimensional projection. Justification for the compressed matrix is the considerable reduction in storage that results: only $2N \times \log_2 (N + 1)$ bits are needed instead of the N^2 bits to store the entire matrix.

A problem with binary projection is the ambiguity that may result when the original data is reconstructed from the compressed version. A simple binary matrix can be considered:

$$0 \quad 1$$
$$1 \quad 0$$

which yields the following horizontal and vertical projections:

$$1$$
$$1 \quad \text{and} \quad 1 \quad 1$$

Such projections will also produce the following matrix:

$$1 \quad 0$$
$$0 \quad 1$$

which is, of course, false.

The ambiguity problem of binary projections has been dealt with on several occasions. These are attempts to reduce ambiguity and loss-of-information problems, which apparently cannot be eliminated completely.

A compression scheme for a binary data base was developed. The original matrix, called Order 0, is compressed by a given factor into successive orders, eliminating unnecessary data. As query complexity increases, the compressed binary method is more efficient than the inverted one, because it works on higher orders of data rather than on the actual matrix.

The binary data base, as a unified view of data, is not without problems. Storage of names or numerical figures is cumbersome in binary form, requiring extensive amounts of storage. For numbers, a solution may be to represent each digit by four columns that correspond to the binary coded decimal (BCD) system, or going all the way and converting the numbers to pure binary values. Storage of names is a problem as well. The specification of 26_n columns for all possible strings of length n is obviously ruled out. However, using $26 \times n$ columns (i.e., 26 for each letter in the name) may be more feasible. Employing a code (e.g., ASCII) to represent the alphabet further reduces the storage requirements to $8 \times n$ columns for names in the binary matrix.

Another issue is how a full record of an individual can be reconstructed from a binary matrix. Such operational transactions may be slowed down with the number of accesses required. A data dictionary, which defines the meaning and association of each column to the attribute, is one solution to ease this problem. In addition, there is the ever-present and still infeasible problem of storing the entire binary matrix in primary memory.

NEURAL DATA BASE

A neural data base is a new model of data storage and retrieval based on existing models of the brain. It views data as a configuration of cell-states in a network-oriented system. Retrieval is therefore achieved by bringing the system into a certain state, rather than actually obtaining the content of any specific cell. The result of such thinking is a major departure from most conventional data base models on hand. The role of nodes and arcs in common data models, respectively representing facts and relationships, is completely reversed in this model. Nodes of the neural data base are the processors, while data is stored over a wide range of cell links. The information content of such a system is the number of link configurations in the network. Both storage and retrieval are performed over the entire network by triggering a dynamic process, given a certain threshold, and letting the system roll until it reaches a steady state. That configuration represents the data as originally stored.

A configuration may be thought of as a route or a flashing that goes through a network of cells, each of which acts as a processor. That route represents the object, entity, or concept stored. Different cells may trigger the same route, which can branch in several directions. In other words, more than one input value—and indeed incomplete or varied input values—can yield the same desired information, portraying the associative behavior of the system.

The model relies on studies in the area of neural networks. It is based on an analogy between a neurobiological model of the brain and the behavior of disordered systems in solid state physics. The analogy of those models seems to be promising not only for computing but for the design of future data base structures able to facilitate associative and parallel capabilities.

The concepts of configuration, storage, and retrieval are summarized as the main ideas of the binary model. Data is stored as network links rather than in the nodes that are the processors, simulating the firing of neuron cells. Retrieval is then performed associatively by content rather than by the usual address search methods.

The system consists of N independent nodes with links among them. Each node i can be in either an "on" or an "off" state. The nodes are denoted:

$$V_i = +1 \text{ (on)}$$
$$V_i = -1 \text{ (off)}$$

A binary matrix defines the connections between any two nodes in the system where the bits 1 and 0 specify the existence or lack of link respectively. A given state of the system, represented by the vector $V = (V_1, V_2, \ldots, V_N)$ of binary digits is called a configuration. The efficiency of the link between node i and node j is denoted as T_{ij} and will be defined later. Such a configuration represents some information as a string of N bits. The entire system participates in the storage of the data, where some nodes have the value zero. The entire system can therefore represent 2^N different configurations.

Each configuration is reached by applying a certain amount of energy E as follows:

$$E = -\sum_i \sum_j T_{ij} V_i V_j$$

which is calculated for the various pieces of information stored in the system.

Storage

The storage of n pieces of information, each of which is a word of N bits, where a word is a configuration, is represented by this simple example:

$$\text{Horse: } V^1 = (V_1^1, \ldots, V_N^1)$$
$$\text{Table: } V^2 = (V_1^2, \ldots, V_N^2)$$
$$\vdots$$
$$\text{Pen: } V^n = (V_1^n, \ldots, V_N^n)$$

Or in general

$$V^a = (V_1^a, V_2^a, \ldots, V_N^a) \text{ for } a = 1, \ldots, n \text{ configuration.}$$

At the time data is stored, link efficiency, represented by the T_{ij} matrix, is calculated. It defines the interaction among the various nodes of the neural system. The values of the matrix are set according to the information to be stored in the system. The matrix is calculated as follows:

$$T_{ij} = \sum_{a=1} \bar{V}_i^a V_j^a$$

Setting the initial values of T_{ij} for the n pieces of information of the system is the process of data storage. It is identical to the learning process that hypothesized that the efficiency of the electrical connections between two neurons changes according to the information learned. Here, too, the storage of data is represented by the T_{ij} matrix that defines the strength of the links among the nodes.

At this stage, the system remembers n pieces of information. In other words, such storage is represented by n configurations, which are the more stable ones that are reached at minimum energy states.

After the data storage state has been reached, the T_{ij} values remain constant throughout the life of the system. At the same time, the system has a dynamic nature by which each node V_i can change its state from on to off and back, using a movement algorithm.

Movement Algorithm

At any given moment in time, the system is found in a certain configuration. As the time cycle advances, each node checks its state and decides what its next state will be. Movement to a new state for each node i, which depends on the values of all other nodes in the system, is expressed as:

$$V_i \rightarrow \begin{cases} +1 > 0 \\ -1 < 0 \end{cases} \sum_j T_{ij} V_j$$

This model seeks to reach a state of minimum energy. Reaching such a state is equivalent to locating a piece of information that was originally stored as such a configuration. In other words, the system is designed in such a manner that the various local minimum energy states reached by applying the movement algorithm are the representations of information initially stored. The problem becomes one of getting to such states, given external input, in the process of retrieval. Exhibit I-2-3 graphically depicts sample data with minimum energy points as the content of the neural-based system. The vertical axis depicts the energy factor calculated for the specific configuration and the horizontal axis represents the range of data values stored in the system.

Further discussion of the neural data base model deals with parameters that increase the likelihood of getting to the right configuration, as well as experiments with storage and retrieval of data in that manner.

APPLICATIONS

Commercial applications of the binary or the neural models to represent full-scale data bases are still far in the future. Hardware constraints, software tools, and storage technology are still too limited for this concept to materialize. However, there are some smaller problems for which the binary data base provides an elegant and feasible solution. One example is the product-ingredient matrix. This application, converging the conceptual, logical, and physical views of data, allows for various, unique operations on data. The inverse query of determining all the products that can be made of ingredients on hand is a case in point.

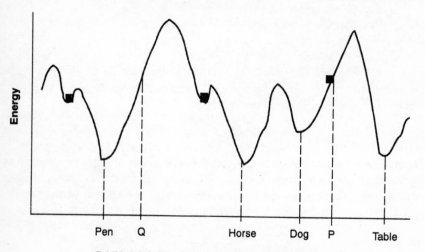

Exhibit I-2-3. The Energy Graph of Configuration

The binary data base can be useful in the same way for matching and controlling flights and crews in an airline work schedule. Here, the binary matrix provides for checking the work plan by adding rows and columns to verify that flights are fully staffed and crew members are performing their jobs. Constraints on the schedule (e.g., certain people not working in the same flight), can easily be represented as 0 bits in the appropriate column-row intersection. A recent application has applied the binary data base to research methodology and classification methods. The binary matrix is used to represent the knowledge about subjects of a study characterized by observed attributes. The binary string representing each subject is then used to calculate a similarity index among subjects in order to group them.

CONCLUSION

This chapter has discussed two possible methods for arriving at a unified view of data to bridge the gap between the structure and content views and operations on data. Conventional methods and strategies used to support managerial operations on data bases designed with a structure-oriented approach were reviewed. Those approaches resort to mapping techniques to facilitate content-oriented managerial operations.

The binary data base concept emerged as a possible solution that may support both transaction types. It unifies the logical and physical views of data in a way transparent to the user. Initial analysis shows that this approach to data storage seems to have advantages in processing complex queries. The approach has some drawbacks when operational transactions are concerned—storage of names and numbers and reconstruction of entire records are cumbersome and slow.

The storage of data in binary form matches computer hardware, which is a promising avenue of further study relating to data base machines and increasing the efficiency of data base work. In addition, methods must be developed to reduce the size of the binary matrix, which is typically quite large and contains a significant number of 0s. This can be done by compression techniques or by rearranging the columns and rows of the matrix (as they are independent) so that the 1-bits migrate to one area.

The neural data base is still in its initial stages. Most of the work done in neural networks concentrates on processing abilities; little has been done in the area of data storage and retrieval. Several avenues of future research are of course needed. Among them is a study of the effect of such parameters as system size, density of storage, and input accuracy on the capacity of such systems. The aspect of partial input supplied by a user needs further study. In all, these new models are a first step toward a unified view of data.

I-3
The Most Fatal Reengineering Mistakes

MARK M. KLEIN

Business process reengineering (BPR) has become the program of choice for achieving business improvement in the 1990s. However, it has been estimated that four out of five reengineering projects are ultimately unsuccessful! Is BPR so inherently risky, or are people and companies making fatal mistakes in planning and executing their reengineering projects? This chapter summarizes results from the author's consulting experience and the research of his company, Gateway Management Consulting, to answer this question.

The technical, management, and trade press are filled with articles on BPR. *The Wall Street Journal* published an entire week's worth of page one articles on BPR. A book on BPR is high on *The New York Times* list of nonfiction best-sellers. In addition, research finds BPR to be the leading improvement program that senior executives have undertaken, or are planning to undertake, to achieve their strategic objectives (see Exhibit I-3-1).

WHY BPR IS SO POPULAR

BPR is not new. There is an example of BPR from the US Navy around the turn of the century. Henry Ford performed BPR on automobile manufacturing in 1910. What is new is the label and a systematic attempt to accomplish breakthrough performance. BPR has become popular for three reasons. First, the three-year global recession has proven to most companies that the business practices of the past are increasingly adequate. Second, disappointment has grown in the ability of total quality management (TQM) to transform companies. Finally, BPR has been advocated by very articulate and entertaining spokespersons.

Why Reengineering Projects Fail

Fatal Mistake No. 1: Unclear Definitions. There have been some genuine BPR projects that were called something else, but many more that have been called BPR that really were not. Exhibit I-3-2 shows the answers to the question "What is BPR?" given by the same executives surveyed in

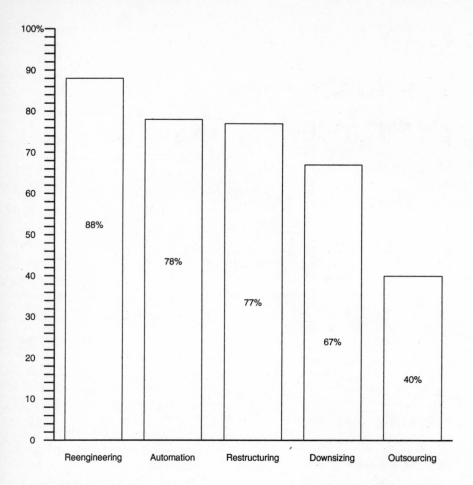

SOURCE: 1992 Survey of Senior Executives

Exhibit I-3-1. Initiatives Taken by Senior Executives for Achieving Strategic Goals 1989–1991

Exhibit 1. While 88% said they were doing reengineering, fewer than half (49%) could successfully define BPR as process redesign.

BPR is not just automation, although it often uses technology in creative and innovative ways. BPR is not just reorganization, although it almost always requires organizational change. BPR is not just downsizing, although it usually improved productivity. BPR is also not just quality, although it is almost always focused on customer satisfaction and the processes that support it.

Rather, BPR is a balanced approach that may contain elements of these traditional improvement programs with which it is often confused—and such

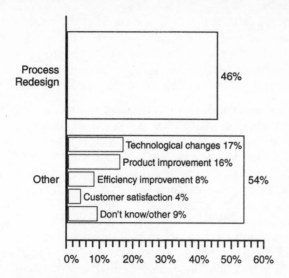

SOURCE: 1992 Survey of Senior Executives

Exhibit I-3-2. Senior Executives' Definitions of Reengineering

---

others as outsourcing, broadbanding, and continuous improvements. But, BPR is more.

First, BPR seeks breakthroughs in important measures of performance, rather than incremental improvements. Second, BPR pursues multifaceted improvement goals—including quality, cost, flexibility, speed, accuracy, and customer satisfaction—concurrently, while the other programs focus on fewer goals or trade-off among them.

To accomplish these results, BPR adopts a process perspective of the business, while the other programs retain functional or organizational perspectives. (TQM does examine processes, but to improve them, not reengineer them.) BPR also involves a willingness to rethink how work should be done, even to totally discard current practices if that should prove necessary. Finally, BPR takes a holistic approach to business improvement, encompassing both the technical aspects of processes (e.g., technology, standards, procedures, systems, and controls) and the social aspects (e.g., organization, staffing, policies, jobs, career paths, and incentives). In other words, BPR leverages technology and empowers people.

The definition of BPR that we use is: the rapid and radical redesign of strategic, value-added business processes—and the systems, policies, and organizational structures that support them—to optimize the work flows and productivity in any organization.

The concept of BPR is a rich and complex one; however, it should be readily distinguishable from the narrower programs. Yet confusion remains. Although 59% of CEOs believe that their companies are currently reengineering, only 40% of their CIOs agree. Because there is no such thing as "stealth reengineering," the CEOs and CIOs must have different ideas in mind.

Fatal Mistake No. 2: Unrealistic Expectations. Perhaps because of the unclear definitions of what BPR is, and perhaps because of overenthusiastic promotion of BPR's benefits, many senior executives have unrealistic expectations of what a reengineering project can accomplish.

Although of 3,000% improvements in performance exist as a result of reengineering, these are exceptions. In some aspects of business processes, tenfold gains may indeed be readily attainable with BPR. But in other aspects, a 30% improvement may well represent a breakthrough, particularly if it involves a broad aggregate measure of performance such as profitability. The point is that BPR can produce performance breakthroughs (of whatever magnitude), while more traditional improvement programs produce only incremental gains.

A BPR project should certainly be undertaken with a willingness—even a hope—for order of magnitude gains. But goals should be set, and expectations conditioned, on the basis of realistic analysis performed during the project.

In addition to unrealistic expectations about the size of the gains from BPR, some executives are mistaken about the domain of its applicability. BPR is applicable to the operational level of a business—not the strategic or even the tactical. It can show you how to do things right, but only in a limited way what are the right things to do. BPR will not identify the markets you should be in or the products you should develop. But it can give you effective processes for making those decisions.

Fatal Mistake No. 3: Inadequate Resources. As with many other corporate projects, BPR projects face the common dilemma that the people best suited to perform the work of the project are usually the ones who can least be spared from their normal duties. It helps to understand that there is no real solution to this problem, and that any accommodation will be a compromise.

Hiring consultants may be a beneficial idea, but they cannot replace your own people on the BPR project. Employees bring to the reengineering team an understanding of current processes, key individuals, and culture that is difficult for an outsider to obtain. They also bring a personal stake in the project outcome.

Outsiders—whether they be consultants, employees from a different division, or new hires—play an invaluable role in BPR. They bring a fresh perspective and the creative naivete to ask, "Why do we do things this way?" Consultants can play another role as well: they can bring methods for BPR and experience in doing it.

Therefore, the first requirement for adequately resourcing a BPR project is to provide a balanced mix of insiders to outsiders (e.g., five or six to one) on the reengineering team. The second requirement is to give the people on the reengineering team enough time to do their work. Some of the people in our reengineering seminars have told us that their reengineering team assignments were for as little as 10% of their time! That's barely enough to account for the loss of productivity from switching tasks.

Full-time assignments are probably neither feasible nor desirable at most companies, because you want team members to stay involved in the processes they will be reengineering. But something on the order of half-time is necessary for meaningful contribution and progress.

The third resource requirement is an adequate budget: for the insiders' salaries, for the outsiders' fees, and for expenses. This should be self-evident, but nearly two-thirds (65%) of companies do not have budgets for programs like BPR.

Finally, and most importantly, it is often not enough to simply assign employees, send them to seminars, and turn them loose. They must be trained and supported. Overall, slightly more than half of companies (54%) are using outside resources to assist their BPR projects. Of those who are not using outside resources, the most common reason given (by 70% of the executives surveyed) was "We have the knowledge and expertise to handle the project in-house."

Interestingly, the larger the company, the more likely they are to use outside consultants (ranging from 43% for companies under $100 million to 71% for companies over $1 billion). This is just the opposite of what one would expect, because the larger companies should have more in-house knowledge and expertise. This is probably a case of the larger companies knowing what they don't know.

Similarly, the percentage of executives who think they have the expertise in-house varies by their functional responsibilities, from a low of 56% for CIOs, to a high of 82% for CFOs. Here, too, this may show that the CIOs (who would be a lot closer to the BPR project) are more likely to know what they don't know.

Fatal Mistake No. 4: Taking Too Long. Many BPR practitioners believe that reengineering projects should take three to five years. Yet few executives have that kind of patience. Exhibit I-3-3 gives their answer to the question, "How soon do you need to see results?"

To a certain extent, this reflects their pressing need for the performance improvements that BPR can bring. This could mean favoring low-risk projects with near-term payback over projects with more substantive returns, but it need not. Gateway's Rapid Re™ methodology, for example, divides a BPR project into phases, each aimed at realizing a "subvision" with specific, tangible results.

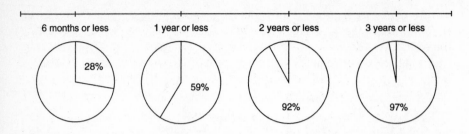

SOURCE: 1992 Survey of Senior Executives

Exhibit I-3-3. Reengineering Programs: How Soon Do Executives Need to See Results?

Fatal Mistake No. 5: Lack of Sponsorship. Meeting senior executives' expectations for results (fatal mistake no. 2) and their tolerance for delay (fatal mistake no. 4) are certainly necessary to retain their sponsorship—as is satisfying their appetites for cost and risk—but one must obtain that sponsorship in the first place. BPR cannot be driven from the supply side, as much as information systems, industrial engineering, and internal consulting professionals might wish it.

Senior management must sponsor BPR for several reasons. First, the impact of BPR is so broad that only senior management can sanction it. Second, BPR usually involves a shift in culture, and it is uniquely senior management's role to set the culture. Finally, BPR requires leadership of the most visible sort.

How to obtain that sponsorship? An executive generally has to go through four stages—awareness, curiosity, interest, and belief—before he or she will commit to sponsorship. Most senior executives are already at the awareness or curiosity stages, at least. As of January 1993, 80% of CEOs and COOs (but only 50% of human resources executives) were familiar with BPR, and the numbers are certainly higher now.

To move to the interest stage, an executive has to have two things. The first is credible evidence that BPR has worked for others. The second is recognition of a need that BPR might satisfy.

Companies do not undertake BPR because it is trendy or because it is elegant. They do so (often as a last resort) because they need to. This need is, in our experience, driven by one of three things: pain, fear, or ambition. Companies feeling pain (e.g., low profits or shrinking market share) have to do something now. Companies feeling fear (e.g., aggressive competition or changing markets) have to do something soon. Companies feeling ambition (e.g., expanding market share or entering new markets) have to do something now to realize their ambition soon. If an executive doesn't feel the need for BPR, he or she won't be interested in it.

To convert that interest into belief, the executive must be convinced that BPR will help meet the need. One way of accomplishing this is by showing the executive a demonstrated success within the company. Another way is by showing the executive exactly how you propose to carry out the BPR project. For it is not so much whether BPR can work, that he or she questions, but whether "we" can make it work.

Fatal Mistake No. 6: Wrong Scope. Sometimes we hear people say, "We're reengineering the company" or "We're reengineering the department." Our new AMA seminar is called Reengineering the Information Services Organization.

Actually, you cannot reengineer an organization—you can only reengineer its processes. And many processes are interorganizational and cross-functional. In fact, one of the main ways that BPR improves performance is by reducing or eliminating the errors and inefficiencies that inevitably arise when processes cross organizational boundaries. When the scope that is chosen for a BPR project is one that includes only part of a process, the opportunity for success is diminished.

By the same token, you need to select the right process to reengineer. Not all processes are equal in importance, or in their contribution to organizational goals. That is why successful BPR focuses on strategic, value-added processes. Strategic processes support the organization's business strategy. Value-added processes are ones that deliver value to the organization's customers.

The question of scope is intimately connected with the question of sponsorship. In the ideal situation, the BPR project would be sponsored by the CEO or COO. In that case, the entire company many be examined to find the most strategic and most value-adding processes to reengineer.

Sometimes, however, the sponsor is a business unit head, a general manager, or even a department head (e.g., a CIO). In that case, the project scope must be made congruent with the sponsor's span of effective influence, and the processes selected for reengineering should be the ones that are most strategic for the mission of the sponsor, most value-adding for the sponsor's customers, and wholly, or mostly, within defined scope.

Fatal Mistake No. 7: Techno-Centricism. Another thing we hear people say is "We're reengineering; we've acquired image processing" or "We're reengineering; we're moving to client/server platforms."

Certainly technology is a key enabler of BPR. But technology is not BPR. BPR changes the business processes—the way the work is done. Applying technology to current processes has been rightly called "paving the cow path."

This mistake is often associated with mistake no. 4. Although some technologies (e.g., desktop computers for personal productivity or mobile telephones) are quick and easy to install, technologies that support and enhance a process as a whole are often more complex and difficult to implement. By contrast, the social side of processes—empowerment—usually can be implemented faster, and often provides the majority of the benefits.

Many of the most successful BPR projects have been ones in which new technology was delayed to later phases. This is not to say that the social changes are easy, just that they are faster to implement. In fact, the opposite is true—the social change is almost always harder than the technical change.

Fatal Mistake No. 8: Mysticism. Inasmuch as BPR requires a willingness to rethink how business processes should be performed, there has been a lot of attention pain to the process of rethinking. For example, a student of BPR reads, hears, and even sees (there are actually training films on the subject) much about paradigm shifts, breaking frame, and out of the box thinking. The trouble is, one can't shift paradigms; one can only experience a paradigm shift.

By the same token, some of the published materials on BPR could lead one to believe that BPR is entirely a creative act, requiring an intuitive jump or some kind of transcendental experience. This is simply not so. BPR is an engineering discipline, although a new one. It can be practiced by the average intelligent manager or business professional.

Just as the human potential movement of the 1970s taught many ordinary people how to transform their personal lives, BPR can enable people to transform their business lives. Although both movements sometimes use mystical terminology, both are based on a discipline and specific methods for achieving the breakthrough.

Fatal Mistake No. 9: Lack of An Effective Methodology. A BPR methodology provides the discipline and specific methods needed to break out of the old narrow way of thinking about the business, envision a better way, and realize that vision. For example, the methodology my company uses consists of five stages:

1. *Preparation.* Mobilize, organize, and energize the people who will perform the reengineering project.
2. *Identification.* Develop a customer-oriented process model of the business.
3. *Vision.* Select the processes to reengineer and formulate redesign options capable of achieving breakthrough performance.
4. *Solution.* Define the technical and social requirements for the new processes and develop detailed implementation plans.
5. *Transformation.* Implement reengineering plans.

These five stages consist of 54 specific tasks that lead the reengineering team from original recognition of the need to reengineer all the way to obtaining the performance breakthrough. A good methodology provides a road map for reengineering. In other words, it enables an organization to select the most appropriate destination, and then to find the best route to get there.

There are many ways to use the methodology, and each organization will have to select the approach that best fits its need. Some will resequence the tasks, or omit some entirely. Others will adapt tasks to their own style and culture.

Without a good BPR methodology, however, organizations are left with the "what" but not the "how to." Without a methodology, reengineering projects run the risk of deteriorating into, on the one hand, brainstorming sessions and quality circles, or, on the other hand, more of the same old automation or operations improvement projects.

CONCLUSION

Business process reengineering projects are no more risky than other types of corporate projects with similar ambitions. Indeed, BPR may be the only way, in the long run, to achieve really ambitious operational goals.

Failures in BPR projects have usually come from mistakes in defining, organizing, or conducting the project. To avoid these mistakes, follow the nine commandments of BPR:

1. Be clear.
2. Be realistic.
3. Be prepared.
4. Hurry up.
5. Have a champion.
6. Focus.
7. Technology yes, but people first.
8. Don't get snowed.
9. Follow a methodology.

I-4
Achieving Information Integrity

MADHAVAN K. NAYAR

U ser departments expect correct information. When embarrassing information mistakes occur, the result is the loss of credibility, business, and
customer confidence. This chapter reviews the causes of incorrect and inaccurate information, examines existing solutions to data quality problems, and
discusses the importance of information integrity as the cornerstone to achieving total quality management, business process reengineering, and automated
operations objectives.

A STRATEGIC IMPERATIVE

In the computer age, it seems ironic that information errors even occur. After
all, by definition and design, computers automate manual tasks to eliminate
human errors. Even more ironic is the fact that many companies verify the
accuracy of the information processed by computers with manual efforts. In
spite of these efforts, however, many errors often go undetected until the
magnitude of the error commands attention.

For example, an $8.7 million phone bill stunned an Illinois Bell customer
who only called her sister a few times. According to a company spokesman, a
manual error (made while typing a correction into the computer system)
caused the mistake. The customer's phone bill should only have been $87.98.

In the spring of 1992, the brokerage firm of Salomon Brothers, Inc., felt
the sting of inaccurate information when a clerk misconstrued an order to sell
$11 million worth of stock as an order to sell 11 million shares of stock. A
second clerk failed to check the order. The computer system detected the
error too late. The mistake created confusion among traders and turned a Dow
Jones rally into a loss for the day. Estimates quantified the error at $500
million.

Information errors have beleaguered the credit industry. TRW, Inc., Equi-
fax, Inc., and National Data Retrieval, Inc., have all made headlines as cases of
data errors came to light.

As alarming as these examples sound, information errors happen every day in seemingly small ways. Data problems as innocuous as the wrong scanned price at the checkout counter can occur unnoticed to most shoppers. Information errors can include duplicate utility bills, dated and mailed within days of each other for nearly identical amounts. Data inaccuracies may also occur on credit card statements as wrong charges or incorrect calculations. So-called computer errors may inadvertently cancel insurance policies or lead to multiple claim payments. The General Accounting Office (GAO) provides another example of an everyday data problem, citing the miscalculation of 20% to 30% of adjustable-rate mortgage loans at a cost of $8 billion to borrowers. As this last example suggests, in the aggregate, seemingly minor data problems are not so minor after all.

The cost of errors large and small goes beyond the costs of lost credibility, customer confidence, and revenue. The costs of poor data affects IS operations daily. To correct errors, IS departments incur the costs of reruns, lost production time, wasted paper and forms, and employee overtime. To detect errors, IS staff and user departments often rely on practices that are too limited in scope to ensure confidence. These everyday costs can amount to hundreds of thousands of dollars a year.

INFORMATION INTEGRITY DEFINED

When the information is unreliable and incorrect, serious and costly problems can occur. The examples given have one factor in common: a lack of information integrity. Information integrity means that information is accurate, complete, and timely; that information is exactly right the first time, every time.

Many organizations recognize the problem. In a 1991 Massachusetts Institute of Technology survey, researchers found that of 50 CIOs at large companies, half of them doubted the integrity of their corporate information. They believed the information was less than 95% accurate and, as a result, limited in its usefulness.

Another survey of IS professionals revealed that 70% of the respondents believe corrupted data had delayed business, that 69% find their company's data inaccurate, and that only 56% have systems in place to detect these inaccuracies. Possibly more alarming to IS managers is the fact that, more often than not, business executives, not the IS department, discover data problems when critical management reports contradict one another.

Benefits of Information Integrity

Although poor data quality can wreak havoc for an organization, the attainment of information integrity within an organization and its IS operations offers bottom-line results and the ability to more effectively achieve other strategic initiatives. Organizations cannot overlook the quality of information because information affects the quality of all decisions and processes. Indeed, organizations should view information integrity as the cornerstone of a total quality management program. Malcolm Baldrige Award–winner Motorola, Inc., has taken this view toward information integrity by expanding its goals for six-sigma quality to the IS area, particularly in the financial systems. Instead of measuring defects per million parts, IS strives for no journal voucher errors in all financial systems.

The confidence of knowing that criticial business decisions are based on accurate data represents one of the greatest benefits of information integrity. Information integrity also improves the level of customer service the data center provides to both internal customers (e.g., user departments) and external customers. With no time delays for verification or reruns, users find the online systems ready and available each morning. External customers find that billing statements are accurate and policies are correct.

The IS department also benefits from information integrity. By eliminating reruns, wasted paper and forms, and employee overtime, costs fall. The resulting increase in automation associated with information integrity brings additional cost reductions and productivity gains. Information integrity also paves the way for greater automation initiatives.

WHY ERRORS OCCUR

No organization intends for information integrity failures to occur; however, for a variety of reasons, they do. System design accounts for many information errors. Many so-called computer errors actually fall into this category. For example, when a customer receives an incorrect bill, often the customer service department blames the computer. However, poor program logic is usually the culprit.

Nearly all organizations try to build controls into their applications to detect information errors. Poor design plays a role in the inability of internally developed controls to ensure information integrity. Programmers find it difficult, if not impossible, to code controls for every potential information error. As a result, inflexible controls are developed that fail to provide consistently accurate data and that require significant modifications as applications, hardware, and user requirements change.

For many organizations, errors occur because old systems cannot meet current demands. Overburdened systems and applications face the difficult task of doing more than they were designed to do. In addition, controls sufficient a decade ago have become obsolete in light of increased amounts of data processed, more complex systems, greater variety in hardware, and more extensive legislation.

Organizations are also sometimes unwilling to take steps to ensure the quality of their data. Until faced with a disaster, many companies do not consider information integrity as a priority for scarce or overextended IS resources. Underestimating the seriousness of information errors only increases the probability of errors occurring.

Financial Impact

Poor-quality information can cost business greatly and seriously impact the economy as all industries are interrelated in a world economy. Errors in calculating loan and investment interest as well as missing transactions can mean huge losses for a bank or a savings and loan institution.

The insurance industry risks enormous financial penalties for incorrect information. Fraud costs insurers $16 billion each year. With better controls on the information integrity of claims, insurers could reduce much of this cost. Payment of false claims or making multiple payments can cost insurers even more. Regulation now makes insurers liable for damages in cases of claim payment errors and mishandled claims, so insurers face the possibility of paying multimillion-dollar awards.

Manufacturers and retailers have known for years that poor information regarding inventory, shipping, and production can hurt the bottom line. To stay within tight margins, retailers require reliable inventory numbers, accurate shipping and transfer data, and correct orders. For manufacturers, raw materials purchasing and production decisions depend on the accuracy of information to prevent surplus inventory, spoilage, and production shortages and downtime. In many cases, manufacturers cannot afford a single error, because one mistake, especially in purchasing, could cost millions of dollars.

Perhaps the best example of the cost that an organization paid for inaccurate data comes from the advertising industry. Because of a six-figure billing error, Geer, DuBois, a New York advertising agency, lost a client worth $25 million in annual media billings. The agency failed to credit the amount to the client's account during the installation of a new computerized system.

Other Liabilities

More interfaces, platforms, and systems within the IS operations provide increased opportunities for information errors to occur. The greater use of electronic data interchange (EDI) and electronic funds transfer (EFT) also increases the possibility of errors. For example, in banking, increasingly online transactions are processed, files updated, and information made available to depositors via ATMs before IS personnel can check or verify the integrity of customer account information.

Automated operations and lights-out processing continue as popular objectives among IS professionals. The IS department can process and distribute the data faster, but the integrity of that information often remains suspect. Speed in processing offers nothing to the IS department if the information processed is unreliable and inaccurate. Automating operations may represent a critical initiative for improving productivity and quality; however, automation alone, without ensuring information integrity, handicaps the entire automation effort.

Finally, the lack of information integrity comes down to one simple issue: liability. IS managers can now find themselves legally liable for the wrong information their departments process and distribute. The courts, no longer intimidated by computer technology, seem more inclined to hold IS organizations responsible for information errors. The likelihood of lawsuits being brought against IS managers is worth considering. One computer law attorney estimates that one out of six corporate IS organizations will be embroiled in a lawsuit in the years to come. Information integrity is not exclusively an IS issue; it is a serious business concern.

THREE LEVELS OF INFORMATION INTEGRITY

The greater use of client-server architectures, distributed processing, and local and wide area networking holds new challenges to address. However, current technology can solve and eliminate the information integrity problems in three areas: file, process, and data.

File Level Integrity

At the file level, information integrity issues focus on correct file use. Because information starts at the file level, so do the opportunities for errors. Is the data center actually using the file it expects to use? Did the right job create the file? Did the right run create the file? Has someone inadvertently altered or used the file? Has a job used a file that should not have been used? Current solutions exist to address and resolve up to 17 file use errors.

File integrity issues manifest themselves as a variety of problems, all of which can corrupt jobs later in the job stream. For example, when the file created by the accounts-receivable update job is used in place of the file from the accounts-payable update job, erroneous customer bills result. Payrolls will not balance when IS personnel mount last month's commissions tape instead of the current month's tape. Wrong generations of data sets, **FILE NOT FOUND,** and **NOT CATLDG2** errors waste production time and corrupt information. File errors may seem obvious and avoidable, but as IS production staff knows, they continue to happen. Reruns because of wrong files occur in IS departments much too frequently. File integrity constitutes the first step to ensuring the information integrity of all information systems.

Process Level Integrity

Process integrity issues also affect information integrity. If an error exists in the process, an error will occur in the information. Process errors may occur relatively infrequently, but their impact can be severe, causing a myriad of problems such as wrong totals or subtotals on reports, incorrect carrying of figures to the next application, missing record counts, and misplacement of data fields (see Exhibit I-4-1).

5–10 Corporate Summary

		Deductions				
	Gross Pay	Federal	Fica	State	Other	Net Pay
Prior YTD	$759,503.33	$200,277.32	$47,939.32	$22,649.58	$11,901.98	$476,735.13
Current Period	$51,470.65	$10,294.13	$3,242.65	$1,544.12	$802.94	$35,586.81
New YTD	($810,973.98)	$210,571.45	$51,181.97	$24,193.70	$12,704.92	($512,321.94)

5–17 Corporate Summary

		Deductions				
	Gross Pay	Federal	Fica	State	Other	Net Pay
Prior YTD	($810,973.98)	$210,571.45	$51,181.97	$24,193.70	$12,704.92	($512,321.94)
Current Period	$45,069.45	$9,308.12	$2,878.03	$1,353.00	$705.68	$30,824.62
New YTD	$856,043.43	$218,879.57	$54,060.00	$25,546.70	$13,410.60	$543,146.56

Have the totals been carried forward correctly from one week to the next? If not, incorrect program logic could be the cause.

Exhibit I-4-1. Verifying Process Integrity

System design often comes into play with process errors. As mentioned previously, incorrect logic in a program's code can create errors. In addition, programs cannot account for every possible set of circumstances that can corrupt data accuracy. Changes to application programs may create information errors within that application or others downstream if programmers forget or fail to make other modifications related to that change. Moreover, as applications become more complex, it becomes increasingly difficult for application programmers to make modifications without affecting interrelated processes. Process errors can also include data entry errors if no controls are programmed to check the accuracy of the inputted data.

Although process problems may occur only occasionally, most IS professionals have experienced the errors that result and the reruns that follow. An incorrect number of records or missing totals may reveal faulty feeder systems. Incorrect program logic may incorrectly carry forward report totals from one month to the next. An example of this type of problem occurs when the previous total on the current month's report does not equal the new total on the previous month's report. Incorrect logic could also create incorrect calculations within programs and reports. If the process causes incomplete processing, faulty information is guaranteed.

Data Level Integrity

Data integrity issues affect information at the most detailed level, and as a result, can be the most difficult to detect. Issues at this level can be caused in part by process integrity issues.

Data-level errors appear on customer bills, statements, and employee paychecks instead of within programs and on reports. However, data integrity issues can sometimes point to specific nonrecurring information errors.

Problems at this level include unusual data fluctuations, inconsistent data trends and patterns, errors in transactions, and specific items or transactions that cause incorrect totals and subtotals. Similar to process integrity problems, incorrectly figured calculations and amounts can be carried forward in error at the data level.

Data fluctuations frequently signal an information error. For example, a medical provider's claims fluctuate significantly higher one month than the average. Further investigation shows the provider submitted the claims twice. Calls going through a communications switching station do not follow the usual pattern of heavy day volume and light evening and weekend volume. A quick check reveals missing data transmissions.

Data integrity issues also illustrate how totals and subtotals on reports can appear correct while detailed data, specific items, and transactions are wrong. A general ledger report total corresponds to totals on other financial reports. However, an entry error inadvertently shows a debit from an investment account not a cash account to cover the weekly payroll. This example demonstrates how information can seem correct when actually it is not. As another example, for more than 21,000 customers, Prudential Securities Group, Inc., either overstated or underestimated customers' investment income. Claiming computer glitches, Prudential executives confirmed that 12,499 investors paid taxes on as much as $8.9 million in overstated income while 8,972 failed to pay taxes on as much as $8.5 million. Overstated and understated income in total nearly offset each other, but individual investor accounts were in error. Only investigation of information at the data level can reveal such a mistake. Currently negotiating with the IRS, Prudential hopes to avoid alarm among investors by not having to send the corrected income information. Exhibit I-4-2 lists some of the problems that data analysis detects. The examples are categorized by industry.

AVAILABLE SOLUTIONS

Manual Verification

Ensuring information integrity is not an easy task, but solutions are available. Most companies rely on some type of manual verification efforts, usually called manual report balancing. Done in either the IS department or more typically in user departments, staff members manually look through reports, checking

Industry	Data Analyzed	Potential Integrity Problems
Banking	Volume of transactions by branch	Higher than average number may reveal multiple postings of transactions
Insurance	Number of canceled policies	Large fluctuations may indicate inadvertent cancellation of policies
Manufacturing	Inventory figures by part number	Sudden change when compared to production may show incorrect inventory
Telecommunications	Switch volume	Hourly or daily volumes less than 20% of average may reveal switch leakage
Retail	Amount and quantity of orders by store	Sharp decrease can show missing orders, sales problems, or wrong shipments
Credit Card	Average daily transactions by cardholder	Increases over average (dollar or number) may reveal stolen card or fraudulent use

Exhibit I-4-2. Data Analysis Examples

control totals in hopes of detecting an error. More often than not, in spite of their diligent efforts, balancing clerks miss errors. Ironically, some manual balancing efforts reveal false errors.

Relying on manual efforts to discover information integrity problems requires significant amounts of time and labor. Many people may spend hours every day verifying the quality of information processed the night before. A reactive, after-the-fact activity, manual efforts check information already processed and printed on a report, in paychecks, or in invoices. As a result, an error necessitates reruns and the printing of new reports and forms. Manual efforts also cannot verify all of the information processed. At best, an organization can hope for random checking or limited verification of only the most sensitive information.

In addition, manual verification can mean delays in processing information. Often, processing shuts down completely while balancing personnel verify output. Conversely, batch processing may continue during the night only to necessitate a rerun of the entire job stream if manual efforts find an error the next morning. As is more commonly the case, manual balancing or reconciliation only ensures the halting of automated processing, not the verification of data integrity or the correct identification of errors. Manual report balancing can be compared to an anchor dragging behind modern data centers.

Customizing Controls

IS departments can address information integrity by building custom controls internally in new applications. However, these efforts often fail to account for the numerous possibilities of information integrity errors. The first problem with custom-built solutions appears early during development. The development and maintenance of internal controls is expensive. Coding and writing controls that address all the areas where information errors can occur would demand an incredible number of hours from programmers. To avoid prohibitive development costs, however, programmers often include only the most obvious and essential controls, which limits the flexibility and usefulness of the controls developed and keeps programmers from meeting the objective for which they created the controls originally. In addition, such controls lack uniformity because they are nearly always application specific and do not address the information integrity issues between applications and systems. Retrofitting applications with controls is an even more difficult task. Only when development crawls, deadlines are missed, or costs skyrocket does IS realize the impossibility of the task. At that point, the IS department may scrap the entire effort or only implement any controls already developed.

Standard Software Solutions

Standard solutions offer advantages to the data center and user departments alike. As the name implies, standard software solutions provide uniform procedures for every job, application, and system. Because any job in the data center can use them, standard solutions offer comprehensive controls; because they require no programming development, standard solutions are cost-effective. An automatic audit trail is another benefit to the use of a uniform, complete, and documented solution. The resulting increase in automation can lead to cost reductions and productivity gains in both the data center and user departments. Standard solutions provide the opportunity to implement other data center automation objectives with a degree of confidence.

Standard solutions are universal, ensuring information integrity within all applications from data transmissions to customer invoices. Standard software solutions can ensure information integrity between any and all applications and systems. For example, software can verify totals between billing and accounts payable, between accounts payable and the general ledger, and between inventory, purchasing, and production. This ability to verify information between all applications and systems ensures integrity within an entire enterprise. Departments, divisions, and subsidiaries can all depend on the accuracy and interdependency of their information.

As information passes from one enterprise to another for use in the other's systems, each enterprise can verify the information integrity of that data. For example, a bank transmits funds to a manufacturer for its accounts receivable, payroll, and cash systems. The manufacturer sends tapes of customer payments to be credited to its account. Inter-enterprise integrity allows the manufacturer to ensure the quality of the information passed between the bank and its own systems. It also allows the bank to ensure the accuracy of the payments in the manufacturer's account and to verify that specific account against other bank systems.

Standard automated software solutions eliminate human verification efforts, maximize hardware and software use, and accelerate the distribution of online and reported information. As a result, IS can consistently meet service levels and reduce expenses. Savings also include a reduction of worker hours, programming effort, rerun time, and paper costs. Quality improves and IS gains the ability to detect errors at the source and avoid the potential embarrassment of an error snowballing throughout an organization.

As essential as standard solutions are for eliminating information problems, only a small percentage of organizations have implemented them. Of all the IBM MVS data center sites in North America, only about 12% rely on a standard software solution to automate manual report balancing, the most common method to ensure accurate information. Similarly, worldwide estimates approximate that only 9% of MVS shops use automated balancing. Exhibit I-4-3 is a self-test IS managers can take to determine their organization's readiness to confront problems related to information integrity.

A STRATEGIC IMPERATIVE

Information executives must recognize the importance of information integrity and carry that through to their IS departments. The bottom line of information integrity is that it improves an organization's business. As such, it becomes a strategic imperative. Total quality management remains an important objective for business today. However, quality in IS processes means little if the information lacks integrity. An organization interested in significantly raising its level of quality and excellence should also concern itself with the quality of its information by asking: Is information accurate? Is it complete? Is it timely? Moreover, quality decisions at all levels of the organization, in all areas, depend on accurate information. Therefore, to achieve total quality management throughout an organization, quality initiatives need to address the fundamental issue of information integrity. Better information means better quality.

Business process reengineering also promises improved productivity, quality, and efficiency. The same applies to the processes—both manual and computerized—that affect the integrity of information. By improving the process, the number of errors decreases and information integrity increases. Standard software solutions help reengineer those processes to ensure information integrity, and as a result, provide the benefits of better productivity and efficiency.

Automated operations also ranks high as an objective of most IS managers. Instead of using automation to simply speed up processes, however, IS managers should view automation as a means for improving quality, including the quality of their organization's information. Ensuring information integrity becomes the focal point of automated operations and of gaining the resulting increases in productivity and reductions in costs.

Answer each of these questions using a scale of 1 to 5 (1 meaning never and 5 meaning always) to determine your organization's information integrity quotient.

1. Data center or user personnel spend many hours each day manually balancing report amounts and totals.
2. Several or more reruns each month are due to data errors.
3. At least eight hours are spent each month investigating data errors.
4. The average monthly costs of reruns (including paper and overtime) from data errors is unnecessary and prohibitive.
5. A majority of applications do not include coded application controls.
6. Controls that are coded in applications are limited in their ability to detect and prevent data errors.
7. Over the past year, your organization has experienced the following type of data error at least once a month (rate each on the 5-point scale):
   - Multiple payments, checks, or payrolls.
   - General ledger.
   - Missing data transmissions.
   - Missed credits or posted transactions to accounts payable or receivable.
   - Others.
8. Your organization made news because of an information error.

Scoring. Total the number of your ratings to determine your quotient.

Quotient

12–20 *Excellent.* Your organization is either lucky, or it has implemented a standard information integrity solution.

21–36 *Average.* Like most organizations, information problems and data errors have occurred, probably in spite of manual efforts to verify data. The costs of these errors may be more significant than IS management is aware. Your organization runs the risk of having serious information problems.

37–48 *At Risk.* Your organization has experienced information problems before and has probably incurred major costs. Most likely, frequent data errors seem inevitable and specific manual procedures are in place to try and detect errors. A standard solution should be implemented to reduce unnecessary expense.

49–60 *Dangerous.* Your organization's information integrity quotient is extremely low. Your organization has experienced serious problems and incurred significant and damaging costs from data errors. Immediate action should be taken.

Exhibit I-4-3. Test Your Information Integrity Quotient

Information integrity is not just an integral part of total quality management, business process reengineering, and automated operations; it is the cornerstone upon which to achieve these objectives. Gaining information integrity is the first step to bringing these other goals to fruition. Information integrity is a strategic imperative, a prerequisite not only to the success of the IS department but to the continued prosperity of business.

CONCLUSION

Information integrity represents an important issue to anyone who depends upon the accuracy of information. CIOs, CFOs, data center managers, sales managers, and auditors (to name a few) know that the consequences of poor quality data and unreliable information can range from embarrassment to a loss of revenue. A global economy so vitally dependent on information cannot tolerate a lack of information integrity. Information integrity becomes a strategic imperative for organizations looking to achieve total quality management, to reengineer business processes, and to automate their operations. Although manual verification and custom-built application controls attempt to address information integrity issues, standard software solutions offer the key benefits of cost reductions, flexibility, uniformity, and universality that allow an organization to attain information integrity within and between its applications as well as in inter-enterprise systems.

Section II
Cultural and Political Issues

Elevating business information to its proper place on the corporate pedestal has ramifications, of course. For one thing, organizations want to quantify and capitalize on their data administration functions. The best way to do this accounting is to perform a data administration assessment. As explained in Chapter II-2, "Assessing a Data Administration Program" involves targeting problem areas so that the resources needed to rectify them can be identified.

Most IS departments grapple with cultural changes when they try to integrate object-oriented technology into the IS environment. The transition to object-oriented methods is rife with trial and error for many organizations. Most organizations have little trouble identifying the many objects germane to their business—it is when they try to precisely define these objects that they encounter problems. The establishment of a data dictionary is one of the day-to-day challenges and practicalities of using object technology. Chapter II-2, "Lessons in the Move to Object-Oriented Systems," discusses this specific issue and others.

General approaches to managing change are at issue in Chapter II-3, "Getting Ready for Strategic Change," and Chapter II-4, "Corporate Downsizing and Rightsizing." The lessons on business change discussed in these chapters should hopefully strengthen the business case for increased attention to data management.

II-1
Assessing a Data Administration Program

JENNIFER LITTLE

A data administration assessment is a method of gathering concrete evidence and identifying and capitalizing on the benefits gained from an organization's data administration program. In addition, an assessment makes it possible to target problem areas and specify the resources needed to rectify them. This chapter highlights the advantages of an effective data administration program, and details the step-by-step method of conducting an assessment of an organization's current situation.

CHARTING A NEW COURSE

Data administration program assessments are performed for many reasons, which determine the assessment's perspective (i.e., internal or external). Some of the more common reasons include the following:

- To help keep the data administration program on track.
- To quantify and publicize the benefits of data administration.
- To help justify the existence of the data administration function during tight financial times.
- To expand data administration in terms of its responsibilities, the scope of the data that is managed, or its level of authority.

The goals originally established for any particular data administration program usually take years to accomplish. In addition, it is not feasible to try to list every day-to-day data administration task that must be performed to reach those goals. Broad objectives are specified for the program, and the subsequent day-to-day activities are expected to fall under those objectives. It would be easy to stray from the course initially established if several mid-course corrections were not made. A program assessment provides the information required to determine where the program is and where it is headed to make the course corrections.

Making a mid-course adjustment does not signify that judgment errors have been made. Data administration programs are often affected by many different organizational factors (e.g., budget constraints, customer demands, organizational mission changes, and technological advances). Data administrators must take advantage of the positive factors and cope with the others as best they can. Some activities that an organization is involved in may not be seen as traditional data administration functions. If these activities are characterized by high visibility and strong resources (e.g., funding and people), however, important benefits can be achieved.

When data administrators participate in nontraditional data administration activities, it is like a captain taking the furthest-reaching tack to reach a buoy in a boat race. Speed may increase, but this tack is further from the straight line to the target. The environmental factors are the current, the wind, and the other boats. These factors prevent a straight course to the target. Nontraditional data administration activities include helping design an application system and using modeling workshops to assist in reorganization planning. Nontraditional data administration activities differ among organizations.

At other times, data administrators perform their core data administration activities so that they may be on the tighter tack. Speed on this tack is slower, but it is closer to the straight line to the target. Speed may be slowed because of lack of adequate staff to provide all the necessary training or to write all the necessary policies. Progress toward the long-range data administration goals is likely to be a combination of activities that are considered to be on both the faster but not as direct tack and the more direct but slower tack. Data administrators must assess and adjust the variables over which they have control to reach their targets.

The more experienced data administrators, like the more experienced sailing crew, see more opportunities and know how to take advantage of them. The maturity level of the data administration program affects an assessment in several ways. It influences the reasons for conducting an assessment, the format of the assessment, and the results of the assessment. As data administration programs mature, assessments are more likely to expand the data administration function in terms of its responsibilities, the scope of data that is managed, or its level of authority. This is part of institutionalizing the data administration function. For data administration programs to mature successfully, the data administration functions must be institutionalized within the context of the other organization activities.

INSTITUTIONALIZING DATA ADMINISTRATION

Like many disciplines, data administration benefitted from separating itself somewhat from mainstream IS management functions to develop its own techniques, methods, tools, principles, rules, policies, and goals. A mature data administration organization, however, must be able to work with the broader IRM environment to produce data administration benefits. Data administration cannot remain isolated any longer. Data administration activities must be well integrated into the entire information systems planning, development, and maintenance activities as well as with other nonautomated information management functions (e.g., forms and document management).

Institutionalizing data administration activities throughout the organization is similar to the way in which personnel management functions are integrated with other organizational functions. It is understood that human resource divisions are responsible for establishing personnel policies, coordinating personnel actions and training, and monitoring the organization's compliance with personnel laws and rules. Many personnel actions are performed by everyone in the organization, however, and the personnel specialists in HR divisions provide training and assistance to the rest of the organization so they can perform those functions. For example, the HR division does not unilaterally:

- Decide what skills are needed.
- Advertise for certain kinds of professionals.
- Interview and hire the candidates.
- Conduct performance evaluations.
- Lay off or retire people.

The way in which personnel management is accepted and integrated into the everyday workings of the entire organization is the situation that data administration should be evolving toward. For that to happen, data administration organizations must determine exactly where they are along their evolutionary path now. A program assessment can help do that.

Part of institutionalizing data administration is ensuring that data administration does not become a bottleneck to the rest of the development activities. When a data administration department consists solely of inspectors who review products after the fact, it is not an integral part of the process. This is not to say that the policing aspect of data administration should go away. But there are different ways of providing review services, and customers react to them differently.

A data administration function can be performed in a way that appears to be either helpful or controlling. Current functions that are viewed as controlling can be changed so they are viewed as helpful. For example, a data administration department may be responsible for ensuring that systems development and maintenance teams develop data elements that comply with standards. Data administrators may currently require the development team to construct the data elements on their own. The data administration department may check the data elements after the software version has been released to tell the development team which data elements were not constructed properly. The same function could be carried out in a helpful way if the data administration department helps the development team create standard data elements during the analysis and design phases so when the software version is ready to be released, the data elements are already in compliance with the standards. Data administration departments that provide helpful services are going to be more successful institutionalizing data administration in their organizations.

THE DATA ADMINISTRATION CUSTOMER

This brings up the question, who are the recipients of data administration services? What they want? Do data administration departments listen to their customers and understand what they need? A program assessment will help document a baseline of customer opinions of the services they receive that can be used to identify potential changes to the data administration program.

Organizations have applied total quality management principles to their business functions and have determined what their value chains are in part to get each employee to understand how what they do affects the customer. Some municipal motor vehicle offices have instituted customer service representatives that are trained to take a customer's problem, issue, or request and complete all the steps necessary to resolve it; the customer is not sent from window to window or from department to department.

Who is the data administration customer? Is there one customer or more than one customer? Is the data administration customer the immediate, next-in-line customer (e.g., a data base administrator or systems project manager)? Is it the end-of-the-line customer (e.g., the information requestor or systems users)? Is it the end of the end-of-the-line customer of the information system (e.g., a consumer or employee)? Where is the data administration program money coming from? Is that the customer? Should it be the customer? If it is not the next-in-line or end-of-the-line customer, should the money come from one of them instead?

The interconnection of customers is complex, and most data administration departments will find that they have several different kinds of customers. There are advantages and disadvantages for specifying any combination of these as the primary customer. For purposes of conducting a data administration program assessment, it would be better to keep the number of types of customers small, but significant. The groups included should have an awareness of the data administration program well before the assessment is going to be conducted. They should have been participating in some data administration-sponsored activities for some time. They should be positioned within the organization in such a way that their opinions will carry weight with the main audience for the assessment results.

While identifying the customers, data administrators should ask themselves, are we listening to our customers? These are some examples of customer complaints that the data administration organization may hear:

- My system does not work!
- Someone changed MY data!
- These reports are wrong!

- How can I figure out how many employees are eligible for this?
- Why does it take so long to make changes to the system?

Some may think that these customers do not care about data administration when they make these kinds of complaints. It may be that the data administrators are not listening to them correctly. Most customers will not be able to explain their requirements in data administration terms. So data administrators must translate what the customers are saying into the implications for data administration. That is not to say that the entire customer requirement is a data administration issue, or even that all customer requirements have a data administration aspect to them. However, data administrators must pay more attention to the customers' complaints and figure out how to address them from a data administration point of view.

Data administration is a service function. Its general goals are to improve quality and accessibility of data. At the same time that data administrators need to listen to customers complaints correctly, the customers must be able to see data administration listening to them and taking appropriate actions. A program assessment is one way of bridging the gap between the two groups.

ASSESSMENT FORMATION

Once the customers have been identified, the assessment format must be chosen. There are several ways of structuring the assessment: measuring the progress toward the original goals, comparing the program to what the data administration experts prescribe, or comparing the program to other similar programs. If the program goals and objectives were not originally established with measuring them in mind, it will be more challenging, but not impossible, to find adequate measurement techniques.

Most data administration programs have evolved over the years to look different from the way they were originally intended. A program assessment can compare the current program to the original plan and measure the degree to which the original planned activities have been accomplished. That would not take into account the accomplishments that were not in the original plan, however, nor would it address advances in data administration tools and techniques. Another alternative is to compare the current program to what some of the data administration experts recommend. These could be such experts as Ron Ross, Bill Durell, Arnold Barnett, or Clive Finkelstein. Their recommendations, however, may include activities that are not practical to implement in all organizations. A third alternative is to compare the current program to data administration programs in other similar organizations. To some extent, this type of comparison is happening constantly as data administrators meet in such forums as the Data Administration Management Association (DAMA) and Data Administration Users Group (DAUG). These forums provide a feel for how one data administration department stacks up against another, but a structured comparison would be more valuable to include in an official data administration program assessment. It would be time-consuming and costly to visit several data administration departments in other companies or agencies and collect the detailed information necessary for a thorough comparison. A different way to compare programs is to use the results from assessments or surveys of data administration programs that have already been completed. This approach and some sample surveys are discussed later in this article. A combination of the three approaches will probably serve most data administration departments best.

STEPS TO CONDUCTING AN ASSESSMENT

If a data administration program has been created with program assessment in mind (i.e., designed with program assessment and feedback into program planning included in its functions), each of these steps should be much easier. These steps will also be easier for data administration programs that have reached higher maturity levels. To get there, they have had to struggle through many of these issues (e.g., operationally defining their goals to achieve them). Unfortunately, many data administration functions are not even recognized as programs. They may have evolved over time from some other function so they do not have the underlying structure that a program charter and roles and responsibilities would provide. For those data administration programs, these steps will take longer. They will be building part of that structure they lack, however, so at the end of the assessment they will have more than just a report card. The following sections detail what is involved in each of the six steps.

Step 1: Deciding What to Assess. The first question to ask here is, what is going to be measured? If initial goals were set for the program, the program's progress toward those goals can be measured. For example, if one of the program goals is to improve data quality, the current data quality levels can be measured and compared to the initial data quality levels. If no formal goals were originally established for the data administration program, some general goals should be inferred from the original purpose and intent of the data administration program. Measurements can then be made against the inferred goals.

Step 2: Deciding How to Assess. If progress toward program goals has been selected as the what, there are many possible hows. They depend on the operational definition of the goal. The goals of most data administration programs are general and broad, but they must be more specific to make actual measurements. Operational definitions provide the specifics required to make measurements; they link the abstract concepts included in the goal to real-world observable facts. For example, improving data quality may be a program goal. To measure data quality, a data administration program may have developed metadata to capture data quality requirements and implemented a data quality measurement process. The metadata may be timeliness, accuracy, and completeness. For this data administration program, the operational definition of data quality is the metadata they developed. Although data administration programs that have not already operationally defined their goals will not be able to develop elaborate arrangements like metadata to capture their data quality requirements, they could still measure their progress toward their goal to improve data quality. They could select specific problem data that existed before the data administration program went into effect and collect opinions about the quality of the current data from the users. This will not produce a result as scientific as the data administration program that has the metadata to measure the data quality for all its data, but it is a workable operational definition.

Step 3: Developing Measuring Instruments. Surveys are frequently used as measuring instruments to collect information from a wide group of participants. Surveys can collect opinions and facts (e.g., dates, numbers of data elements, and models). Many professional services are available to create and conduct surveys. If these services are not feasible, and the data administration staff decides to create the survey themselves, they should at least consult with some survey reference materials for assistance. Survey validity, clarity, structure, and format are likely to suffer from the lack of professional involvement. Software is also available to help develop the survey, collect measurements, and calculate results. The survey should be designed to collect the measurements that have been decided upon in the what and how steps. Data administration staff members should be warned against only including opinion-type questions in the survey. They should resort to collecting opinions only when there is no reasonable method to collect facts. Opinion-only survey results contain the biases of the participants and may not portray a realistic view of the situation. If the goal is to collect customers' opinions of the data administration program, customer comment cards can provide the opportunity for them to comment on every interaction with the data administration program. This way, collecting customers' opinion would be a part of the data administration function instead of an added function that is only done once every four or five years.

Step 4: Collecting Measurements. One-on-one interview meetings can be used to administer the survey to executive-level or functional area project-system sponsors. These are often the assigned data stewards or custodians, and that may be a new role for them that they are just learning about. A data administration staff member or a survey expert can perform the interviewer role. The data administrator should attend this meeting too, so the interviewer can concentrate on collecting the information and the data administrator can answer questions about the program. A notification letter should be sent to the interviewees beforehand to prepare them. The notification should include the purpose of the assessment, provide a copy of the assessment schedule with the high-level assessment activities, and indicate when and in what form the final results of the survey will be made available.

A wide variety of ways to collect measurements are not included on the survey. For example, the program that has the goal of improving data quality and the data quality metadata will simply collect the measurements that already exist. Data administration programs that have operationally defined all their goals in this way would be able to conduct an assessment of their program at any time.

Step 5: Collating Information and Calculating Results. Storing the raw data collected in a data base allows the data administration department to use it in the future (e.g., for comparison with future assessments or for other program uses). A program assessment is likely to be a large investment—one that must be protected. If a survey software package is used, it will likely support the long-term storage of the survey itself, the raw measurements, and the compiled results. Several statistical analyses can be performed on the results. If unfavorable results occur from running the statistical analyses, they should not be ignored. If they are accurate, no matter how unpleasant, they are revealing something significant about the program. Data administrators should take this opportunity to address them with assertive solutions.

Step 6: Reporting Results. This step is imperative. It is worse to conduct an assessment and not report the results than to not perform an assessment. If the results are not flattering, it should be used as an opportunity to focus on how to improve things. If the results are flattering, data administrators should shout them from the rooftops and send a copy of the results to everyone. One of the final products of the assessment should be an updated data administration program plan. It should document the data administration program accomplishments, provide the rationale for dropping any tasks from the original plan, and forecast the strategies and tasks for the outyears.

USING RESULTS FROM OTHER SURVEYS

The ideal situation would be to conduct periodic surveys and keep the results to compare year after year. Few data administration programs are old enough to have had this luxury. They can simulate that situation by using the results of other surveys. Some example surveys include:

- DAUG, "Data Administration Survey Report."
- GUIDE "Selling Data Administration for the 80s and Beyond."
- Center for Information System Research, MIT, Sloan School of Management, "Managing the Data Resource: A contingency perspective." This paper presents case studies of 31 data management efforts in 20 different firms.
- Database Newsletter, "Results of the 1991 Advanced IRM Survey Part I." The survey collected information from US and Canadian firms.

When using the results of a previously conducted survey, it is important to determine the similarity of the responding organizations. The surveys mentioned here reported background statistics on the responding organizations that show a wide variety of type and size organizations participated. Unfortunately, none of these surveys reported correlations between those background statistics and the respondents answers to any of the other questions. Another difficulty in working with results like these is that the same category of information may have been collected, but the specific operational definitions are often not compatible. Even with these drawbacks, results of other surveys can be very useful in performing an assessment.

Some similarities exist among the lists of the important data administration functions constructed from the responses to these surveys. It would be valuable to correlate the organizational characteristics of the data administration programs to this information. For example, are the data administration offices that have only been in place for a short time the ones that see data modeling as the most important function and the more mature data administration offices are focusing on supporting system development? Unfortunately, this cannot be determined from the information as presented.

The results from other assessments or surveys can be used to assess a data administration program's maturity level. Its relative level of maturity can be estimated before the assessment to compare it with other data administration programs, or its level of maturity could be judged after the assessment using the measurements collected to show comparisons when reporting the results. There are different sources of information that can be used to calculate the maturity level. One specific maturity model that could be used is a six-stage maturity model. This may be useful because it looks at the evolution within the data processing environment and recognizes that even with advanced technological tools, data processing shops can be in any of these stages.

CONCLUSION

An assessment can assist an organization in identifying and capitalizing on the benefits it has gained from its data administration program. It can also help target problems areas and specify the resources necessary to rectify them. Like any important undertaking, an assessment must be well-planned and it needs management's support and commitment. Whatever the results, it will also help anchor the data administration department in the organizational structure. Therefore, proper preparation and planning for different outcomes before the assessment is conducted is crucial.

II-2
Lessons in the Move to Object-Oriented Systems

MICHAEL JESSE CHONOLES

Many software development organizations are currently facing the challenges of making the transition to object-oriented technology. The focus of mainstream software development has inevitably moved from the evaluation of object-oriented technology to the implementation of this technology. Although there are many excellent sources of information and training for object-oriented concepts and methodologies, there is little available that addresses the day-to-day challenges and practicality of applying object-oriented technology.

Established organizations making the transition to object-oriented technology find that many of the procedures and practices that they traditionally relied on are no longer suitable. They stumble into barely adequate replacements and alternatives largely through trial and error. However, a development organization can be too quick to throw out all existing procedures and current best practices and erroneously assume that everything must change with the switch to object-oriented technology. Especially on their first object-oriented project, analysts and developers usually want to jump headfirst into object-oriented models and abandon any proven analysis or design techniques they may have practiced. The most successful course of action usually lies somewhere in between these two extremes—some procedures must change and others must remain as they have been.

This chapter discusses some lessons in object-oriented analysis learned by the Advanced Concepts Center of Martin Marietta while helping its clients make the transition to object-oriented technology. Although these lessons focus primarily on analysis phase activities, many carry through into the later phases of development as well. The guidelines examined in this chapter include:

- Managing the pace of the transition.
- Identifying systems boundaries early.
- Defining terms.
- Establishing an operations concept.
- Keeping previous implementation objects out of current analysis.
- Having users participate.

- Avoiding too much change.
- Not skimping on analysis.

These guidelines may seem traditional, but they require updating and refreshing for object-oriented projects. They can help organizations to avoid the most common pitfalls of the transition to object-oriented technology and to experience more quickly the benefits of using object-oriented technology.

MANAGING THE PACE OF TRANSITION

As with any major change, an organization undergoing the transition to object-oriented technology must be steered carefully through many opposing currents. Within the organization, there are often strong forces attempting to delay, detour, or derail the transition. Equally dangerous are the forces that attempt to rush or accelerate the transition more than feasible and expectations that object technology can solve all the organization's problems. Ignoring any of these forces does not make them less dangerous. Ultimately, the conversion will occur, but the transition will most likely be slower, more painful, and more expensive than anticipated.

Identifying the origins and symptoms can counter these forces. Software development organizations that have been very successful with pre-object-oriented methodologies usually have taken their time in progressing through the conversion. They have decided that a major conversion would be disruptive and believe that the gain obtained from object technology may not be significant. They do have a point, after all—why mess with a good thing? It is hard to persuade them to speed up the pace. They study, plan, debate, and produce numerous white papers, but because they will not get their hands dirty, their deliberations will not touch on practical issues. Unless they produce real deliverable, marketable products with object-oriented technology, the organization cannot get the practical experience needed, and study efforts are mainly wasted.

An organization stuck in the old paradigm exhibits some of the following symptoms:

- Wanting to follow previous procedures or schedules.
- Still requiring the production of reports and documentation related to old method.
- Not realizing that old way of managing and doing business had evolved along with methodology.
- Investing too much in old methods and procedures.

Overcoming Status Quo

To counter this complacency, the organization needs to understand what it does well and the conditions that enabled it to succeed. Management needs to do an honest assessment of the organization's strong points and competitive edges, as well as its weak spots.

For each capability, whether a forte or a flaw, the organization needs to understand the effect of current market, business, and technological trends. For example, an organization may excel in mainframe batch technology but find its market is moving quickly to client-server technology. Another strong point may be configuration management procedures; the organization may find that as long as it keeps its personnel satisfied and turnover low, it may be able to keep its edge in that area.

After this sort of self-analysis, most organizations find in this time of rapid change, that it is unwise to rest on their laurels. Market forces are driving them to more reliable, more portable, and more maintainable products, which require shorter development cycles. Previous areas of valuable technical expertise are becoming backwaters and lessen the marketability of the product and the enthusiasm of the development teams. Organizations generally find that they have a developing consensus for modernizing their methodology.

Reasonable Risk versus a Team Approach

Once an organization that has been suffering from foot dragging actually starts to convert to object-oriented technology, it commonly takes a horizontal approach in which each horizontal activity or phase is converted to object technology (see Exhibit II-2-1). Typically, an organization timidly attempts to go to object technology by moving its programmers to an object-oriented language (e.g., from C to C++). This is mistakenly perceived as significantly cheaper and less risky than the vertical approach, which converts all the phases of small project to object-oriented technology (see Exhibit II-2-2). In the horizontal approach, after converting to object-oriented programming, the next step is

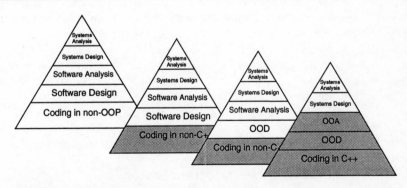

Exhibit II-2-1. The Horizontal Approach to Making the Transition to Object-Oriented Technology

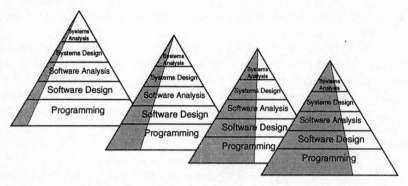

Exhibit II-2-2. The Vertical Approach to Making the Transition to Object-Oriented Technology

to move the design phase activities to object-oriented design, then the analysis phase activities to object-oriented analysis, and so on up the chain of phases.

Starting the transition to object technology by converting to C + + is often seen as a reasonable risk management approach because it gives the project an object flavor but does not create too much change. It saves on training costs because only programmers, not analysts or designers, have to be trained. If the programmers started out knowing C, even that training cost could be skimped on or minimized. It also saves on tool costs because only tools for the end of the life cycle need to be bought. This approach is best on small programs, which require limited analysis and design phases.

However, this approach avoids the real transition costs and learning the real lessons and produces systems that are not very good. The programmers do get some experience, but the programs produced without real object-oriented training typically encapsulate only the implementation, misuse inheritance, and have only an object veneer. Because the object-oriented analysis and design phases were skipped, the structure of the system is still not object oriented and is very sensitive to requirements or design changes.

In addition, the discontinuity between phases causes confusion and re-work. The analysts and designers speak a language different than the programmers speak, which results in confusion and potential organizational discontent. Because senior staff members are typically designers and analysts, the horizontal transitional approach brings the senior staff on board near the end of the transition. The organization loses the benefit of senior staff members' insight on how to make the transition and faces their opposition over a longer period.

The vertical approach to making the transition is usually more appropriate. This approach begins by developing a small subsystem or program using object-oriented technology. For many projects this is an object-oriented analysis, object-oriented system analysis, or object-oriented requirements analysis phase.

In this approach, representatives of all the activities get to develop and test object-oriented versions of their standard procedures. If possible, user representatives should also be involved in the conversion. Instead of just the programmers getting experience, now the organization as a whole gets the experience.

A team approach not only allows for concurrent engineering, which can produce a higher-quality product, but facilitates buy-in from the key senior technical people. The organization gets insight as to where bottlenecks are. Tools and procedures for all the phases can now be evaluated. Because a consistent object-oriented approach was used, the end product is more robust and tolerant of requirements or design changes.

IDENTIFYING SYSTEM BOUNDARIES EARLY

Traditional methodologies have long promoted the value of determining system boundaries early in the project. Unfortunately, many object-oriented methodologies seem to ignore the process of identifying system boundaries altogether or include it almost as an afterthought, deferring it until the object model is complete. There are significant advantages to taking a preliminary look at the system boundaries before beginning any work on the object model. By using the system boundaries as a guide, analysts can decide which objects are within the system and which are not, as well as which objects need to be analyzed in detail.

Context Diagrams. Two different ways can be used to identify system boundaries. The first, an object context diagram, is part of the functional model and has its origins in the context diagram used in the structured analysis process. An object context diagram indicates all the external interfaces for an object. By treating the system as a whole as an object, a systems-level object context diagram can be created. As in the traditional context diagram, the system is represented by a centrally placed circle or an oval surrounded by the external entities, which are often called terminators or actors.

As shown in Exhibit II-2-3, a simplified medical insurance system accepts receipts and forms from insured patients and also receives bills directly from

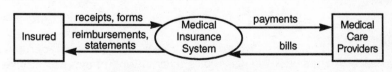

Exhibit II-2-3. System Context Diagram

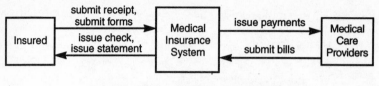

Exhibit II-2-4. System Event Flow Diagram

medical service suppliers. The system can reimburse the insured and may directly pay the medical service suppliers. In this example, the insured and the service suppliers are the actors. The named arrows represent the data (i.e., objects) that flow across the system boundary.

Event Flow Diagrams. System boundaries can also be identified by using a systems-level event flow diagram as shown in Exhibit II-2-4. The event-flow diagram is part of the dynamic model of the system. It captures events and signals that flow among objects. The arrows are labeled to indicate events, signals, messages, or operations that cross an object's boundaries. The systems-level event diagram captures the events that cross the system boundaries as a whole. Actors are represented by class boxes in both diagram forms, which emphasize their object nature. Depending on the nature of the system and its interactions with the outside world, either type of diagram may be appropriate.

Determining which objects are inside the system and which are not is important to place appropriate analysis emphasis. However, objects that represent the actors often appear within the system. For example, in the example medical insurance system, the insured is an actor, but it also appears as a very important object within the system.

Most actors have surrogate objects within the system that are used to track changes to the actor, accumulate historical state information, or buffer input and output to the actual actor. Actors may also have related objects added during design to encapsulate their interfaces. These surrogate objects are only passive and do not need to capture the total behavior of the external object.

If the system boundaries are not determined beforehand, much time can be wasted in detailed analysis of objects that are not actually part of the system. It seems surprising that the importance of determining system boundaries needs to be reemphasized. It appears that in converting to object-oriented analysis, even good system analysts are tempted to jettison this important step.

DEFINING TERMS

Few object-oriented methodologies place adequate importance on the development of a data dictionary (i.e., defining all objects, classes, attributes, roles, operations, messages, events, and other terms used in modeling requirements). Although most organizations have little trouble identifying many objects germane to their business, they often have problems with precisely defining them. Forcing the analysis team to define these objects uncovers many inconsistencies and prevents potential misunderstandings.

Difficulties in defining the terms often arise because no team starts without inheriting some description of the application domain. Significant problems may arise when different functions in business name the same objects differently or, worse, use the same name to refer to different objects. Often the common meaning of the term differs from the internal business meaning, or perhaps the connotation is subtly different.

Some organizations have the advantage of a standardized enterprisewide or domainwide analysis model or are developing one. Even if these models are not object oriented, their standardized common vocabulary is very useful to analysis teams. However, many users and reviewers may continue to use old, non-enterprise-wide, or idiosyncratic terminology. It takes time for an organization to achieve wide levels of acceptance of standard terms and definitions.

Because it is important to ensure that every member of the analysis team understands and accepts these terms and that they are documented for the future, the best approach is not to make assumptions. Analysts should not rely solely on the enterprise model's data dictionary and should provide a data dictionary or glossary for the analysis models that they developed.

It is important that analysis teams recognize the potential for multiple meanings and define precisely all their terms. The most effective approach to establishing consistent and accurate names is to develop a data dictionary from the start of the project and to keep it up-to-date while the analysis models develop. This is difficult because most analysts look upon data dictionaries as part of the dreaded activity of documentation and not as part of the analysis process.

Because the data dictionary is so important to a project, it is well worth the extra effort to initiate its development in an attractive manner. Instead of making the updating of the data dictionary a tedious responsibility assigned to one analyst, project management should make it a team effort to review names and meanings. Although the first team meeting to review proposed definitions may be approached apprehensively by the participants, it usually turns out to be a very productive meeting; many objects are renamed, many terms receive new or modified definitions, and exciting discussion ensues. Also, everyone understands a great deal more about the requirements.

The Role of the Data Dictionary

Most object-oriented computer-assisted software engineering (CASE) tools have a data dictionary that is integrated with the model diagrams and allow users to retrieve instantly or edit the data dictionary entry in context. However, the level of sophistication of these data dictionaries is still weak, and a fully linked hypertext dictionary is most desired. It may be useful when using the more limited CASE tools to keep the data dictionary in a separate tool (e.g., a commercial database or hypertext authoring tool).

The Art of Naming. Although the data dictionary is necessary to capture precise and consistent meanings, it is important to pay attention to the process of selecting names. Precise naming is an art. Poorly chosen names can result in misunderstandings during review of the analysis models and hinder their acceptance. They can also add to a general confusion about the analysis models and add difficulty to their use.

Names need to be short, distinctive, unambiguous, and even politically and emotionally corrrect. It does not add to the acceptance of the models if the terms are unpronounceable, humorous, diagreeable, or radically different from accepted use.

ESTABLISHING AN OPERATIONS CONCEPT FROM THE USER'S VIEWPOINT

Good analysts have always known that an important part of defining a system is defining the operations concept. An operations concept is a description of the overall system from the users' perspective without reference to internals. It is often known by such other names as operational scenarios, scripts, threads, traces, or user modes. The operations concept has the following components:

- The externally visible major system processing modes.
- The identification and description of all users, including operational and maintenance users.
- The roles of all users.
- High-level system scenarios.
- Routine processing.
- Responses to anomalous conditions.
- Periodic or cyclic processing (e.g., daily, monthly, and yearly processing).

It is important that the operations concept also include an estimate of the number, education level, training, and skills for the personnel required to maintain and run the system.

At a high level, it gives a general description of the intended look and feel and the pattern of interaction with the users. In the case of a highly interactive system, the high-level description may be in the form of sample input and output screen images instead of descriptions of the user patterns. An alternative form for interactive systems is an actual running prototype of the user interface. The exact format that the operations concept takes depends on the nature of the system and the extent of user interaction.

Benefits of an Operations Concept

There are many advantages to developing an operations concept for a system. The operations concept helps in identifying external system interfaces and provides a starting point for the development of the system dynamic models and test cases. It helps identify many objects that will be part of the system (e.g., browsers, controllers, and interfaces) and that may have to be included in the analysis-time object model. Other objects identified will need to be added and refined during the system design phase. For large systems, the operations concept is also key to understanding system life-cycle costs as it defines the ongoing staffing needs for operations and maintenance.

The roles identified in the operations concepts should be converted to objects in the object model for which attributes, operations, and associations can be specified. These correspond to job position, task descriptions, and responsibilities for the users and operators. Because system needs in this area are otherwise not apparent until the system is about to be delivered, early insight into cost of operations is very valuable.

Perhaps the greatest value obtained from producing the operations concept is forming a consensus on how the system will operate. Although analysis concentrates on understanding the problem domain and on requirements development and avoids design issues, this bit of system design from the operations concepts can be a great practical help. It is a vision statement that drives the team and generates buy-in from developers, managers, users, and customers. By making the system more real, by providing an image of what the system will be like, the analysis team and all involved can test proposed requirements and features against a more solid plan.

Despite all these benefits, an operations concept is frequently overlooked as a product of the analysis phase, especially in object-oriented projects. Object-oriented methods, of course, tend to be more data oriented than procedure oriented, especially when compared to functional methods. Somehow, this change in emphasis often leads developers to skip this important step. Because the benefits of developing an operations concept early in the analysis phase are so significant, it is apparent that a formal incorporation of this step into all object-oriented methods should soon occur.

Influencing the Choice of Methodology. The integration of this step into the methodologies is a significant factor influencing the choice of methodology for a project. For example, the Object Modeling Technique (OMT) methodology has always emphasized scenarios and event traces, and the Advanced Concepts Center of Martin Marietta has increased the role of the operations concept in the OMT methodology. For projects with very extensive user interaction, a more formal and extensive development of this approach can be found incorporated in the Objectory methodology, with its central emphasis on the Use Case.

KEEPING PREVIOUS IMPLEMENTATION OBJECTS OUT OF CURRENT ANALYSIS

The first step in many object-oriented methodologies, including OMT, is to identify objects, particularly, real-world objects from the application domain.

These are identified before classes or other features. After the real-world objects are identified, the process of abstraction or classification is performed to identify classes. This emphasis on real-world objects is intended to focus the analyst on properties of the actual objects rather than on preconceived notions or distinctions not appropriate to the current problem.

The process of identifying the class hierarchy is postponed until later. Producing the class hierarchy is a mix of generalizing the existing classes to make superclasses and specializing the existing classes to make subclasses. The process of producing the class hierarchy is called generalization, which highlights its bottom-up nature. The analysts' attention is thus directed toward the application requirements and away from design or implementation objects.

Although this works successfully to produce appropriate class hierarchies, it is not always effective in keeping out the taint of existing design and implementation objects from the analysis. Users and analysts, even those new to object-oriented technology, have little difficulty after appropriate training in identifying the many objects in their application domain. Although rudimentary, the identification of objects by examining the concrete nouns of the problem statement gives surprisingly good results, especially when supplemented by real-world knowledge.

However, when the new system is a replacement for an existing system, the choice of analysis objects is likely to be compromised by the previous implementation's objects. It is important to remember that the objects found in the old system are only implementation objects and may bear no relationship to the underlying requirements. An extra test on each object identified for replacement systems should be performed to verify that the object forms part of the natural discourse of the system used by people unfamiliar with its implementation.

There are times when including preexisting implementation objects is appropriate. Not every object model must be an analysis model; sometimes an existing system must be modeled for reengineering, migration, or documentation purposes. Including objects that fail, the natural discourse test may then be acceptable. Even in these circumstances, however, it is important that objects are justified. Including objects because they have always been included simply perpetuates the past without progress.

HAVING USERS PARTICIPATE

One of the advantages of using object-oriented techniques to develop systems is their suitability for user participation during development, especially during the analysis phase. It has been a longtime goal that users of a system be extensively involved in the development of system requirements. The advantages of their participation are that they are more likely to understand, accept, and ultimately benefit from a system that they themselves have helped to define. Because no one knows the actual requirements better than the users, their active participation can enable analysis to progress on systems with initially vague or incomplete requirements.

Although there is nothing specifically object oriented about this practice, using object-oriented techniques during the analysis phases enables the work to proceed using application discourse terms, keeping the focus on requirements, and inhibiting premature design.

Adding users to the analysis team does not always guarantee a focus on requirements. Some end users are also developers or maintainers themselves. It is these end users who are most likely to be assigned to help develop a replacement system. If the users are also programmers, especially maintenance programmers of the existing system, they usually think primarily in design or implementation terminology. They are accustomed to thinking in terms of fixes rather than in terms of requirements. Analysis as a separate phase from design may be foreign to them and they may be frustrated by the pace of the project and wish to get on with the implementation.

It is still important to keep the analysis team focused on requirements while not frustrating any of the team members to the point that they are no longer productive. Whenever a digression into design is recognized, the domain-oriented requirements should be separated from the design approaches. Only the domain-oriented requirements should be used for the analysis models, but suggestions concerning design or implementation should not be ignored. These suggestions should be recorded as notes or annotations attached to the analysis models for consideration later. Not only does this minimize frustration by allowing contributors to feel that their input is important, but it also captures potentially good design ideas from experienced users.

Although object-oriented analysis makes it easier to bring users and analysts together than structured analysis does, it does not solve all the problems. A close correspondence between analysis objects and the real world (i.e., between analysis terminology and domain discourse) does not necessarily cause a close correspondence between the goals or expectations of the users and analysts. Especially on the first attempt, differences in goals and approach of the team members may seem insurmountable. It is often useful to have a neutral facilitator lead the analysis. A facilitator can encourage team development by evaluating and incorporating input from all members, as well as keeping the team focused on the needs of analysis.

AVOIDING TOO MUCH CHANGE

Besides making the transition to object-oriented technology, many organizations are also moving away from traditional mainframe projects. Development is now often on a PC or workstation, and the target environment may be client/server or even a distributed environment. New user interfaces, operating systems, languages, and tools are also sweeping the development organization.

This is a whole lot of change to integrate at once. If a project fails in some way (e.g., is not completed or completed over schedule and budget), it is easy to blame object-oriented technology, though object technology is just one of the new technologies being used.

Encapsulating New Technology. It is very difficult to manage the process of technology transfer. Because changing even a single technology is painful and changing many technologies can be disastrous, the best strategy is to introduce new technologies or approaches gradually, one at a time. Unfortunately, this is not always possible—there always seems to be good business or technical reasons for wanting to leap into the future. It is important, then, to take advantage of the object-oriented techniques to encapsulate the new technologies and hide areas of potential change and uncertainty.

Of course, management must plan for sufficient training in all the new technologies, not only financially but to include the training and learning curve in the schedule. The promises of performance and productivity improvements from the new technologies may eventually be realized, but they usually are not available on the first project.

NOT SKIMPING ON ANALYSIS

When applying object-oriented techniques on their first project, many developers become concerned about the amount of time spent in the analysis phase. It is natural to be anxious about the schedule, and they want to begin design and start coding soon. In some organizations, there never has been a separate analysis phase. In others, where an analysis phase based on structured techniques was performed, they became accustomed to building just one model of their system during analysis. Most object-oriented methodologies require several models to be built (i.e., object, dynamic, and functional). The extra time required to build these three models may be seen as unnecessary.

What some developers do not realize is that more upfront effort spent in analysis and in understanding the requirements is more likely to yield a system that is actually a success. Failed or significantly delayed systems or extreme cost overruns are not caused by analysis paralysis. One of the major factors seems to be incorrect or inconsistent requirements. If the requirements are wrong, the system built from them is also wrong. It is best to understand what the requirements are and what the customer really wants at the start of the project than to have them painfully understood at the end of the project.

Object-oriented analysis increases the amount of time spent in the analysis phases. Exhibit II-2-5 illustrates typical distribution of efforts for object-oriented and non-object-oriented projects. Increasing the amount of time spent during analysis actually benefits the entire project. Time spent thinking about what needs to be done before doing it is a sound investment. Problems found early in the systems life cycle are much easier and cheaper to fix than those

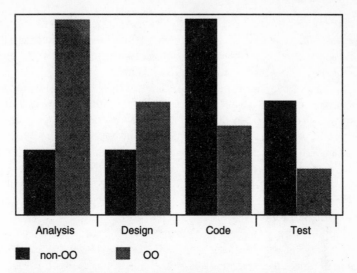

Exhibit II-2-5. Effort by Phase: Non-Object-Oriented Development Versus Object-Oriented Development

found later. Also, when problems are found in object-oriented systems, they are easier to diagnose and fix. Despite the increase in the time for analysis, time to complete does not usually increase for object-oriented projects.

It appears that as the organization's experience with object-oriented development increases, and the organization's library of reusable objects grows, the total time to complete a project may significantly decrease. The extra time spent in analysis is often a significant problem for the first few object-oriented projects that an organization attempts. The problem is not of technical origin but of managerial origin. Managers and users often become impatient with any delay of design and coding because of their expectation of the traditional effort required in the later phases of development. Sometimes management even gets the idea that because object-oriented development is so highly touted, analysis should be faster than before. Pressure from these forces can prematurely cut short the analysis phase, which always spells trouble, but can be more problematic with the extended object-oriented analysis phase. It will take several successful projects to convince all concerned that the proportion of effort required for each phase has permanently changed.

Overcoming Resistance

There are some strategies that might help. With object-oriented development and its use of application domain terms and concepts with a simple consistent notation comes the increased possibility for user input and interaction. The developers should take advantage of this opportunity to enlist customer forces in the project. If they identify with the project and understand the progress being made they will become allies of the development team.

It is also necessary to develop interim milestones so that the worried can review progress without waiting until the end of the analysis phase. For example, in large projects one can do enough analysis to get a preliminary cut at subsystems and set a review at this time. Another approach is to separate the analysis phase into domain analysis, application analysis, system requirements analysis, and software requirements analysis. Not only are reviews at these points politically necessary, but they meet the need for periodic in-depth technical reviews and feedback. These reviews can become an important component to successful analysis.

Another strategy is to reexamine the development model. Most organizations use variations on the traditional waterfall development model, which increases the time until the analysis milestone is met. Alternatives include several parallel waterfalls, the spiral, or the fountain development models, which are very well suited for object-oriented development. These development models also encourage the development of prototypes, especially user-interface prototypes, which can demonstrate progress and are good analysis tools for refining requirements.

Prototypes are particularly suited for object-oriented development because object-oriented interfaces are more stable and less dependent on implementation, and advance development in key areas runs less risk of needing rework later. These techniques enable an organization to demonstrate successful progress while it establishes a standard object-oriented development baseline.

CONCLUSION
Action Plan

When an organization faces the challenges of making the transition to object-oriented development, it should remember that though many traditional concerns of the analyst remain the same, they may need to be updated. The guidelines discussed in this chapter include the following:

- Knowing which objects are in the system and which are not.
- Carefully naming and defining objects.
- Understanding how the objects and users work together.
- Keeping previous implementation objects out of current analysis.
- Soliciting users' knowledge for the objects models.
- Using objects to encapsulate change.
- Preparing for a longer analysis phase.

Organizations may find that they need to formally document their existing procedures and the changes needed to adapt them to object-oriented technology. Less formal organizations may still need to document the changes in some manner. The first cut at these procedures and processes often undergoes considerable changes as it matures in a fashion suitable for the organization. By documenting the process and allowing for feedback and changes, the organization embarks on the path of continuous process improvement. Using experienced staff members and outside mentors expert in object-oriented technology, each organization must develop its own object-oriented practices and procedures reflecting the history, education, and experience of its staff.

II-3
Getting Ready for Strategic Change

ROCCO W. BELMONTE • RICHARD J. MURRAY

Recent statistics show that less than 45% of companies that try business process redesign are successful at achieving their intended goals. This may seem surprising, but change management specialists assert that fewer than one in five endeavors to implement major change initiatives in companies succeed. Because business process redesign (BPR) represents major organizational and cultural change, organizations should not be discouraged by this low rate of success. Businesses can succeed at redesign if they are deliberate and if they conscientiously understand what they are undertaking.

Nolan, Norton & Co., which has wide-ranging BPR experience, has identified five factors that companies must satisfy to succeed at redesign. These include:

- Understanding the company's need for BPR and defining new levels of performance in business terms that will focus the design.
- Assessing the readiness of the business to undergo strategic change.
- Organizing a campaign that carefully incorporates change management in the process.
- Carefully examining how information technologies can enable new decision-making capabilities.
- Understanding the pitfalls other companies have encountered in their approaches to BPR.

Companies can no longer afford to forego strategic change if they want to sustain competitive advantage in global markets. And in this environment, business processes are more important than ever before. In his book *Head to Head: The Coming Economic Battle Among Japan, Europe, and America,* Lester Thurow comments:

"In the past economic winners were those who invented new products. But in the twenty-first century sustainable competitive advantage will come more out of new process technologies and much less out of new product technologies. Reverse engineering has become an art form. New products can easily be reproduced. What used to be primary (inventing new products) becomes secondary, and what used to be secondary (inventing and perfecting new processes) becomes primary."

DEFINING BUSINESS PROCESS REDESIGN

Like any new management practice, BPR means different things to different people. Some describe BPR as an intelligent alternative to downsizing and a means to translate vision into action. The common elements used to describe BPR are:

- Radical redesign.
- Dramatic improvement.
- Process integration (rather than process independence).

BPR is radical because it challenges the assumption of status quo and the need to perform a process. It deals with innovative approaches to business processes rather than incremental improvements to business operations. In contrast, continuous process improvement strives to incrementally enhance the performance of an existing business process.

The term "reengineering" is frequently used to describe BPR, implying that existing processes were once designed. Actually, most of today's business processes evolved with little or no design embodied, and without consideration of the opportunities provided by technology. Many processes were developed in response to business paradigms that may no longer be valid.

Dramatic improvement means quantum gains of 5 to 10 times compared to incremental improvements of 20% to 30%. BPR achieves radical business performance improvements. These improvements are generally characterized in terms of time reductions (such as faster time to market, reduced process costs, or improved product or service quality.) Many times these are not independent variables, and the goals usually include improved quality at one-half the current cost.

In short, BPR is the practice of designing new paradigms. Specifically, existing paradigms are frames of reference expressed through rules, policies, procedures, structures, values, and beliefs. These filters, or frames of reference, must be recognized, challenged, and transformed. An effective technique for achieving paradigm breakthroughs is by establishing stretch goals—that is, goals that seem impossible today and can only be achieved by challenging current assumptions about the business and its processes. Unless companies set goals and develop future visions, they may roam aimlessly in redesign efforts.

DEFINING NEW PERFORMANCE GOALS IN BUSINESS TERMS

Corporate America is facing unparalleled challenges to its once unsurpassed prosperity. Global competitors are entering US markets, profit margins are shrinking, industries are deregulating and re-regulating, and products are experiencing shorter life cycles. Customer demands are increasing, and most companies' abilities to meet these expectations are only incrementally improving. Many companies realize that unless they take corrective action to address these new challenges and meet these expectations, they may not survive in the new global marketplace.

The first step toward success is recognizing the need for change. Strategic threats have a way of accentuating management awareness of the need to change. Benchmarking against best-in-class companies is a way to reveal the extent of change needed. Corporations or divisions of major corporations facing these threats are obvious candidates for BPR. There are also many companies that must anticipate future performance levels and design toward that end. In the case of General Motors, for example, management didn't anticipate performance changes soon enough or react to the strategic threat once it was apparent. Ford did, and it is continuing to progress.

Peformance goals must be described in business terms that energize the organization's thinking. For example, for one company, time-based competition may mean trying to become a superfast innovator who introduces new products to market in shorter time frames. It may also mean trying to introduce more features to existing products faster. For some companies time-based competition means becoming superfast producers by putting existing products in the customer's hands in ever-shorter time frames. For other companies, it means reducing service order cycle times from days to hours, or shipping orders in days instead of weeks. Each organization must define stretch goals in terms of cycle-time-reduction at favorable cost positions.

Many companies today pursue such solutions as BPR or Toal Quality Management (TQM) without understanding future performance level goals. They apply the processes to intangible targets. Often, they inadequately define root causes of business problems. It is important to delineate between means and ends. BPR is a means rather than an end in itself. Future performance targets are a way to focus the efforts and ensure a higher potential for success.

ASSESSING YOUR READINESS FOR BUSINESS PROCESS REDESIGN

Understanding the need for BPR is just the beginning. Another step is to assess the organization's readiness to successfully undertake the challenge of redesign.

Two components of this readiness analysis are today's management systems and organization capabilities, and the organization's capacity for change. Taken together, the management system and organization structure is a BPR issue; the capacity for change is a change management issue. Both need attention in BPR. Following are examples of some elements that can be measured within each of these components.

- Management systems and organization structure criteria include:
  —Capability for process thinking (cross-functional analytical abilities).
  —Clarity of business vision and direction.
  —Suitability of current organization structures (nonrigid hierarchy).
  —Relevance of performance measures and reward systems.
  —Knowledge of and sensitivity to customer needs.
  —Level of employee involvement and empowerment.
  —Ability of information technology to deliver quality products and services in a timely manner.
- Organization capacity for change criteria include:
  —Degree and quality of sponsorship and commitment to change.
  —Cultural alignment with change.
  —Level of resistance to change throughout the organization.
  —Effectiveness of change agents to enable and support change.
  —Track record for undertaking major change in the past.

Exhibit II-3-1 illustrates an analytical framework Nolan, Norton uses to understand and manage BPR readiness. Business need is plotted against readiness in order to calibrate the criticality versus the risk of BPR. Understanding your organization's readiness and taking corrective action to prepare for the journey is a large part of getting the organization where it wants to go.

Positioning in a quadrant is a first-cut look at how to proceed. Quadrants I and II represent the Critical Zone, where a BPR effort needs to be launched

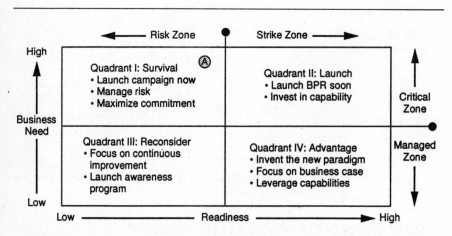

This framework can be used to determine how critical major innovation and change is at the present time and how ready your organization is for successful BPR.

Key: Ⓐ Your company

SOURCE: Nolan, Norton & Co.

Exhibit II-3-1. BPR Need/Readiness Analysis.

as soon as possible. Quadrants III and IV represent the Managed Zone, where there is less urgency for business process redesign and any effort should in fact be approached carefully. Quadrants I and III represent the Risk Zone, where significant effort should be focused on preparation and managing risk. Quadrants II and IV represent the Strike Zone, where launching a BPR effort has a high probability of yielding strategic advantage. The quadrants are further described as follows:

- *Quadrant I.* Labeled Survival, to indicate it is critical to improve business performance as soon as possible. Quadrant I endeavors are high risk and require maximum sponsorship commitment and a heavy investment in risk management.
- *Quadrant II.* Labeled Launch, to indicate it is critical to improve business performance. Because there is only a moderate risk to engage in BPR, companies would benefit from investing in the development of BPR capabilities and launching an effort soon.
- *Quadrant III.* Labeled Reconsider, to indicate the company is healthy and has a low need for dramatic improvement at this time. Companies in this quadrant are also not well equipped for BPR. Such companies should reconsider launching BPR and instead focus more on continuous process improvement.
- *Quadrant IV.* Labeled Advantage, to indicate that although there is no urgency for dramatic improvement, there would be a strategic advantage in undertaking a BPR initiative. Companies in this quadrant are prepared for BPR, but undertaking such an effort requires an aggressive vision that seeks to create new paradigms.

Senior Management's Involvement

Critical to successful BPR is the involvement of senior management in the redesign process. Redesign requires the collective intellectual capacity of senior management and the energy of employees. If there is one common failure, it is the failure of key management to get involved and stay the course. This is a change for senior managers. Therefore, the readiness of senior management and the organization to undertake the strategic change of redesign should be assessed. If the organization is not ready, it is better to wait until the understanding, commitment, and participation needed from your business can be ensured. After the need and readiness for the BPR effort are addressed, an informed go, no-go decision can be made.

CHANGE MANAGEMENT: ORGANIZING THE CAMPAIGN

Business redesign is synonymous with change or transformation. One executive's perspective is that process redesign is akin to changing a flat tire without stopping the car. That analogy certainly conveys a message of risk and complexity. Thousands of books have been written on the discipline of change management. Change management is a science in itself. With process design, the organization must grasp the extent of direction of change. In other words, what is the organization trying to create?

Organizational change presents equal and opposite resistance to process redesign implementation efforts. As a result, some subliminal human factors must be addressed. At any point in time, people have varying capacities to assimilate change due to personal and business circumstances. If process redesign is to be sustained over the long run, the capacity for change needs to be measured and steps taken to remove natural barriers. The goal of process redesign is not just to implement a new way of doing business, but to internalize it and improve the process going forward. BPR creates change on two fronts: designing the process and then implementing the process.

Design

Designing new business processes involves a team of people chartered to transform the way business is conducted. It involves changing the perspectives of individual people and includes:

- *Systems thinking.* This defines the whole process (as opposed to any individual part) of adding value. It focuses on internal and external interdependencies of suppliers, employees, and customers. The team must understand how each of the steps in the process influences the whole process of creating value.
- *Understanding how value is created.* This perspective focuses on customers and, most important, includes defining what value is in the eyes of the customer.
- *Employee empowerment.* People should be encouraged and able to initiate innovative ideas, make decisions, and change management decision-making processes to make the company more flexible and responsive.

Implementation

The second front must consider the change necessary to implement the new process design. It must deal with nontraditional or new:

- Organization structures that are cross-disciplinary.
- Job content and skills.
- Responsibilities and accountabilities.
- Performance measures and incentive systems.

Any approach to BPR that does not have an integrated approach to managing organizational change will have a lower probability of success. Furthermore, if the ability or resources to manage the change process are not available, the organization needs to acquire the capability through specialists. Questions to address at the outset of redesign efforts include:

- Who from senior management owns the change agenda as new processes are designed?

- Who manages, focuses, and executes the process for change? Is it the design team, the executive committee, or the organization design group within the human resources function?
- What is the business risk of not succeeding with strategic change?
- What is the change management campaign and how is it integrated into the process design approach?
- How can the business and the information technology group change together?

Because BPR results in innovative business transformation, existing paradigms are challenged. Changing the way work is performed, as well as the job content and skills of individuals, are natural outcomes of a redesign effort. Change must be confronted by your organization. Therefore, management of change must be an integral part of the process. It is also an integral component of risk management. It is a means to ensure desired results are achieved within established time frames.

A carefully orchestrated game plan must be developed for each front of the redesign campaign. Each phase of the campaign must be delineated by time and required logistics. You must define which beachheads to secure before another phase of the campaign can proceed. Business process redesign is a strategic change event in the history of a business. It is limiting and dangerous to view BPR as a project.

Three important fronts to the redesign campaign that must be addressed are:

- *Process.* The steps and activities associated with creating customer value. What are they and what will they look like in the future?
- *People.* The quantity and skills of individuals needed to support the new process. What are the new skills, capabilities, and competencies of the business?
- *Technology.* The technology needed to enable process transformation. How will information technology be deployed to support the new business processes?

INFORMATION TECHNOLOGY: THE ENABLING FACTOR

Innovation and major improvements in performance are difficult to achieve without leveraging the potential of information technology. Information technology often enables BPR, and in many cases, business processes cannot be restructured without it. Therefore, it is important to understand the role of IT in business process redesign.

Applying process redesign without considering technology usually yields marginal business improvements. In fact, over the past 20 years, industry has done just the opposite. Businesses have assumed they improved business processes by automating rather than redesigning them. Today, organizations must redesign business processes before automating them.

To succeed, business and IT managers must view business process design and the deployment of information technology as mutually supportive and synergistic. There has been limited success with business process redesign when IT leads the effort. It is not a question of capability, but one of credibility in the eyes of the business. IT management must be an integral member of redesign teams because it is on the critical path in redesign efforts. However, because the business management team members inherit the new processes, it is appropriate that they be responsible and accountable for the results.

In many cases, IT needs to redesign itself in advance of the business. The IT group should focus on developing a clear technology infrastructure strategy. New applications and support services are required to support more highly integrated and interdependent business processes.

COMMON PITFALLS TO AVOID

Occasionally, the best way to provide insight is to describe how other companies have stumbled while attempting process redesign. Collective experience reveals some common pitfalls.

Pitfall #1: Guru Trap. Senior management is lured into BPR by eloquent and dynamic experts who write and speak about the promised land of BPR. However, most of these experts rarely manage or even participate in the redesign efforts they sell. When they leave and the redesign begins without experienced consultants, results fall short of expectations. Inflated expectations and inadequate attention to the company's readiness for BPR are the causes. Many experts and consultants are reluctant to frighten clients by telling them the truth about all the areas that should be addressed when undertaking the BPR commitment.

Pitfall #2: Poor Methods. Some people believe methods have more to do with actual outcome than do objectives. Few cookbook methodologies exist for performing BPR today because it is a relatively new management discipline. BPR is a creative design process. Creative energy and thinking "outside the box" is needed. Formal methodologies rarely provide creative thinking and usually provide a false sense of comfort. Yet there is a place for descriptive methods. There are many techniques, tools, and frameworks that can be applied to stimulate thinking, analyze processes, and simulate new designs. Candidates include:

- *Value chain analysis.* To analyze how customer value is created.
- *Stretch goal setting.* To force thinking beyond today's paradigm.
- *Process modeling tools.* To describe processes.
- *Simulation modeling tools.* To dynamically change process designs and see resulting implications.

The methodology used for BPR must also integrate with the methodology for change management.

Pitfall #3: The Wrong Team. The wrong team or time commitments from team members usually generates less than adequate results and impedes future redesign efforts. There is no substitute for securing the right people to perform redesign. It is essential that a team represents the various business constituencies affected by redesign. It should comprise the organization's best and brightest people. Team roles should be clearly identified and a strong team leader who has the prestige to get things done within the company must be chosen. Teams should also include analytical systems thinkers who have BPR expertise and are willing to challenge the status quo. This often requires outside assistance from people who can objectively challenge the team and facilitate the effort.

Pitfall #4: Inadequate Management Commitment. Management commitment and active involvement are essential for successful redesign. Active involvement means there are certain nondelegable tasks in which the sponsor must participate. For example, when setting product stretch goals, corporate executives should be included because they are often best suited to define the future product development life cycle time. If executive sponsors are truly committed, they will invest in the new design and be willing to discard traditional rules and structures.

Pitfall #5: Short-Term Results Orientation. It is important to achieve near-term benefits in order to build the momentum for change. If too much pressure is exerted for immediate results, however, the potential for strategic change is limited. In today's business climate, it is much easier to launch a BPR effort than it is to sustain the effort. In some cases, there is extreme pressure on executives to improve performance immediately. To achieve the big payoff BPR can bring, organizations must set and manage expectations on the longer-term results. Effective BPR teams identify quickstrike opportunities that can be implemented within a few weeks or months, knowing that most major benefits will be realized in two or three years.

Pitfall #6: Ignoring the Impact of IT. Although business process redesign is not an IT-led activity, IT does provide a critical role in enabling the new design. If management is unwilling to acknowledge the role of IT, or does not consider how IT can provide support for radical new ways of doing business, the results will be less than dramatic. It is nearly impossible to reach stretch goals without effectively using information technologies.

Pitfall #7: Inadequate Preparation. A reasonable portion of the BPR effort must be spent in preparing to launch a successful process. It is important to develop a clear and compelling business case for action and to heighten the level of awareness about BPR throughout the business. Once shortcomings are understood, corrective action can be taken to build a more prepared team. The "ready, fire, aim" approach, without appropriate training, will certainly lead to undesirable consequences.

Pitfall #8: Focusing Solely on Cost Reduction. Most BPR efforts today focus primarily on reducing costs, which ultimately translates to large staff reductions. This is a natural tendency, because BPR is viewed by many as an intelligent alternative to downsizing. The pressure on companies to be more cost-competitive is real; however, focusing only on cost meets with much greater resistance by employees and ignores even greater business opportunities for strategic change. Innovative, breakthrough thinking related to new products and services, new market penetration, or the development of new distribution channels must be designed into the process.

Pitfall #9: Letting IT Managers Lead the BPR Effort. Although the IT function can be the catalyst for introducing BPR into the organization and for supporting the analysis, the process owner must assume sponsorship of the initiative. BPR efforts led by IT have a high failure rate because of IT's inability to address the policy, procedures, and organizational issues critical to successful redesign. However, IT professionals can be a valuable asset to a BPR team; they understand process analysis more easily than do people from most other business functions. Effective redesign requires executive management support and a functional head to be the primary sponsor of the effort and to take charge of implementing the required changes.

CONCLUSION

These guidelines may seem simple, but even the most experienced practitioners of process redesign testify to how difficult it is to avoid the common pitfalls. Ideally, an organization wants to get the approach totally correct. Realistically, it must strike a workable balance. Only experience can tell when the balance is appropriate. Companies that are serious about BPR must be prepared to launch a campaign, not just fund a project.

To sustain enhanced business performance, companies must ultimately create learning organizations that thrive on change—organizations that are flexible, adaptable, and responsive to a changing competitive landscape. The characteristics of a learning organization are comprehensively defined in Peter Senge's book *The Fifth Discipline: The Art and Practice of the Learning Organization.* In short, a learning organization is one that rapidly adapts to change in competitive forces or the environment. More advanced learning organizations anticipate and prepare for change. The most advanced learning organizations actually create change to their competitive advantage. Learning faster than your competitors is the primary force. If companies can accomplish these goals—and many can with the help of BPR—staying on the leading edge will be simpler.

II-4

Corporate Downsizing and New Technology

MAX H. MIRANDA • NAOMI A. TELLERMAN

Business conditions influence corporate decisions to restructure the organization. The influence that corporate restructuring has on IS is discussed in the context of decisions to adopt new technology such as CASE and in the description of a failed CASE implementation at one oil and gas company.

The current trend to redirect the strategic direction of corporations has led to the elimination of activities of low-value contributors in a company. IS is not exempt from this review. IS departments are increasingly pressured to estimate the value of information systems and information technology to the point that their survival depends on their effect on the corporate bottom line.

In the enterprisewide information management model, information systems are justified by the users of the applications.[1] Information technology is, however, a need justified by IS management in order to achieve the ultimate information needs of the corporation. Computer-aided software engineering is one of the technologies generally designed to improve the quality, quantity, and speed of the work done by systems analysts and programmers. Traditionally, the IS department justifies its projects on the basis of the cost versus benefits. The estimate of benefits is usually provided by the user. To enable IS to achieve the client's requirements for software, the tools are usually justified by IS management according to its technical knowledge and experience with and perception of the corporate strategic direction.

This chapter shows the major hurdles IS managers must overcome to implement technology such as in a CASE restructuring corporation. An understanding of the obstacles may help IS managers assess the value of CASE and the method most likely to be successful in implementing CASE technology in today's environment.

BUSINESS AND INFORMATION TECHNOLOGY FACTORS

Several business and information technology-driven factors must be considered. Business factors include:

- The nature of the business.
- The environment and business situation.

- The availability of packaged applications.
- The economics of CASE.

The information technology domain includes factors such as:

- IS management vision.
- Attitude to new technology.
- The maturity of the IS department.
- The IS planning horizon.

Nature of the Business

Most IS departments have built applications over the years in response to business demands. As business expanded, so did the number of applications and the size of the IS department. The nature of the business has a bearing on the strategic importance of information technology. For example, if the business is in the consumer industry, such as banking or transportation, the use of IT is demonstrably strategic and can be shown as directly affecting business performance. In the resource sector, such as the oil and gas industry, the IS function is usually regarded as nonstrategic except as it applies to exploration analysis and processing. Commercial applications are characterized mainly by recordkeeping or accounting processes. The application of IT is not critical to the performance of the company. Therefore, the IS function is nonstrategic to the corporation.

IS is positioned in corporations in direct relation to the importance of its applications. The strategic direction toward in-house development versus packaged software determines the extent of the use of CASE. Companies whose IS function is actively pursuing internal development are most likely to benefit from the use of CASE technology to achieve data standardization, improved design quality, higher level of control, documentation, flexibility, and productivity increases in the long run. Ultimately, general function modules can be reused for various applications, thereby decreasing development time and increasing the IS function's ability to deliver the right system at the right time. This condition occurs if the business depends on information technology to be successful. CASE is likely to make inroads where the IS portfolio is strategic to the successful operation of the corporation.

The Environment and Business Situation

In a period of declining production, price volatility, high interest, high overhead, and environmentalism, organizations continue to formulate strategies to survive and compete effectively. Corporations are looking inward and reevaluating their operations. Information technology increases the speed of feedback mechanisms. The resultant effect has been increased pressure for corporations to respond to indices of performance. This pressure of competition has so far meant that minimizing the cost of production is critical and that companies are concentrating their efforts on their core business and on measures to increase profitability. This effort has led to the elimination of redundant positions, including most existing support functions.

Nonstrategic IS departments are in a vulnerable position, especially if they rarely contribute to the corporate bottom line. If they are perceived by senior management as a necessary evil, a support function that is neither efficient nor effective, they become candidates for budget cuts. This perception is the product of a history of unfinished projects, projects whose costs doubled or tripled from their initial estimates, and projects that after implementation were rejected by users for not meeting their business needs. As a result, IS is seen as expensive and is put increasingly on the defensive.

Outsourcing, or obtaining information technology application services from outside the corporation, is becoming an attractive option. The extent this alternative is used ranges from replacing one specific function to abolishing the entire IS development department in favor of third-party systems developers.

Cost control and reduction is not the only reason for outsourcing the IS function. In some cases, the maintenance function is contracted out so that the efforts of IS resources can be concentrated in new development. It is a reality IS management must contend with today. The IS manager has to be as flexible as a business executive.

In a situation of total outsourcing, management's goal is to establish a contractual agreement that can provide a fair return on the service contracted. The focus is on deliveries on time, on budget, and as specified at a set price and, most important, on a lights-out implementation. Quality is not pushed aside, but as long as the product meets the user requirements, the methodology used is not an issue. Therefore, it is mostly up to the contractor to decide on the methodology. CASE methodology is likely to be promoted by the corporation only if it intends to add to or modify the application. Outsourcing does not dictate the use of CASE. A combination of business needs, the extent of outsourcing, and the IS methodology in place at the time of outsourcing all provide the parameters to select a methodology that is acceptable to the business and that provides the contractor the tools to meet its obligations successfully and economically.

Availability of Packaged Applications

Business professionals and their IS counterparts are often confronted with the choice between developing new applications internally or selecting an application package from a third-party vendor. The number of available software packages for all platforms has grown, with the microcomputer area presenting the highest activity. Packaged applications provide an option for quick implementation of solutions. This alternative to internal development is also less risky when the package can be readily demonstrated and the vendor has a track record for supporting it. The less strategic orientation the IS department has, the more attractive packaged applications are perceived as a primary method of delivering solutions.

Although the IS structure and its supporting technologies influence the decision of which package to purchase, the availability of packaged solutions drives the user's decision. Users know what is available and understand how to apply third-party software to their advantage. This new generation of application users is increasingly demanding from IS the quick delivery of instant-gratification software. Software vendors offer sophisticated software at reduced prices and have scaled-up user support functions to satisfy the increased demand. This support includes their own IS professionals working together with the application user to ensure a successful installation. The downsizing of corporations directly translates to increased purchasing of packaged software because IS personnel and budgets can be reduced and the company can concentrate its activities in its core competence.

Economics of CASE Technology

The cost of instituting CASE in the IS department mitigates against successful implementation. Currently, the entry cost is high relative to what can be gained. CASE tools composed of planning, analysis, design, and construction modules sell on the average of $50,000 per set for starter kits. Hardware requirements must include an inordinate amount of memory, resulting in expenditures ranging from $15,000 to $25,000 per practitioner. The cost of training adds a minimum of 10% to the software cost.

Depending on the size of the CASE application, it is reasonable to expect to invest from $100,000 to $1 million. For the benefits to be worth the costs, productivity gains must at least equal this expenditure. The science of measuring the benefits of IT is not yet fully developed or understood. In IS, budget savings may be extracted from either hardware costs or salary and benefits. The cost of CASE tools have to be borne by the reduction of salary and benefits expense. If the payback period is one year, a 25% reduction for a $4 million IS payroll is required to save $1 million. IS managers cannot guarantee that CASE can increase quality output—but rather it can run up training costs and lower productivity during implementation because of the learning period. Downsizing strategies usually decrease the budget for retraining employees.

IS Management Vision

If the benefit is that the IS function's contributing to the business is nonstrategic, the management vision will provide solutions at the lowest cost available with a short-term view. Older equipment is considered attractive as long as it works. Maintenance activity is high but overall cost is low because equipment costs are not significant. This is a vision for low-risk takers. Little time is allowed to gain the benefits from developing new applications. The IS team is risk averse; the department works within two extremes: high-payback projects with short duration or low-risk projects with unnoticed high duration.

Strategic-based IS shops have a longer-term vision. IS management believes that new technology can yield significant benefits and invests in these ventures. Research and development money is included in the budget. In this situation, CASE is looked upon as a means to increasing IS value contribution to the organization.

These are the extreme ends of the spectrum: the ultraconservative function that is almost grinding to a halt and the visionary risk taker that is looking for the big payoff. As a leading-edge technology, CASE attracts those with expertise and confidence who can afford to wait for the payoff.

Attitude Toward New Technology

It is an accepted observation that programmers and analysts become comfortable in their expertise in the languages, system software, and data base management system they are accustomed to working with. The trend to standardize in DB2 and SQL environments has divided the community of programmers. CASE vendors design their tools to work with DB2, SQL, and procedural languages such as COBOL and PL/1. This has two drawbacks. First, the IS staff resists throwing away its expertise, especially if its technical know-how is not in the mainstream technology. If their expertise is in a procedural language, IS staff members feel that their knowledge is better than the CASE expert system. If their experience is in a 4GL, CASE is anachronistic in its preference to generate COBOL code. The design tools are based on designing DB2/SQL systems. Therefore, CASE has a problem to overcome in the community of practitioners that it is supported to help. A closed attitude no doubt stops any movement to apply new technology.

Maturity of the IS Department

Organizations at the start of their charters are filled with dynamism and evolve to the growth and maturity stages. The growth phase reaches the maturity stage when the thinking can be exemplified by the phrase "all systems that will ever be developed are developed." Sometimes, organizations reach this stage artificially, and IS is no exception to this.

Mature IS shops stay with the same vendor or with one version of software, claiming that the cost of change is formidable. This is artificially justified when capital is conserved by not acquiring new technology; instead, maintenance (expense) dollars receive priority and are perceived as sunk costs. In this environment, CASE is not favored. In the growth phase, however, new tools and technology are viewed as potential benefactors to the information processing effort. This is the moment rich for technology breakthrough. This is the proving ground for CASE technology. Optimism in a growth environment is healthy for adopting new information technologies. Organizations closer to the marketplace have the most to gain from CASE technology. Software application vendors on the leading edge point to CASE technology as the basis for their competitive strength.

IS Planning Horizon

A corporation's planning horizon affects the IS horizon. Planning horizons used to expand five to ten years with reviews done annually, but clearly, as feedback of performance is hastened by newer, faster, and better systems, the planning horizon is shortened. Therefore, IS must produce output in a shorter time frame. Users cannot wait for four-year projects; they want solutions that are operational today or they demand waiting periods no longer than six to nine months. This puts the onus on IS for finding faster solutions. CASE must prove its worth if it is to compete with packaged turnkey solutions. CASE has an edge if no package is available and internal development can be accomplished within a time frame acceptable to the application user. This shortening of the planning horizon is influencing the promised deliverable for CASE technology.

A PRACTICAL SCENARIO

These business and information technology factors that influence decisions about CASE use are further explained in the case study described in the following paragraphs.

Nature of the Business. The company is a fully owned subsidiary in the oil and gas industry and makes most of its money upstream, in the exploration and production of oil and gas properties. The company's IS function was perceived as not strategic to the business. The information was decentralized and difficult to share across applications. Management appeared to have mixed feelings about accepting this prevalent condition.

Availability of Packaged Applications. The mandate was to replace an aging accounting system. Initially, a consulting firm was contracted by the user to identify vendors of accounting packages. The oil and gas industry's downturn resulted in the project being scaled back to an accounts-payable system only.

The project was later revived and led by users with a preference for packaged solutions. The availability of packaged software made this option a contender for solving the user problem. A review of products was held with product demonstrations. Following these activities, a package was selected. Technically, the package did not fit the company's computer environment; however, the users were convinced of the package's fit. The package selection and installation was by all accounts a user-driven process.

Economics of CASE. The newly hired project manager was a proponent of CASE technology and convinced the company to purchase one physical workstation and three information engineering modules (i.e., planning, analysis, and design) and to budget for training for four staff members. The total expense amounted to 1% to 2% of the IS budget.

The expectations were that CASE technology would reduce the development time by three to eight times compared to traditional systems development estimates. CASE technology also promised that the corporate data base modeling/planning activity would be simplified; that systems maintenance would be reduced, requiring less personnel; and that documentation would be complete and maintainable.

The Environment and Business Situation. Because of the oil and gas industry downturn, the company was asked by its parent to review its operation with downsizing as an objective. The outcome of this business introspection was a significant reduction in the company's staff, the appointment of a new president, and the reorganization of all departments.

IS Management Vision. The vision of the IS management in the company was aligned with the organization's strategy at the time. The organization's direction was to limit the span of problem resolution and, wherever possible, to reject new projects. The project manager believed that involvement with CASE technology would keep the department abreast of current trends. The timing for a change on IS strategies, however, was inopportune. Although IS management recognized the benefits of CASE, staying in tune with the corporate view of providing lower-cost, short-term solutions was the overriding priority and was in contradiction of the CASE project. The vision had narrowed while the verdict on CASE was still out and undecided.

Attitude to New Technology. The IS personnel included in its ranks a significant proportion of people who were comfortable in older technologies already in use in the department. The IS practitioners' prevailing approach was to solve issues with existing, familiar technologies. This was expected of a function whose predominant activity was fixing and maintaining code.

Maturity of the IS Department. The IS department was small and stable and concentrated its efforts on maintenance. New development was rare; small-scale enhancements to existing software was the rule. This financial accounting project was a major development. After this event, everything was of a maintenance nature. IS expertise was limited to mainframe technology while users led the introduction of microcomputer technology and the implementation of packages.

IS Planning Horizon. The planning horizon was three years. The corporate restructuring led to more dynamic planning and the horizon shortened to 12 months with monthly updates. IS had to respond with faster and cheaper solutions. Users opined that a purchased package appeared to be the answer to these new demands.

The Outcome

Accounting functions were supported by an in-house-developed batch system. This system was 17 years old and running under the DOS/VSE operating system. The software was developed in COBOL. Five full-time programmers performed the maintenance function.

The need to replace the accounting system had been identified by the users and approved by the corporation. A package that met most of the accounting function was selected. To make use of the current VM/CMS and ADABAS technical environment, extensive modifications were required. As a result, a joint application development between IS and the vendor was recommended and approved.

The possibility of using CASE to perform reverse engineering was considered, but because of the vendor's lack of vision and expertise, the idea was abandoned. In addition, the vendor had developed the original package using a traditional life cycle development methodology and opposed the reverse engineering idea because of its self-imposed time constraints in delivering the product. This was the first time mainframe installation for the package and the vendor wanted to implement it as soon as possible to expand its business from a System 36 customer base.

Modification of the package could have minimized the new system errors, but it would have required a more disciplined project staff to deliver on schedule. Consequently, the software was installed even though it lacked a part of the business requirements, which had to be added at a later date. This resulted in higher project cost. The quality of the final product was compromised and high maintenance and enhancement costs were incurred.

As generally suggested by CASE advocates, a noncritical application was selected as a first CASE project. During the implementation of the package, the need for a subsystem that had to be integrated to the new accounting system was identified. Because of the nature of the subsystem, the application users and the IS team decided on in-house development. The analysis phase was completed using the Information Engineering Workbench CASE tool from KnowledgeWare, Inc., but the design and construction phases could not be performed because the tool was not compatible with the NATURAL and ADABAS data base environment. In addition, the entity descriptions could not be transported to the PREDICT data dictionary unless additional funds were spent for a tool to bridge the CASE output to the data dictionary. The entire entity descriptions had to be input again.

On the positive side, the use of CASE technology contributed to a well-documented subsystem, to better quality analysis, and to a successful development. However, this subsystem was not implemented in the production environment. Why? Because it was nonstrategic, of low priority, and replaceable by a manual process. The choice of a nonstrategic system as a pilot for CASE was a mistake. The user had higher-priority items to implement and could perform the function without the system's help. Therefore, it was inconsequential to have a CASE-delivered product.

Other factors influenced the outcome of the pilot. The entry cost was too high for a small IS department; the company was reorganized and its operations reduced; expenses that did not contribute to the exploration effort were questioned and trimmed; the IS department had successes using its own methodology, so there was resistance to the introduction of the information engineering methodology. This resistance stemmed from a strong bias toward the current environment and the conservative approach to fix broken systems with proven technology, in this case COBOL, PL/I, NATURAL, and ADABAS.

What Went Wrong?

The implementation of CASE was based on two goals:

- To determine whether development time and quality of the final product could be improved.
- To prove the low-maintenance advantage of CASE technology.

This experience opened up a hornet's nest. It polarized the IS groups. Users ignored the technology's favorable points. IS management was left with the perception that the introduction of CASE causes dissention in the ranks and requires retraining the development staff. The company was not committed to increased training costs, which further gave the impression that CASE was a natural and easy-to-learn methodology. In a business where IS is not strategic, the use of CASE was not critical to satisfying the users' demands. It only satisfied IS needs to be current technically. It was IS management's opinion that future systems requirements would mainly be satisfied by extensions or enhancements to existing computer applications and by providing programmers to users. The technology is not yet capable of adapting existing applications to CASE in a seamless fashion. More important is the fact that CASE is difficult to implement in an environment where software development is a craft or a nonstandard activity.

CONCLUSION

In the case study described in this article, the modus operandi has been to assess the contribution of each function in the organization and its value with respect to the new strategy. The IS department and the application of new information technology have not escaped this reassessment. The success of CASE technology was dependent on two major parameters: the strategic significance of information technology and the cost of information systems to the corporations. Exhibit II-4-1 illustrates the relationship between these variables. This experience in implementing CASE technology and the degrees of success in proposing CASE solutions bear this out.

In nonstrategic IS departments, solutions lead to high average costs because of a philosophy of crafting programs. Because it is a visible cost and a quantum leap for organizations where IS is nonstrategic, new technology is seen as too high a price to pay. IS shops with nonstrategic vision commit to nonstandardized data models and a menagerie of applications that the IS department manages by riding the business cycles.

The next best alternative is to acquire packages. In most cases the vendor's quoted price is perceived as the only cost to be included in the approval

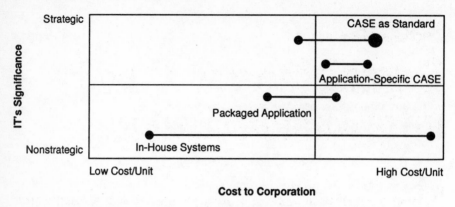

Exhibit II-4-1. Degrees of Success in Proposing CASE Solutions

process. Consideration for the hardware and software required to run the application is kept to a minimum. These piecemeal projects proliferate until the IS department is unable to move to state-of-the art technology. The IS department is seen as an inflexible and slow bureaucracy.

Strategic-oriented organizations identify the key areas for their success. When the organization is in a growth stage and confidence exists in its competitive ability, the IT strategy is in line with business strategy. Serious efforts are undertaken to use information technology to advance the cause of business. The investment is high and the outlook is excellent for long-term projects that include the use of CASE, especially object-oriented CASE tools that support code reusability and allow semiautomatic development. When handled correctly, commitment leads to integrated data architectures and standardized data models as data objects. Code is reusable for application development and data is standardized. With the current restructuring of corporations, this scenario should become predominant as managers succeed in presenting their case for CASE.

Notes

1. M.M. Parker and R.J. Benson (with H. E. Trainor), *Information Economics: Linking Business Performance to Information Technology* (Englewood Cliffs NJ: Prentice-Hall, 1988).

Section III
Organizing for Quality Information Systems

N ew data-oriented roles and responsibilities, new organizational structures and relationships, and new ways of looking at the total scope of and trends within business data—these are the key subjects in this section. Horizontal strategies that integrate the business and its data are pivotal.

Information collection and the timely delivery of decision support capabilities are replacing applications development as the IS organization's prime directive. Chapter III-1, "Organizing for an Enterprisewide DSS Architecture," presents an infrastructure for worldwide decision support that relies on business-focused information delivery teams.

The use, structure, and relationship of process-oriented methodologies and data-oriented methodologies are discussed in two chapters: Chapter III-2, "Enhancing Structured Analysis to Consolidate Data," and Chapter III-3, "Integrating Process and Data Models into the Horizontal Organization."

Data found in master files, tables, and transaction files is an excellent source of information about an enterprise. By examining this production data, it is possible to compose a complete picture of the existing business practice and policy and to faithfully portray data values used in the organization's information systems. Chapter III-4, "Domain Study: Analyzing Production Data," details this technique. The results can be used as a starting point to construct an ideal business model for the future.

III-1
Organizing for an Enterprisewide DSS Architecture

ROBERT L. SLOAN • HAL H. GREEN

The two most important responsibilities of leadership are to establish a vision or strategy for the organization and to put in place the systems, processes, and structures that enable the organization to progressively achieve that vision. One of the structures used by manufacturers to create competitive advantage is integrated information systems. Competitive advantage, including cost and differentiation, can be won or lost by marginal differences in the speed, accuracy, and comprehensive nature of information being delivered to decision makers.

An organization's competence in timely decision support capabilities has been given impetus by the total quality movement: the Malcolm Baldrige criteria state that "the ability to access and act on timely, reliable business data is requisite to the achievement of quantitative continual improvement in the delivery of products and services."

Michael Porter has described the importance of horizontal strategy as the interrelationship between business units. Integrated information and control systems support horizontal strategy, enabling independent business units to share key product and process information along the whole supply chain.

HORIZONTAL BUSINESS INTEGRATION STRATEGY

Manufacturers are providing increased service levels in response to competitive pressure and to create differentiation in product offerings. One trend is toward smaller, custom lot sizes on the part of the process manufacturer and custom product configurations on the part of the discrete component manufacturer.

As manufacturing assumes these higher levels of service, the strategic model of the manufacturing organization is moving toward a professional context, in which the operating work of an organization is dominated by skilled workers who use procedures that though difficult to learn are well defined. In this model, empowered workers are given greater decision latitude. In other words, with increased automation of the manufacturing processes, the nature of the work in the plant or factory shifts from manually effecting the independent processes to using information systems in support of customer-driven operating objectives related to production. The empowered worker equipped with business operating objectives makes decisions using information that previously was the purview of manufacturing management. Information systems, integrated with factory automation systems, therefore enable both differentiation and flatter organizational structures.

Compared with the conventional machine concept of the manufacturing organization, empowered or high-performance work teams typify a more people-centered, organic culture. This new manufacturing organization depends on high-speed access to high-quality information. For example, total quality management prescribes the use of statistical quality control (SQC) techniques. Manufacturers use SQC software to help workers process the sheer quantity of data required by the application of SQC principles in manufacturing, further illustrating the affinity between strategy, organization, and information technology.

The IS organization within the global manufacturing enterprise must understand the impact organizational strategy has on the information technology (IT) infrastructure. Furthermore, it must determine and create the optimum IT architecture to best support a horizontal business integration strategy.

DIFFERENTIATING INFORMATION SYSTEM PRODUCTS AND SERVICES

Historically, the IS organization has delivered custom computer applications to business functions to improve effectiveness and reduct cost. System projects were justified on their standalone return on investment. The IS management structure reflected project team independence and aligned applications development teams with their respective customers (i.e., manufacturing, finance, or distribution). This approach to systems development avoided the long-term need to integrate data between applications. Viewed separately, each system met its functional objective. Viewed collectively, they presented a set of conflicting interfaces and incompatible information, thereby constraining a horizontal business integration strategy.

As businesses flatten their organizations, their dependence on integrated information flow across worldwide boundaries increases. The IS organization must find ways to remove the functional and technical incompatibilities of existing computer systems that are barriers to business-centric information access.

Trends in Manufacturing

More business managers recognize that information-related service extensions to their product/service mix can affect their companies' ability to compete favorably in international markets. They are also beginning to recognize that existing computer systems were designed in a way that is inconsistent with the view of information as an asset to be managed by the corporation, which has led to concerns about the return on investment for older systems.

Plant-level information systems, once the domain of process control engineers and production personnel, are being drawn into the scope of the IS function from the standpoint of integrating the operational data in these systems with horizontal supply-chain business strategy. The span of the IS organization's responsibility may expand to include multiple operational (e.g., manufacturing) systems from which enterprise information is collected and delivered. The charter of IS becomes focused on assimilating and combining manufacturing-process data with other forms of business data to enhance the quality of customer service, to support integrated operations objectives, and to provide value-added decision support across the corporation.

QUANTITY OF MANUFACTURING DATA

Information systems are pervasive across the manufacturing supply chain. The entire manufacturing supply chain uses information, but the epicenter of IT in a modern industrial manufacturing company usually exists at the manufacturing plant site. Here, a variety of systems, using data at different levels of abstraction, are employed to control manufacturing processes, provide decision support to operations, and perform planning functions such as those offered by material requirements planning (e.g., MRPII) systems.

The problem of functionally integrating manufacturing software applications is exacerbated by the total volume of data employed in manufacturing. In the case of the process/batch manufacturer who employs process control systems, extensive quantities of process data may exist within the process control applications. Most of that data is needed by other parts of the manufacturing organization. It is common, for example, for a process manufacturing plant to generate 8 to 10 million pieces of information every 24 hours.

A central concern when manufacturing-process data is integrated into enterprisewide information systems is the requisite changes necessary to derive information from elemental process data. For example, a Fortune 100 diversified chemical company needs to maintain a complete history for each lot or batch of material made, including details of the processes used to make any given batch. A maker of an automobile safety device needs similar detailed information for each discrete component and assembly produced. In addition, the customer, the automotive industry, and proper business practice all specify that the detailed information be maintained indefinitely and be available on demand during the anticipated 20-year life of the product.

NATURE OF MANUFACTURING DATA

The problems outlined in each of these situations can be understood when the nature of manufacturing data itself is examined. Exhibit III-1-1 identifies four categories of data that exist in manufacturing:

KEY ATTRIBUTES OF DATA / CATEGORIES OF DATA	Example Data	Typical Orientation	Typical Use	Integration Scope	Typical Volume
Multisite Decision Support	Lot/Batch Quality Summary	Subject/Table	Multisite Read Only	Business	Low
Cross-Area Integrated Operations	Lot/Batch Quality Detail	Subject/Table	Transaction Driven	Site	Medium
In-Area Operations	In-Area Quality Result	File/Field	Event Driven	Area	Medium
Process/ Machine Control	Process/Quality Parameter	Tag or I/O	Real Time	Machine/Process Step	High

Exhibit III-1-1. Manufacturing Data Framework

- Derived data needed for longer-term business decision support.
- Transaction-driven, product-oriented data.
- Event-driven, operations-oriented data.
- Real-time, process-oriented data.

The columns of Exhibit III-1-1 contrast the key attributes of these different data types. Non-site-specific positioning of derived data is critical to successful horizontal business integration for the multisite manufacturing enterprise.

Process data possesses the lowest level of integration in manufacturing, whereas decision support data has usually been integrated or summarized to afford the user a basis for broad business and planning decisions. These two extremes can be illustrated by considering the questions the business user of manufacturing data might ask as compared with those asked by a process engineer concerned about the problem of manufacturing process optimization.

Business users of manufacturing data might want to know about the yield for a given product manufactured at all sites during the previous month. A typical process engineer might inquire about the historical trend of temperature for one or more tag (i.e., input/output) values, related to a particular piece of equipment or process. Both questions have equal relevance and potential merit, but they are fundamentally different, being based on the type of data needed to render a valid response.

The process-related question requires access to manufacturing (i.e., process control) data at its lowest atomic level. The product yield question requires access to data stored at a higher level of abstraction. Process data such as lot/batch yield must be collected and derived uniformly into a value for product yield at each site. This type of query represents a significant change in the level of abstraction and integration of the data across multiple plant sites.

The operations data presented at the middle levels of Exhibit III-1-1 reflects the transformation of data from process (tag) to subject (table). An operations data base often provides a repository for manufacturing data that is clearly outside the process domain but is still necessary for manufacturing. Operating conditions, procedures, recipes, and specifications, organized by product, equipment/cell/area, or manufacturing team, are often candidates for operations data. If MRP is employed, the operations information data base is also often used to provide the MRP system order-operations as they are completed by product, line, or plant.

DATA-DRIVEN MANUFACTURING APPLICATION FRAMEWORK

Past efforts to computerize manufacturing focused on the automation of isolated process steps or organizational functions. The success of the global manufacturing enterprise depends on new application architectures predicated on data integration, and the availability of derived production data for use in multisite business decision support. Using the categories of manufacturing data

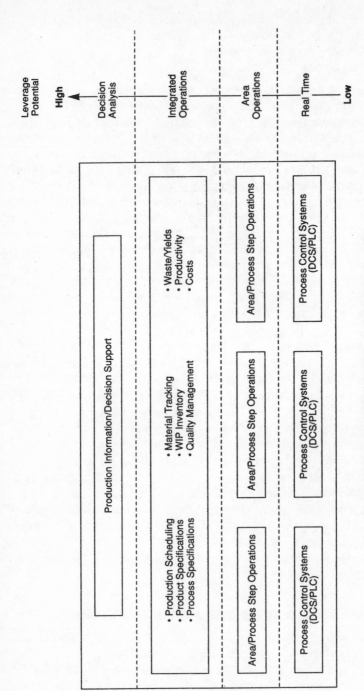

Exhibit III-1-2. Data-Driven Manufacturing Application Framework

from Exhibit III-1-1, a data-driven application framework can be constructed for a typical manufacturing site (see Exhibit III-1-2). This framework takes advantage of the existing differences in data, provides for the horizontal separation of multiple manufacturing process steps, and recognizes the need for operational integration. The upper level in this manufacturing site application framework supports the business need for horizontally integrated, multisite production information access.

Adoption of a consistent manufacturing site application framework both enables multisite integration and presents a major cost-reduction opportunity. The lack of a consistent framework for site applications all too often results in unique site applications requiring expensive life-cycle support. Use of a consistent framework enhances the prospects of multisite applications development (or commercial purchase), which significantly lowers life-cycle support cost.

EFFECTIVE INFORMATION DELIVERY

In view of the strategic use of IT and the vast quantity of manufacturing data now available, what should be the product of the IS organization? What should be the role of IS in the world-class manufacturing organization?

The manufacturing IS organization is required to reduce total cost of ownership of software systems, reduce lead times, increase flexibility of developed applications, deliver integrated (i.e., customer, supplier, and internal manufacturing) information to a wide variety of users across the enterprise, and develop and acquire applications suitable for multiple sites. The manner in which these conventional business objectives and their implied information needs are provided must improve for the manufacturer seeking integrated information and control systems.

Information collection and delivery is replacing applications development as the IS organization's prime responsibility. The advent of consistent manufacturing site application frameworks and the growing availability of commercial applications to satisfy operational needs can reduce over time, the IS role in the development and support of operational applications. As a result, IS can focus on the development and support of a new infrastructural layer of decision data services and networks built above the existing base of manufacturing site and centralized order entry/product distribution systems.

Infrastructure for Worldwide Decision Support

This infrastructural layer is designed to collect and position the requisite information for horizontal supply-chain integration and worldwide decision support. William Inmon's unified data architecture with data warehouses holding decision support information separate from operational systems is gaining acceptance in manufacturing and nonmanufacturing industries alike. The IS organization's prime responsibility is to implement and maintain this secure worldwide decision support infrastructure (see Exhibits III-1-3, III-1-4) and to provide business with effective information access and delivery mechanisms.

The IS organizational model has evolved so far to optimize its traditional primary product: custom applications development. To accomplish worldwide information delivery, the IS organization must adopt a model that reflects its new primary product.

As the IS organization changes from a custom manufacturer to a product distributor, with enterprise information as its essential product, the central focus of IS becomes information supply, inventory, regional warehouses, and business delivery mechanisms. The responsibility for this nonoperational data storage, structure, and content must be separated from applications development and controlled centrally or regionally, driven by the need for data integration, end-user data access, and enterprisewide data integrity (see Exhibit III-1-5). Distributed information storage and access mechanisms, predicated on the use of client/server technologies, can be implemented to insulate both the business users and decision support system (DSS) developers from the incompatibilities of existing operational applications.

New or reengineered operational systems are required to pass selected data from manufacturing sites and centralized order entry/product distribution operational systems to the infrastructure layer, thereby taking advantage of the infrastructure's ability to provide data to DSS applications. New operational systems can be downsized and optimized to best meet the immediate operational tasks. History, nonoperational analysis, and reporting could be accomplished as extensions of the infrastructure layer using commercially available analysis tools. Such a strategy allows users to select analysis tools according to their own business needs, with IS ensuring the integrity of the data managed within the infrastructure layer.

Delivery Teams

A consistent set of development policies, principles, methods, and tools is needed to govern the secure development and delivery of information products and services. Online metrics relating to the performance of the infrastructure layer need to be made available to determine who is using information, as well as when, why, and where information is being used. A single (i.e., logical) DSS environment can provide insulation from underlying hardware and operating system in incompatibilities. Decision support applications can be accomplished as a unified effort by IS or others, independent of the facilities or physical location of the developer.

A new IS business-focused organizational model emerges in which internal technical support teams assume the responsibility to design, build, and support the infrastructure layer. Radiating from the core are information delivery teams working directly with the businesses to identify information needs and ensure information delivery. Exhibit III-1-6 details the relationships among the different members of the business-focused information delivery team. Exhibit III-1-7 shows the overall organizational model for optimizing information delivery.

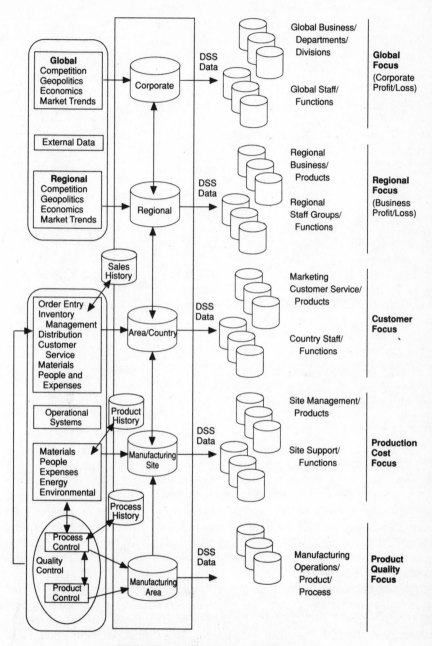

Exhibit III-1-3. Data Delivery Architecture

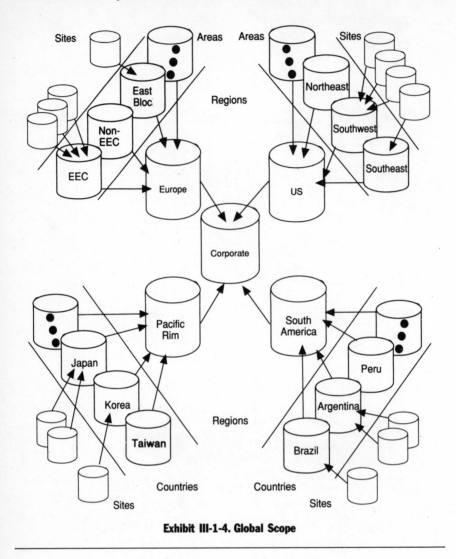

Exhibit III-1-4. Global Scope

ACTION PLAN

The actual steps required to move an IS organization toward the described information delivery paradigm depend on current IS business practice and how quickly the IS and business cultures can accept change. Although the individual paths forward will differ, the overall goal is to establish sustainable change in both the IS technology and the people processes.

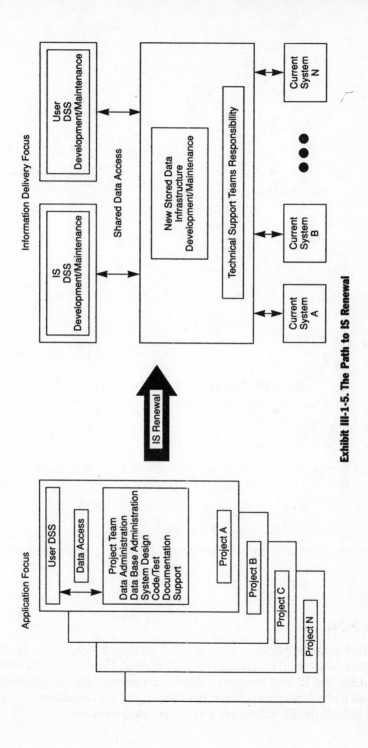

Exhibit III-1-5. The Path to IS Renewal

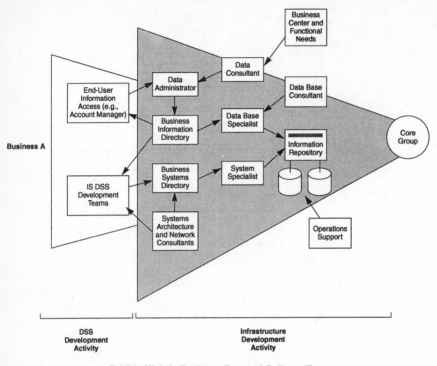

Exhibit III-1-6. Business-Focused Delivery Team

Organize Around Information Delivery. If the IS function is to be a provider of information as opposed to a provider of automation, change is a prerequisite. The IS culture can begin by defining its purpose as that of empowering its user community through access to information.

Existing IS organizational structures that optimize custom applications development should gradually be replaced with structures promoting cross-application integration. Decision support capability should be removed as a task of individual applications development teams and organized as an enterprisewide infrastructural activity. Employee recognition and reward mechanisms must be redesigned to reinforce and sustain these new IS directions.

Develop and Implement an Enterprisewide Architecture. The plant sites of the global manufacturer are often littered with locally optimized IT solutions that defy integration into a multisite supply-chain strategy. The standalone nature of these solutions reflects the fact that no shared business rules or IT framework exists to provide the technical integration ground rules.

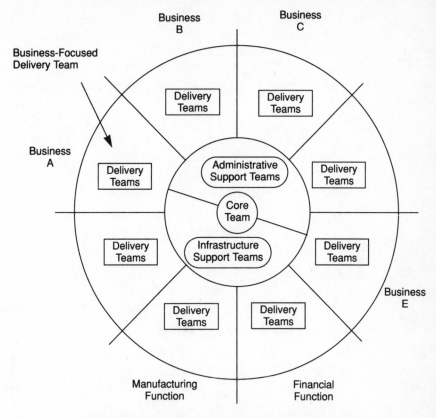

Exhibit III-1-7. Business-Focused Organizational Model

An essential IS path forward is the establishment of the architectural framework that provides a consistent technical context for horizontal business integration strategy. This framework should provide specific guidance for both existing and proposed applications, technology, and data. Not only is data a valid architectural consideration, it is fundamental to establishing integrated information delivery mechanisms. The data models resulting from data architecture development become the product catalogs for the IS function's information delivery business.

Information strategic planning (ISP) offers a valid approach to designing the overall enterprise architecture. The deficiency in information engineering has been a lack of recognition of the fundamental differences and uses in manufacturing data at different levels in the architecture. Exhibits III-1-1 and III-1-2 reflect these differences and their implications for manufacturing systems. Exhibits III-1-3 and III-1-4 reflect the logical placement of the data warehouses in the global manufacturing architecture. The use of encyclopedia-based CASE technology is strongly recommended in the development of the enterprisewide architecture. The distributed nature of this technology allows IS to both automate and share reusable software assets while teaming across geographical boundaries.

III-2
Enhancing Structured Analysis by Consolidating Data

SASA M. DEKLEVA

As currently practiced, structured analysis is a process-oriented methodology, and its principal documentation technique is data flow diagramming. Data stores can be represented on these diagrams at any level in the hierarchical model generated during structured analysis and are freely introduced when required by individual processes. Such an approach results in a highly redundant representation of data stores, and a formal procedure for data consolidation is recommended to eliminate these redundancies. This chapter describes a five-step procedure of data consolidation to remove redundancies and discusses each step's operations and sequencing. An additional benefit of this procedure is that it generates a system data model from the process model.

Information systems development methodologies generally recognize processes and data as the two key systems components, and these methodologies are oriented toward the analysis and formulation of either processes or data stores. In both cases, the secondary component is also analyzed and specified. Developers who use process-oriented methodologies recognize data as an essential systems component; similarly, processes are equally important to those who use data-oriented methodologies.

THE ORIGINS OF PROCESS- AND DATA-ORIENTED METHODOLOGIES

Process-oriented methodologies have their origins in those methodologies developed in the early years of IS development, when computers were used predominantly to automate routine, manual procedures. Program development mainly involved the study, documentation, and possible automation of manual processes. During the 1970s, process automation was improved by methods that used a top-down approach for systems development. These methods started at the top by modeling the entire process, which was continually broken down into individual structures. Process-oriented methodologies today are commonly known as structured analysis and design of software engineering. Because this chapter focuses only on the analysis phase of systems development, the term *structured analysis* is used to refer to process-oriented methodologies.

Data-oriented approaches have more recent origins and were developed for the design and implementation of data bases and complex, integrated information systems supporting unstructured decision making. The development of unstructured systems (e.g., decision support systems), in which processes cannot be defined in advance, is one reason for the increasing popularity of data-oriented methodologies.

Another reason is the recognition of data as an important organizational asset that needs to be carefully organized and managed. Therefore, consolidation of corporate data has become a central activity in IS development. Data-oriented methodologies are commonly called logical data base design or information engineering, and data consolidation is one of their major activities.

Despite the increasing popularity of data-oriented approaches, structured analysis remains a valuable methodology. It is more effective for the development of well-structured and process-intensive systems. It is also better known that data-oriented methodologies, and the majority of systems developers have been trained in structured analysis.

Structured analysis uses data flow diagramming as the main documentation technique for the functional specification of information systems. Data flow diagrams (DFDs) are grouped hierarchically to model a system. DFDs can represent four components of an information system: data flows, processes, data stores, and optional external entities. Consequently, most CASE tools that support the early stages of IS development support data flow diagramming as well as functional decomposition, which are techniques essential to structured analysis.

Despite its primary orientation toward processes, structured analysis also entails the definition of data structures, which are implemented as files or data bases. Data stores are, however, perceived as repositories of data that support processes rather than as organizational assets. They are introduced on DFDs because individual processes manipulate those specific data items. Some processes update and input data to data stores, but the majority of processes retrieve data for editing, manipulation, or output generation. Data is structured according to the requirements of the individual processes, and data stores are introduced on DFDs whenever a process requires access to data. This practice, however, causes the data stores to be scattered throughout the hierarchical model, and data is consequently represented in a redundant manner. Structured analysis possesses no mechanism to discourage such treatment of data stores, and redundant specification is actually encouraged, if not necessitated, by this type of analysis.

Representation of data stores in a hierarchical set of DFDs may be inappropriate for three reasons:

- A data store may contain redundant data.
- A data store may be a copy of another data store elsewhere in the model, or it may contain attributes common to other data stores.
- Similar data stores may already exist in operational files or data bases.

To correct these problems, data must be consolidated.

DATA CONSOLIDATION: A FIVE-STEP PROCEDURE

This five-step procedure for consolidating data (see Exhibit III-2-1) originates in current data base theory, but research continues to reveal the best method for consolidating data. For most practical situations, however, the following five steps can transform data into nonredundant form:

1. Consolidation of attribute names.
2. Definition of data dependencies.
3. Local decomposition.
4. Global synthesis.
5. Balancing of data stores.

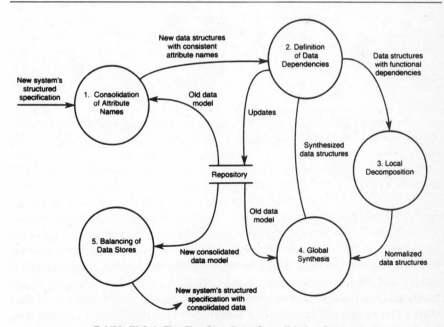

Exhibit III-2-1. The Five-Step Data Consolidation Process

The first two steps are performed in sequence. Steps 3, 4, and 2 (in that order) are iterated, and step 5 concludes the process. Each of these steps and their sequencing is discussed in the following sections.

Consolidation of Attribute Names

Data cannot be streamlined unless attribute names are consistent throughout the model as well as within existing files and data bases. Consolidation of names is often a difficult task, because systems analysts and end users often use different names for the same attribute (i.e., synonyms) or the same name for different attributes (i.e., homonyms). To eliminate redundant data, it is necessary to ensure that each attribute is named consistently.

In manufacturing, a product is given at least a particular code and often a particular name. This is done so that each product can be easily identified and distinguished from other products. For the same reasons, each distinct data item in a data model should be equally identifiable. An attribute name rather than a code is used to distinguish a piece of data. Therefore, this name must be unique and consistent throughout the model. For practical reasons, structured analysis often allows the use of synonyms. When a synonym is used, each distinctive attribute has two or more unique names, which are all recognized as references to that particular attribute.

Attributes serve two functions. One is simply to denote a part of the real world that is being modeled, and the other is to identify an object. Sometimes these two functions are combined; such attribute names identify other attributes and relate information about an object or event. A consecutive order number, for example, is just an identifier; it does not relate information about the order it identifies. A zip code, on the other hand, not only identifies a region but contains information—it denotes the location of that region. A birth date conveys no information by itself and is meaningful only when paired with a person's identification.

Naming should therefore reflect the nature of data attributes. Names of identifying attributes communicate the fact that attributes function as identifiers and should also state the object or event they identify. Examples of this type of attribute name include:

- Customer identification number.
- Department code.
- Order number.
- Shipment number.

Names of descriptive attributes identify an object or event by describing and identifying it. Examples of such names include:

- Customer street address.
- Department street address.
- Order due date.
- Item unit price.

An understanding of the environment that is represented by the data is required to properly name attributes and recognize such naming anomalies as synonyms and identical names for different attributes. Suppliers, for example, may be called vendors by the market research group and suppliers by purchasing personnel. The attribute called address can have different meanings to a customer-service officer and a personnel manager. For the staff that services customer orders, the term *address* may refer to such different items as headquarters address, billing address, and shipping address.

Because the environment influences attribute naming, those in charge of naming attributes must possess general knowledge of the overall environment that the information system models. Specifically, they must consult different functional experts with whom they need to communicate effectively. The task of naming attributes is usually performed by the data administration team. To successfully accomplish its task, the data administration team must be centrally organized even when the IS system and hardware are distributed. Data administration is not only a technical activity; care for data models and data names is a permanent activity of data administration.

An Example. In the inventory reordering system example in Exhibit III-2-2, several attribute names were used inconsistently. Although production planners called attribute-identifying items part numbers, they were called item codes by purchasing personnel. Similarly, what was known to production planners as **On Hand Quantity** was called **In Stock** by purchasing staff. After some consultation, the names **Part Number** and **On Hand Quantity** were chosen because they were considered more appropriate by the majority of concerned employees. Alternative names, **Item Code** and **In Stock,** were recognized as synonyms, but their use was allowed only until a five-month transition period had expired.

In addition to these synonyms, several homonyms needed redefinition. For example, the **Order Quantity** attribute in the data store **Open Orders** represented a quantity that had actually been ordered. **Order Quantity** from the **Supply Market Information** data store referred to the quantity of an item packed into a box and represented the minimum order quantity. Alternative names **Quantity Ordered** and **Minimum Order Quantity** were chosen.

Definition of Data Dependencies

The second step in the data consolidation process is the specification of associations among attributes. In particular, the dependence of certain attributes on other attributes, known as determinants, must be specified. Determinants are attributes that can identify other attributes; a single determinant can often determine the value of more than one other attribute. In addition to identification information, a determinant can also contain its own information.

Only when an attribute is matched with its determinant does the data

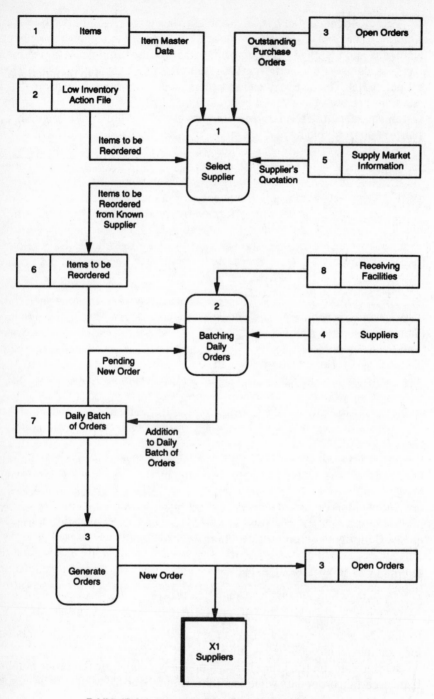

Exhibit III-2-2. Inventory Reordering System Overview

contained in an attribute become meaningful. Sometimes an attribute has to be matched with more than one determinant to have significance. For example, an order quantity attribute gains meaning only when both corresponding order number and product number are known. Attributes are said to be functionally dependent on their determinants or functionally determined by their determinants.

To describe data structures fully, attributes as well as the functional dependencies among attributes must be identified. A complete description of attributes is necessary for the successful consolidation of data, and the functional dependencies in all data stores must be identified to carry out the next step in the data consolidation process. The determination of functional dependencies has not previously been recognized as a part of structured analysis, and it is not required or supported by any related documentation standard. (The only related information that is sometimes requested is the specification of identifying or key attributes, which cannot be used to consolidate data.)

In addition to functional dependencies, multivalued dependencies must also be identified. A multivalued dependency occurs when a set of values described by one attribute is related to a determinant. Examples of this type of dependency are the skill and dependent attributes in an employee data structure. An employee may have one or more dependents or skills; therefore, the dependent and skill attributes may contain multiple values. These multivalued attributes are determined by the employee identification attribute; therefore, they have a multivalued dependency on their determinant. Multivalued dependencies are also required to perform the next step in the data consolidation process.

An Example. The structures of the data stores **Open Orders** and **Suppliers** are shown in Exhibit III-2-3. The exhibit also shows the structure of **Offices**, an existing data base file set up by the physical plant department. In the search for multivalued dependencies, it is observed that each order may contain several items, as many as 20 in this example. In such cases, each order number is associated with (i.e., determines) several part numbers as well as several part short descriptions and quantities ordered. The following multivalued dependency is identified (the double-headed arrow designates a multivalued dependency): *Order number* $\rightarrow\rightarrow$ *Part number, Part short description, Quantity ordered.*

Analysis continues with the examination of each attribute (i.e., data item) to find out whether another item or group determines it. An order number, for example, is not determined by any other attribute.

Order date, on the other hand, is uniquely defined by the order number. Using a certain order date while searching through the file would not be enough

Open Orders	Occurs
Order Number	1
Supplier Number	1
Supplier Name	1
Supplier Street Address	1
Supplier City	1
Supplier State	1
Supplier ZIP	1
Supplier Contact Name	1
Order Date	1
Receiving Facility Code	1
Receiving Facility Street	1
Receiving Facility City	1
Receiving Facility State	1
Receiving Facility ZIP	1
Receiving Facility Phone	1
Delivery Date	1
Part Number	20
Part Short Description	20
Quantity Ordered	20

Suppliers	Occurs
Supplier Number	1
Supplier Name	1
Supplier Street Address	1
Supplier City	1
Supplier State	1
Supplier ZIP	1
Supplier Reliability Rating	1
Supplier YTD Purchase	1
Supplier Total Last Year	1
Supplier Contact Name	1
Supplier Contact Telephone	1

Offices	Occurs
Office Code	1
Department Number	1
Office Name	1
Office Street Address	1
Office City	1
Office State	1
Office ZIP	1
Office Area	1
Office Working Days Code	1
Office Working Hours Code	1

Exhibit III-2-3. Sample Data Structures

---

to retrieve a particular order, because many orders are issued every day. Knowing the order number uniquely identifies a certain order and determines the value of the related attribute order date. This association is called functional dependency (i.e., order date is functionally dependent on order number), and the order number is recognized as a functional determinant.

Local Decomposition

Local decomposition is governed by the rules of data base normalization. Basically, normalization is the decomposition of a redundant data store into nonredundant ones. A data structure is decomposed according to the definition of its attributes and the functional and multivalued dependencies of these attributes.

An Example. Application of the simplified normalization procedure on the inventory reordering system example from Exhibit III-2-2 leads to a decomposition of the **Open Orders** data structure from Exhibit III-2-3. Attributes constituting multivalued and functional dependencies are organized as separate data structures. The resulting structures are shown in Exhibit III-2-4.

Normalization results in the separation of attributes participating in multivalued and functional dependencies from the original data structure. Each set

---

Open Orders

Order Number
Supplier Number
Order Date
Receiving Facility Code
Delivery Date

Suppliers of Ordered Items

Supplier Number
Supplier Name
Supplier Street Address
Supplier City
Supplier State
Supplier ZIP
Supplier Contact Name

Receiving Facilities

Receiving Facility Code
Receiving Facility Street
Receiving Facility City
Receiving Facility State
Receiving Facility ZIP
Receiving Facility Phone

Open Order Details

Order Number
Part Number
Quantity Ordered

Items

Part Number
Part Short Description

Exhibit III-2-4. Data Structures Resulting from Decomposition

of attributes forms a separate, nonredundant structure. The determinants of excluded sets also appear in what remains of the original data structure.

Global Synthesis

Local decomposition is performed on individual data structures; it increases the number of data structures that can contain the same data. One goal of data base design is to organize relevant data into a minimal number of data structures. Therefore, the data structures created during local decomposition must be consolidated and subsequently integrated. Algorithms to accomplish this are premised on the integration of all data structures that have common determinants. Attributes with a common determinant describe the same entity or relationship and should be organized into one data structure.

Attribute synthesis algorithms are used solely to synthesize data structures that have the same functional dependency. They do not combine multivalued dependents but leave multivalued dependencies as separate structures in normalized form. Data structures are organized into groups that have the same functional determinant. Each group is replaced by one structure that contains each group's attributes. Care should be taken with the way synonyms are treated; for purposes of synthesis, synonyms should be considered equivalents. Such special cases as determinants with extraneous attributes, redundant functional dependencies, and equivalent keys are not handled properly by simple synthesis.

An Example. The application of this step in the inventory reordering system example demands the fusion of the **Suppliers of Ordered Items** (see Exhibit III-2-4) and **Suppliers** (see Exhibit III-2-3) structures, because both share the same determinant—the supplier number. Attributes from **Suppliers of Ordered Items** are a subset of attributes in **Suppliers**, which is not unusual and simply means that the first structure is redundant and that the **Suppliers** structure is different.

Global synthesis also requires the integration of the **Receiving Facilities** structure (from Exhibit III-2-4) with the Offices structure from an existing data base (shown in Exhibit III-2-3). Receiving facility code is recognized as a synonym of office code. The analysts failed to recognize this during the first step of data consolidation. Both structures are fused to form the **Offices** structure in Exhibit III-2-5. Another example of synthesis is the **Items** structure from Exhibit III-2-4 that is a subset of an existing data base file **Parts**. The **Parts** structure contains both part number and part short description and is therefore a complete substitute for **Items**.

Iterating the Steps

Ideally, data consolidation can be accomplished in five steps. After all data stores have been specified, required attributes are identified and uniquely named. Functional and multivalued dependencies are determined, and data

Offices

Office Code
Department Number
Office Name
Office Street Address
Office City
Office State
Office ZIP
Office Area
Office Working Days Code
Office Working Hours Code
Office Phone

Parts

Part Code
Part Status
Part Drawing Number
Part Short Description
Part Long Description
Part Classification
Part Responsibility
Part Lead Time
Part Cost
Part Reorder Policy
Part Order Quantity
Quantity On Hand
Part Current Engineering Change Number

Exhibit III-2-5. Structures of Two Synthesized Data Stores

---

structures are locally decomposed and synthesized accordingly. To avoid repeating any steps, naming conflicts should be resolved at the beginning of the process, and all dependencies should be determined, *all* meaning not only dependencies among attributes in individual data structures but also dependencies among attributes in the whole model. It is not realistic, however, to expect that no steps will need to be repeated.

As dependencies are identified the first time, each data store is analyzed individually. Functional and multivalued dependencies that make up a particular data store are specified. During local decomposition and global synthesis, structures are decomposed and synthesized. Integration causes attributes other than those from the original structures to be joined, which opens up the possibility that some new, previously undetected dependencies exist. Synthesized structures must be evaluated again to determine functional and multivalued dependencies. Upon the discovery of any new dependencies, the structures have to be decomposed and synthesized again. This cycle continues until no additional dependencies are found.

In most situations, one or two iterations of this cycle are required. Usually, the only determinants are the record identifiers or keys, and these are easily recognized. Integration of these structures results in normal, nonredundant form.

Balancing of Data Stores

In this final step, data stores initially defined in DFDs are replaced by those derived during the data consolidation process. After iterative decompositions and syntheses, attributes from an original data store may be dispersed and contained in several data structures. On the other hand, a number of original data stores may be combined by consolidation into a single store. The replacement of redundant data stores is a straightforward process, which is based solely on attribute names.

This step ensures that processes are given access to the data they require for proper operation. Although manually performing this step may be time-consuming, the replacement process can easily be automated by CASE tools. The complex task is the generation of new DFDs, for which some human intervention may be needed. CASE tools should provide the information required to draw up a new DFD, and the analyst can diagram the consolidated stores according to individual criteria for diagramming.

An Example. Several changes are now needed in the inventory reordering system example. The original data stores shown in Exhibit III-2-2 must be reexamined and the consolidated data stores substituted. The DFD showing the inventory reordering system resulting from the data consolidation procedure is shown in Exhibit III-2-6. The data store **Open Orders** was split into a new **Open Orders** data structure and **Open Order Details**. The data structure **Items** must be substituted with an existing data base file **Parts**. The data store **Supply Market Information** was restructured and no longer contains general descriptive information about suppliers. To compensate, the data store **Suppliers** is retrieved during the manual process number one—**Select Supplier.** Finally, a redundant date store **Receiving Facilities** is substituted with the already existing store **Offices.**

ENHANCED STRUCTURED ANALYSIS

Existing literature on structured analysis suggests that the models of a systems' functions and data should be developed in parallel and that modeling is an independent activity. Both models should then be used to cross-check each other, and neither model should be considered the dominant one.

By using the data consolidation procedure described in this article, analysts can concentrate on data flow analysis and functional decomposition without having to develop a separate data model. A data model can later be extracted semiautomatically from the functional model. Careful naming of attributes, the specification of functional dependencies, and normalization are also required whether the data model is created independently or not. Balancing data stores and generation of new DFDs can be automated if a CASE tool

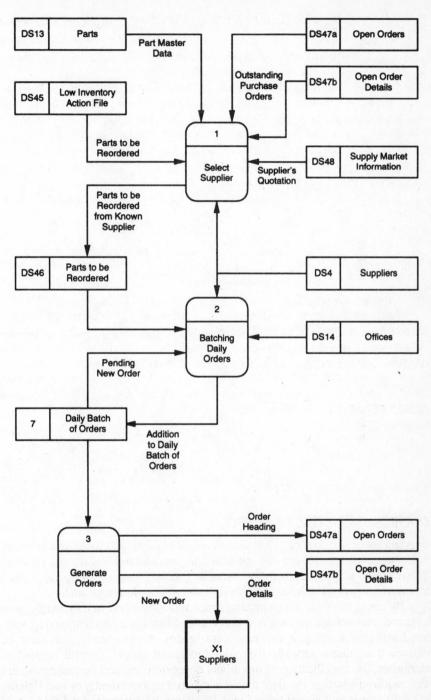

Exhibit III-2-6. Inventory Reordering System After Data Consolidation

supporting data consolidation is available. Advantages are gained, however, by the manual development of a data model; analysts may have better insight by investigating the same system from two perspectives, and they may discover discrepancies by cross-validating the two models.

The benefits of data consolidation often out-weigh its shortcomings. The most important benefit is obvious: a consolidated data model integrated with the previously existing organizational data base. Another advantage of observing a system from only one perspective is that analysts should become more productive. Process-oriented structured analysis is used to model systems that are process intensive and well structured. Analysts model such systems by specifying processes and their decomposition. They can draw supporting data stores and specify their structures without paying attention to data redundancy. Analysts develop only half of the structured specification and extract the data model during the data consolidation procedure.

To automate this procedure, CASE tools should be enhanced to support naming standards, which include the control of synonyms and homonyms. They should be able to specify functional and multivalued dependencies. CASE tools should also perform local decomposition, global synthesis, and related iterations. Finally, they should support or automatically perform the substitution of data stores on DFDs with consolidated data structures. All these facilities should be integrated with the central repository that holds information on the system under development as well as on all existing systems.

CONCLUSION

Current approaches to structured systems analysis and design do not present a procedure to properly treat data stores. Even worse, they encourage redundant structuring and specification of data stores, which can appear anywhere in the hierarchical model. One remedy for this situation is to supplement functional documentation with an entity-relationship data model. The five-step procedure discussed in this article describes a formal procedure to derive a data model from DFDs. This procedure originates in data base theory and can be partially automated.

Designers of CASE tools often ignore the need for consolidating data. Despite this, many tools can support some data modeling and data base design. CASE tools usually do not support the specification of data dependencies and therefore cannot perform local data decomposition and global synthesis. They should be upgraded to perform at least simple decomposition and Bernstein's synthesis algorithms.

The data consolidation procedure can also be performed manually (which is how it must be performed until the proper tools are available). The most difficult tasks in consolidating data are properly naming attributes and recognizing attribute dependencies. These cannot be automated because they require knowledge about the part of the world being modeled for successful completion. Reasonably effective decomposition and synthesis algorithms are relatively straightforward. They can be easily performed manually, and they are not nearly as time-consuming as the continued maintenance of poorly designed data files or data bases.

III-3
Integrating Process and Data Models in the Horizontal Organization

DAVID C. WALLACE

I nformation systems are created to help achieve the goals and objectives of the organization by integrating them with information technology. Information technology is an extensive concept in which all the new technologies from fax machines to multimedia devices to new computer hardware and software are grouped. To be an effective part of an organization, individuals must understand and use information technology within the organization. Therefore, an organization that wishes to be successful must first develop a strategic plan, which involves a systematic way of integrating information systems and information technology.

Currently, the IS field is focusing on developing both new methodologies and criteria for the evaluation and selection of appropriate methodologies. This effort is often completed without regard to new trends within the business organization field. When that happens, the new methodologies may not meet the needs of the business community and produce systems that are flawed.

ALIGNMENT AROUND CORE PROCESSES

IS methodologies have largely ignored the recent trends within the business management area—the gap between research and practice. One of these major trends focuses on aligning organizational resources around essential processes, or core processes. This trend has been identified by Frank Ostroff and Douglas Smith of McKinsey & Company as the horizontal corporation. M. Anthony Burns, chairman of Ryder System Inc, states that the horizontal corporation concept is the wave of the future. From such large profit-centered organizations as General Electric, AT&T, Ryder, and Xerox to such small nonprofit organizations as the Police Department at Illinois State University, there is a movement toward the horizontal organization. Lawrence A. Bossidy, chairman of AlliedSignal Inc, sees a significant increase in productivity as more organizations restructure themselves around this concept.

In this paradigm, the organization restructures its goals and objectives around the essential processes that define the organization's existence and sequential survival. The result is the flattening of the organizational structure into essential processes—eliminating the traditional hierarchy of bureaucratic divisions, departments, or sections. This allows both profit and nonprofit organizations to be more responsive to their clients or customers. The traditional goals of profitability, market share, and shareholders' satisfaction will not be identified as goals but as natural outcomes resulting from the emphasis on tying goals to an organization's essential processes.

Integrating recent trends in the business organization field with an effective IS methodology is a critical success factor for an organization. For a profit-centered organization, this will often provide the means to achieve competitive advantages in the market by enhancing existing products and services, developing new products and services, changing the existing industry and its characteristics, and creating new industries and markets. For a nonprofit organization, the ability to stretch shrinking resources to meet the demands of its constituents is critical to its success. As budget dollars for local, state, and federal agencies are cut, these agencies find they are still responsible for meeting the requirements of their charters. They will also need to integrate their IS structures around proven trends within the organization field to achieve their maximum productivity. Therefore, it is important to develop IS methodologies that integrate these recent trends.

THE HORIZONTAL CORPORATION

The horizontal corporation is an approach for all types of organizations—public or private, profit or nonprofit, corporate or sole proprietorships, big or small. The prerequisites for this approach are to redefine corporate goals around strategic actions that will improve the organization's competitiveness, efficiency, or other strategic actions defined by the organization. One important goal for any organization is to focus on improvement. The organization must know its markets and customers thoroughly to know what it will take to satisfy them. Once these corporate goals have been clearly identified, the organization should be able to identify key objectives that will help them to achieve these goals (e.g., customer and supplier satisfaction). These key objectives are measurable and identifiable for each process and should contribute to the organizational goals.

The next step requires the organization to identify its essential processes. These processes can be characterized by mission-critical applications or core processes. The applications focus on the very purpose or meaning of the organization (e.g., the identification of new markets and new customers, retention of existing customers, and other critical applications). The very purpose or meaning criteria can be answered by focusing on the actions necessary to accomplish the corporate goals. The key objectives identified in the previous step should provide insight into the identification of the essential processes. For example, customer satisfaction can be achieved through customer support, new product development, and sales and fulfillment. The next series of steps involves the actual restructuring of the organization.

Multidisciplinary Efforts

Once the essential processes have been identified, the organization will restructure itself around these processes. Each process will have a manager who helps facilitate the coordination and communication within the process and with other processes. Each process should link related tasks to yield a product or service to a customer or user. Careful attention should be given to the elimination of tasks that do not support, in some way, the related objectives of the process. Training, evaluating, and paying employees should be linked to the accomplishments of objectives of the essential processes. Each process is responsible for all tasks needed to produce the end product or service. This requires each process to be multidisciplinary (e.g., finance, marketing, production, accounting, or sales).

The intent is to localize the necessary tasks for an essential process to streamline operations so that the organization can react quickly to changing conditions. Ideally, each task should harmoniously fit together with the next to generate the end result, thereby eliminating layers of bureaucracy that tend to increase costs and delay actions. All essential processes should harmoniously fit together to achieve all strategic goals of the organization.

The horizontal concept is illustrated in Exhibit III-3-1. The essential processes operate on a horizontal level using the multidisciplinary efforts within each process to accomplish their objectives. Each process is not a standalone entity but is integrated into part of the entire picture where each part communicates and coordinates with each other part.

Realistically, special expertise and strategic direction are needed to monitor changing conditions in the markets and environments in which the organization must exist. These strategic considerations should be accomplished at a higher level. The more operational and managerial considerations would be held at the process level. Downsized support departments (e.g., finance, legal, accounting, and marketing) will exist at the higher level within the organization to provide the expertise needed by the processes. Strategic direction will be provided by a high-level department. The responsibility for this department will be to provide strategic planning and direction for the organization. Exhibit III-3-1 illustrates the relationship between the essential processes and the higher-level support departments. The interactions between the processes, between the support departments, and between the support departments and the processes are shown with double arrows.

Information and the systems that support its capture, transformation, and dissemination are strategic to the survival of the organization. To support

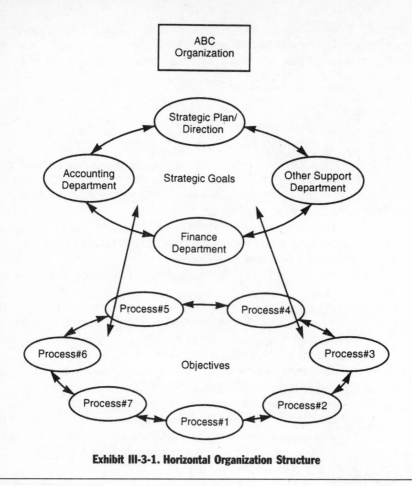

Exhibit III-3-1. Horizontal Organization Structure

horizontal organization adequately, IS personnel must incorporate a methodology that supports the horizontal approach. Without recognizing the recent trends in organizational structure and adopting methods to facilitate their integration, IS resources will not gain full management support and may lose their major impact on the organization.

POPULAR METHODOLOGIES

Integrating IS throughout the organization is a key issue for senior management. Two popular methodologies that can be used to facilitate the integration of information systems within an organization are a data-focused approach and a process-focused approach.

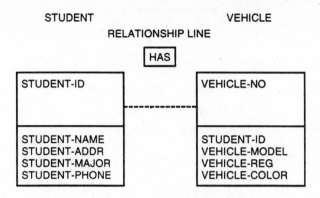

STUDENT   VEHICLE

DATA MODEL

INCORPORATED BUSINESS RULES, BASED ON THE
DATA STRUCTURE AND RELATIONSHIP LINE:

1. A STUDENT IS UNIQUELY IDENTIFIED THROUGH
   STUDENT ID.
2. A VEHICLE IS UNIQUELY IDENTIFIED THROUGH
   VEHICLE NO.
3. A STUDENT MAY HAVE ZERO OR MANY VEHICLES.
4. A VEHICLE CAN ONLY EXIST IN BUSINESS IF IT IS
   ASSOCIATED WITH ONE STUDENT.
5. A VEHICLE CANNOT BE ADDED UNLESS IT IS
   IMMEDIATELY ASSOCIATED WITH ONE STUDENT.

Exhibit III-3-2. Data Model with Associated Business Rules

Data-Focused Approach

The data-focused approach is currently the more popular methodology. Generally, data models are more stable reflections of how an organization uses data and establishes business rules within its various components. By focusing on the types of data and the various attributes and classes they represent, a comprehensive, relational, or hierarchical model can be constructed to reflect their relationships within the organization. This model can serve to help simplify and reduce duplication of data, and validate business rules governing relationships and dependencies. Data-focused models are powerful tools for data administrators but offer little help for senior executives in terms of IS planning unless they are properly presented (see Exhibit III-3-2).

For nontechnical computer personnel, data-focused models are often difficult to comprehend and implement within an organization. Many experienced IS managers and academics do not fully understand the data modeling process and the related topics of object orientation for developing information systems on the project level as well as the corporate level.

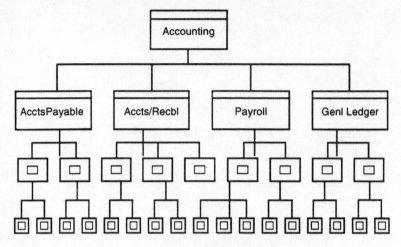

Exhibit III-3-3. Simplified Information System Structure

Process-Focused Approach

The process-focused methodology looks at IS as a series of related activities that transform data into information. The emphasis is on the processes or activities that comprise a particular information system. A model is generated to reflect the hierarchical relationships of information systems within an organization. Therefore, an information system such as accounting can be broken into basic processes (e.g., accounts payable, accounts receivable, payroll, and general ledger). These processes can be further decomposed into smaller processes. For example, payroll can include the following related processes: generating payroll, generating quarterly payroll reports, generating year-end payroll reports, and updating employee records. Each of these processes can further be decomposed into smaller, related processes. The end result is the hierarchical process structure. Exhibit III-3-3 illustrates this hierarchical relationship between the processes.

Each process has a set of objectives that supports the objectives of the next higher-level process, which in turn support the overall goals of the organization. Therefore, each activity or process can be justified by the objectives and goals of the organization. An organizational model can be created to facilitate the process of evaluating activities within each information system and to establish an effective decision support system for management. The evaluation process could be used to identify activities that are not contributing to the goals and objectives of the organization and either eliminate or modify them. One study indicates that the process-focused approach remains (or is being reinstated) as the preferred IS planning tool.

The next important step for the process-focused approach is to integrate it into a corporate structure. Recent studies have indicated that senior IS managers and senior corporate management are looking for information technology that can be elevated to the organizational level.

Both process-focused and data-focused approaches have had a significant effect on the project level, where IS personnel have used each technique to develop information systems for specific applications. Yet, neither technique has had any significant effect on the corporate level. A methodology must be developed that can take the strengths of both process-focused and data-focused approaches and blend them into a corporate model—which can include the recent trends of the horizontal organization. This has been successfully accomplished in industry using the combination of the IDEF0 Activity Modeling and IDEF1X Data Modeling approaches, as well as through the Information Engineering Methodologies of James Martin and Clive Finkelstein.

INTEGRATING THE MODELS: PROCESS MODEL SUPPORTED BY A DATA MODEL

Integrating information systems technology into the corporate organizational structure requires the support of both senior management and lower-level personnel if it is to be successful. It must be a methodology that can be understood and communicated throughout the organization by both computer technical and noncomputer technical personnel to be effective.

Because the horizontal organization concept uses multidisciplinary teams within each process, an effective IS methodology must be simple enough to communicate across disciplines and yet be effective in IS planning. Process-focused modeling relies on simple, easy-to-understand symbols that can be used across disciplines. This methodology must be easy and effective enough to be used by all levels within the organization.

Senior executives identified IS planning and information integration as a key issue for competition and survival in today's market. A process-focused methodology is compatible with modeling tasks and activities at the essential process level as well as strategic activities at the higher level. A process-focused approach has been recommended as an appropriate methodology for an organization structure. The data-focused approach is most appropriate for the data administrator. Therefore, an important consideration is to develop a methodology that can integrate the strengths of both process- and data-focused approaches within an organizational model.

With the growth of computer-aided modeling tools, the complex task of representing interrelated activities and their associated data components can be accomplished much more easily for both the process-focused and the data-focused methodologies. Detailed computer specifications can be generated to alleviate the problems of consistency at each level and between levels within each type of model hierarchy. An appropriate computer-assisted software engineering (CASE) tool can help facilitate the integration of process- and data-focused models. The CASE tool must be very easy to use and comprehensive enough to allow for easy integration between the two models.

Using Dynamic CASE Tools. The diagrams should have simple, easy-to-follow menus that allow the rapid development of each level of diagram. If the diagramming tool is difficult to use to create and modify different symbols, it becomes a more static tool with which systems analysts will tend to create models that they are reluctant to change. The tool should be esthetically pleasing to view, and data flows should flow with arcs, straight lines, and right angles. Finally, the tool should be comprehensive enough to allow the systems analyst to move from the front-end stages (i.e., analysis and design) to the back-end stages (i.e., implementation and installation) smoothly.

When users and systems analysts work with a CASE tool, the process should be a pleasing experience, thereby allowing the tool to be more dynamic or easily changeable. When the people who work with the model are glad that the model has been created and never want to touch it again, a static model has been created. If the model-creation process was a pleasing experience for them, they won't mind changing it—this is a dynamic model. In the horizontal corporation, systems change constantly as a result of changes in the competitive environment. Therefore, it is important that the model be a dynamic model capable of changing constantly.

By using simple, easy-to-understand symbols supported by a comprehensive data dictionary, a process model can be generated to represent detailed information processing as well as more abstract decision making at the higher level within the organization. The ultimate goal of integrating IS methodologies into the horizontal organization is to develop a comprehensive organizational model using a dynamic CASE tool that can handle constant changes. The major component of this model is a process-focused model supported by a data-focused model representing the higher-level support processes and the essential processes within the organization. This organizational model can be used as a blueprint for the restructuring of the traditional hierarchical organization into the newer horizontal organization.

Data Structures. For organizations interested in developing a horizontal structure, the process-focused model can be used to reinforce and enhance communication and coordination within the organization by illustrating the lines of communication, information flows, and coordination (i.e., exchanging of information) between the essential processes and the support departments. The data-focused portion of the integrated model supports the processes by ensuring that the data structures used (and perhaps created) by the processes are in their most logical formats. It will remove redundancy and simplify the actual data structures used within the organization. Exhibit III-3-4 represents the overview of this approach. In addition, more detailed discussions concerning

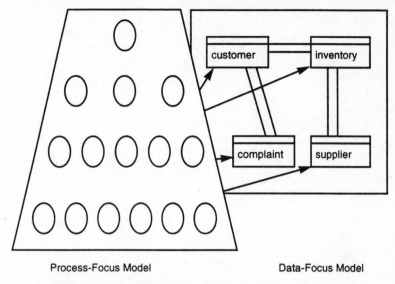

Process-Focus Model   Data-Focus Model

Exhibit III-3-4. Simplified Integration of Process and Data Models

process modeling techniques appear in McLeod's *Systems Analysis and Design: An Organizational Approach* (The Dryden Press, 1994) and other comparable process modeling texts.

The arrows in Exhibit III-3-4 illustrate the interaction or connection between the data structures in the process model and the data structure representation in the data model. Each access to a data structure in the process model is represented by either an object (e.g., customer) on the data model or a relationship between objects (e.g., the connection between customer and inventory, or customer buys inventory). It is beyond the scope of this chapter to provide the detailed process of connecting the process-focused model to the data-focused model. A possible connection can be established between the process and the data models. Once the process model has been developed, the principles of object orientation can be applied to the construction of a data model that will often provide better insight and use of existing data structures. If a particular data structure on the process model is not in its most logical format (redundancy with other data structures, transitive relationships, or other problems associated with data structures), the data model will show the changes and these changes will eventually be incorporated into the process model. Exhibit III-3-5 illustrates the creation of a logical data structure model (entity-relationship diagram) and how it influences the changes in the process-focused diagram.

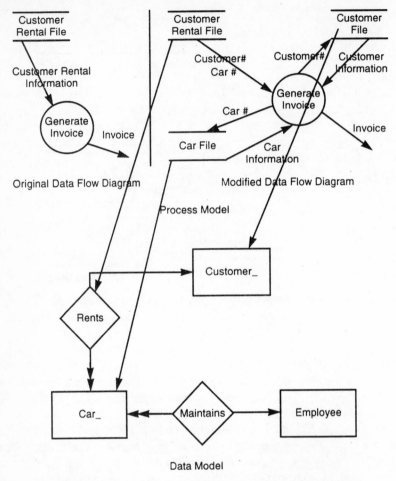

Exhibit III-3-5. Relationship Between Data and Process Models

The original diagram accessed a complex data structure identified as a customer rental file. A normalization process generates a data model that in essence created three entities (i.e., customer, employee, and car) with relationships between the objects where customers rent cars and employees maintain cars. The final result is that the process diagram is modified by the data model. The data model is a quality-control mechanism that ensures that the data used in the organization is in the most logical format. When that format is assured, data can easily be shared throughout the organization to improve both coordination and communication between the essential processes and the support departments on the higher level.

Data can also be easily maintained, thereby ensuring its integrity. It is the business rules in the activities or processes within the organization that establish the relationships between the various data objects. As the process model is applied to the entire organization, the data model is also extended to the entire organization (generally depicted by Exhibit III-3-2). The end product is an organizational process model supported by an organizational data model. The data administrator maintains the data model and coordinates the various processes and support departments to ensure that changes in the process model are incorporated into the data model, subsequently modifying the process model.

CREATING A HORIZONTAL ORGANIZATION

Roles and Responsibilities

To create a horizontal organization by integrating a process model and a data model, the organization will still have to identify the strategic goals of the organization and key competitive advantages (e.g., customer satisfaction and quality-control issues) to achieve these goals. These key competitive advantages will help the organization identify the core or essential processes necessary to achieve the goals.

The next step is the restructuring of the organization. This restructuring involves establishing multidisciplinary teams centered around the essential processes. At this point, the teams will identify key objectives that will help them achieve the overall goals of the organization. Once the objectives have been identified, the essential process can be decomposed into several basic subprocesses that will allow the essential process to achieve its objectives. These subprocesses will often be multidisciplinary, involving accounting, finance, marketing, sales, production, and others.

After the essential processes and key subprocesses are identified, the organization should know what support departments are needed to provide more expertise for the essential processes. Of course, the standard support departments (e.g., legal, accounting, and other basic support functions) will probably be identified by both senior-level management and the essential processes. Each subprocess will be decomposed into smaller processes—each with its set of objectives (that support the objectives of its parent subprocess, as was mentioned earlier) creating a hierarchical IS model.

Again, the process of generating an IS model is not a disguise replacing one hierarchical structure with another. The process modeling concept is the identification of related activities or processes as a means of understanding the various multidisciplinary activities needed for incorporation into an essential process or support department. It shows how the activities within the organization interact, and not necessarily the lines of authority and responsibility often identified in the traditional hierarchical structure. Exhibit III-3-2 shows the hierarchical nature of the process modeling method.

To facilitate the generation of an organizational process model, a steering committee should be established at the highest level of the organization to set such standards and guidelines as naming conventions for data elements and process identification. Each support department and essential process is responsible for developing its portion of the process model. Some overhead training will be needed to provide personnel involved in the development of the process model with basic information about process modeling. Experience has shown that a basic discussion (e.g., type of symbols, use of input data flows, processing, and output data flows) is necessary only to get nontechnical information personnel involved in the development process.

With the advance of group decision support systems, a systems analyst can facilitate the decision-making processes used to generate the key objectives and the subprocesses. As each support department and essential process builds its respective model, the steering committee will provide guidance and coordination between all these components. When each portion of the model (i.e., support departments and the essential processes) is completed, the steering committee will be responsible for bringing each portion together into an overall organizational model.

Once the overall model is created, the data administrator will be responsible for normalizing the data structures and subsequently for generating the data model. The series of steps used to generate the actual data model is beyond the scope of this chapter. But the general concepts of object-oriented analysis and design along with the normalizing process are used to generate this data model. Once the data model is completed, the process model must be modified to reflect the more logically created data structures. Exhibit III-3-4 illustrates generally how data models on the project level change the process model. The same approach is used to develop data models on the organizational level and subsequent changes to the organizational-level process models.

A CASE tool should be used to expedite the development of the subprocesses for the essential processes and for the support departments. The principles for selecting the appropriate CASE tool were discussed earlier. In short, the CASE tool should be process-oriented with the ability to generate data models in support of the process models. The CASE tool should be powerful enough to handle complex organizations involving many levels. It should also be flexible enough to handle the dynamics of change. This decision must not be a trivial decision.

Building a dynamic process and data model is the salient consideration when deciding on an appropriate CASE tool. The methodology that supports the CASE tool is also important. The main point of this chapter is that the horizontal organization can be depicted by a process-focused model supported by a data model. Therefore, a few simple, easy-to-understand symbols are necessary so that both technical and nontechnical IS personnel can use them appropriately. Getting senior management to commit to a CASE tool and methodology is the underlying foundation of this approach. The use of the CASE tool must be a total effort by all personnel. The maintenance of the process model is the responsibility of each essential process and support department. With the help of the systems analyst component of each process, changes will be the constant force that drives the continuous development of the process model. By incorporating users and IS personnel into the process model methodology, a common communications tool (e.g., CASE tool) can be used to help facilitate changes within the organization. All individuals within the organization should be able to visualize their contribution to the organization and its goals by locating their process and its objectives in the process model.

CONCLUSION

Incorporating the horizontal concept into today's organization is an important trend that will allow the organization to be more competitive in domestic and international markets for profit organizations and funding sources for nonprofit organizations. The horizontal organization will reduce the amount of bureaucracy which often generates information delays and failures. Organizations will need to be able to change quickly to meet the challenges of a volatile, competitive environment. IS methodologies should integrate recent trends to be successful and accepted by organizations. An effective approach would be to integrate the horizontal organization into an organizational process model supported by a data model. The process model should focus on the essential processes and the support departments in building its information system model.

The process model will help organizations move logically toward the horizontal organization by ensuring that the activities within each essential process and support department provide overall support for the goals of the organization. The process model will also provide better coordination and communication throughout the organization by integrating the information used within it. The data model that supports the process model will ensure that the information is in its most logical format, thereby allowing the various components of the organization that need information to have it in a timely fashion. With the help of an effective, user-friendly CASE tool as the common communication tool throughout the organization, the process model will become a dynamic tool for change.

III-4
Domain Study: Analyzing Production Data

MICHAEL SCOFIELD

Reverse data engineering is one of many ways of discerning a correct model of the existing enterprise, which is a starting point for constructing an ideal model for the future. Other techniques include examining any previously existing business models (particularly data models), interviewing knowledgeable users and IS staff members, and surveying existing business policy and systems documentation.

Unfortunately, all these sources may yield an incomplete or obsolete view of existing business practice and policy. Models may become stale if not updated. The same can be said for business policy documents and application systems documentation. Most organizations fail to keep these up-to-date. A solution is to examine existing production data. Found in master files, tables, and transaction files, this is an excellent source of information about current practices. But what is the best way to look at this data? A file dump is too difficult to read, and only shows you a few records. The reader cannot see the total scope and trends of individual kinds of data.

THE DOMAIN STUDY TECHNIQUE

At the consumer packaged goods company where I work, we developed the domain study technique of creating an inventory of data values found on production files. Some of the examples of data from our files are altered to protect proprietary data, but the kinds of data values we found are faithfully portrayed.

The domain study is different from a file dump in that it looks at a single column at a time but looks at all the values in that column over all the records (see Exhibit III-4-1). This first level of understanding data behavior in a column is to see what values can be found. But to do so with confidence, we must look at the values in the column.

The domain study uses a query language. In my shop, we have had FOCUS for a number of years and it serves very well, but other fourth-generation languages will probably work equally well. The only requirements are that it

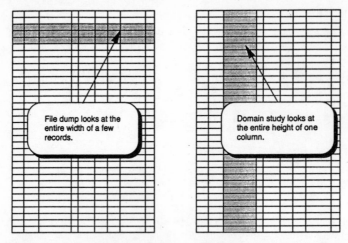

Exhibit III-4-1. The Difference Between a File Dump and a Domain Study

must be a language that is easily manipulated, replicated, and modified and that has a simple file description mechanism that can be used repeatedly in different code. COBOL has been found too tedious for this purpose.

When examining a column to see how the data behaves, we should ask some basic questions:

- How many unique values are observed?
- What are the extremes in the values (i.e., the highest and the lowest values)?
- How is the data skewed?
- What are the most common values?
  What are the most rare?

The extremes in values and the rare values may reveal data anomalies to us. They may reveal unusual subsets of the subject entity described by the file or table. These subsets may be entity subtypes, or totally new entities that must be considered when creating a data architecture. It is these anomalies that are often overlooked by systems documentation and often lost in the oral tradition or information knowledge of the employees.

INFORMATION ABOUT MAJOR FILES

In our shop, we compose domain study books about major files. These consist of one page per column in the file. There are two general page formats: one for many-valued fields and the other for few-valued fields.

Few Valued Columns

The most common type of field in this category is a simple code. Consider gender for example. What values in the employee master file might we find? The FOCUS query below is preceded by a simple three-line declaration of a counter field, one per record to aid our survey:

```
DEFINE FILE EMPLMAST
RECCNT/P5 = 1;
END
TABLE FILE EMPLMAST
SUM RECCNT BY SEX
ON TABLE SUMMARIZE
END
```

The answer provided (either online, or in a paper report) would be in the format shown in Exhibit III-4-2. We may assume (if the master file data is correct) that the employee master file has 1,421 records for males and 947 records for females. This very simple case demonstrates the domain study format and technique. A more complex situation assumes that the customer master file contains three kinds of customers in terms of their progression along a life cycle. This might be found in the documentation as follows:

Status Code	Meaning
A	Prospective
B	Active
C	Dormant (no activity for two years)

A superficial analyst would read that documentation, and go no further. A cynic will look at the data on the master file. Building a domain study might reveal something else:

```
TABLE FILE CUSTMAST
SUM RECCNT BY STATUS
ON TABLE SUMMARIZE
END
```

This report in Exhibit III-4-3 immediately tells us that there is another value in the domain (R) not found in the documentation. Immediately, the domain study has been helpful because R is not in the original documentation.

SEX	RECCNT
M	1,421
F	947
TOTAL	2,368

Exhibit III-4-2. Answer Format for FOCUS

STATUS	RECCNT
A	241
B	1,947
C	482
R	1
TOTAL	2,671

Exhibit III-4-3. Customer Master File Summary Report

Furthermore, the fact that there is only one record with this value is cause for further investigation. It could be an error. If so, the individuals responsible for the integrity of the data should be notified. It could be that a data entry program did not test for valid values.

Another option might be that the R value is legitimate, added to the valid domain by some programmer or analyst after the system had been running for a while, and the documentation was never updated. Whatever the case may be, it is important to understand what is going on.

Many files have foreign keys—that is, code fields that logically point back to the root table or file where the home domain resides. A comparison of the valid values on the master table may be compared against the values found in the corresponding foreign keys of these other files.

In the example in Exhibit III-4-4, the inventory file has a warehouse number field that should contain only values found in the valid warehouse table. Unless you have an effective relational data base with the referential integrity feature turned on, you cannot necessarily assume that the domain of these foreign keys is confined to the domain of the reference table. Most of

TABLE FILE
INVENTORYM SUM
RECCNT BY WHSE ON
TABLE SUMMARIZE END

WHSE	RECCNT
	472
P	1
01	441
02	537
03	522
11	203
12	78
13	42
21	492
A	1
ST	1
TOTAL	2,671

Exhibit III-4-4. Sample Inventory File

the records in this inventory master file have valid and well-behaved warehouse numbers. However, there are many records with a blank in the warehouse number field—perhaps for some business reason. Then, there are three records with what appear to be errors.

This is the basic form of a few-valued domain study—a simple tally or record count. Because it is so simple, it may be worthwhile to enrich the page by cross-tabulating the column under study against the most significant major categorical grouping of records in the file. In Exhibit III-4-2, the life cycle may be the most significant categorical grouping. Some customers (customer records) in status-A may not have the same attributes as those in status-B (active customers). This should occur when something like credit rating is examined. For this, record counts may be shown in Exhibit III-4-5.

Reverse data engineering is an inferential exercise. If the first line of the report represents a blank credit rating and means the absence of a credit rating, the following statements can be made about business policy (or business practice) from the data in Exhibit III-4-5.

- Credit rating 2 is the most common or popular rating.
- Credit ratings have been assigned to some prospective customers. (Should they be?)
- The strange *R* record has no credit rating assigned.

Aside from the blanks in the credit rating code, (which we assume mean not yet assigned) and the anomalous *R* record, the data is reasonably well behaved.

It is important to give serious thought to what the major subdivision of occurrences in an entity (i.e., records on a file) is. When considering using a record type code, it is essential to first question if record types really reflect separate or distinct subject entities. If so, separate sets of domain studies should be done on each record type.

Many-Valued Columns

The approach taken to many-valued columns is slightly different, because the entire domain of values cannot be printed on a single page. Therefore, this

TABLE FILE CUSTMAST SUM RECCNT AND ROW TOTAL
ACROSS STATUS BY CREDIT—RATING ON TABLE
SUMMARIZE END

CREDIT RATING	STATUS A	B	C	R	TOTAL
	225			1	226
1	4	251	51		306
2	10	1,400	400		1,810
3	2	296	31		329
TOTAL	241	1,947	482	1	2,671

Exhibit III-4-5. Sample of Cross-Tabulated Record Counts

applies to columns with more than 40 to 50 values. In this class of columns, we search for the extremes. This is done with a slightly more complex query language routine, which should ultimately be modularized.

On our customer file, we keep an observation of how much total revenue each customer earns in a year (regardless of how much business they do with us). We need to extract a temporary file (**REV 1**) that contains one record for each observed value. Then, we would sort it by those observed values. TOTREV is the total customer revenue for the past fiscal year:

```
TABLE FILE CUSTMAST
SUM RECCNT BY TOTREV
ON TABLE HOLD AS REV1
END
```

In the temporary work file (**REV1**), we have only two fields; **RECCNT** and **TOTREV**. We access that with a query that basically gives us the five highest values:

```
TABLE FILE REV1
PRINT RECCNT BY HIGHEST TOTREV
IF RECORDLIMIT EQUAL 5
END
```

The result appears in Exhibit III-4-6a; it seems to be well-behaved data. A similar second-step extract would provide us with the five lowest values (as

---

FIVE HIGHEST VALUES

TOTREV	RECCNT
4,271	1
3,151	1
2,982	1
2,741	1
2,711	1

a. Highest Values Report

FIVE LOWEST VALUES

TOTREV	RECCNT
4	1
3	1
2	1
1	1
0	421

b. Lowest Values Report

Exhibit III-4-6. Highest and Lowest Values Reports

seen in Exhibit III-4-6b). The query used is:

```
TABLE FILE REV1
PRINT RECCNT BY TOTREV
IF RECORDLIMIT EQUAL 5
END
```

This suggests that there are 421 records (i.e., 421 customers) for which we have no figures on annual total revenue. The value zero could also mean that the revenue actually is zero. Sometimes, in data design, we need ways to distinguish the different meanings of a value; this is covered later in this article.

Another useful statistic is to know simply how many distinct values are observed in a column. This is easily done in any query language. Finally, we want to know the 10 or 20 most frequently seen values. This requires one additional query:

```
TABLE FILE REV1
PRINT TOTREV BY HIGHEST RECCNT
ON TABLE SAVE AS REV2
END
*

TABLE FILE REV2
IF RECORDLIMIT EQ 10
PRINT TOTREV RECCNT
END
```

Exhibit III-4-7 shows the most popular 10 records, but the regular approach is to show the top 20.

Many amount fields in master reference files and transaction files often are skewed like this. The nice round dollar amounts of total revenue suggest that people typically make estimates in round numbers, and this is understandable. This is very well behaved data.

TEN MOST COMMON
VALUES

TOTREV	RECCNT
0	421
100	82
200	49
500	37
300	31
1000	28
400	25
2000	23
5000	19
3000	18

Exhibit III-4-7. Ten Most Common Values Sample Report

TEN MOST COMMON
VALUES

PRODNO	RECCNT
	597
10425	381
59205	322
E4400	289
10592	276
42252	218
52093	205
52091	197
20422	192

Exhibit III-4-8. Sample Product Numbers in the Invoice File

TESTING KEYS AND FOREIGN KEYS

The many-valued domain study is useful for examining the behavior of key fields. Any domain test on what is reputed to be a unique key to a file should yield no more than one record per value. Logical keys should, of course, have certain characteristics that make them easy to use—they should be short, for example. They also should not have any imbedded spaces.

Domain studies of some of our production data files have revealed some surprises. For example, we examined product number in our invoice file. It should be a foreign key, pointing to the product number in our product file (five digits, numeric). Exhibit III-4-8 shows that we discovered 597 records with blank (or a common nonprintable character combination) in the product number field. Were these records representing something other than a product shipment? Then, we noticed the E4400 value and after asking around, learned it was not a product number at all. The product number field in this old file was used, in some circumstance, to carry an account number for some other purpose.

As previously mentioned, looking at the extremes of coded fields often reveals some anomalies, if not ouright errors. An account number's normal format should be an alpha character, followed by five digits (see Exhibit III-4-9).

FIVE LOWEST VALUES

ACCTNO	RECCNT
	4,029
	2,421
A4002	1
A10031	3
A10042	5

Exhibit III-4-9. An Account Number's Normal Format

FIVE LOWEST VALUES

CLAIMNO	RECCNT
C425253	1
A001402	1
A001573	1
A001843	1
A002047	1

Exhibit III-4-10. Sample Claims File with a Leading Blank

In the file shown in Exhibit III-4-10, we found two distinct values that were nonprintable. One was probably blanks, and the other may be low values. They were probably put there by different programs in a legacy system with a long chain of cascading files. The third line of the report in Exhibit III-4-10 shows what is probably a keying error. It also suggests that there was inadequate validation in the screen software when this was entered (i.e., if it had been entered online).

Although examining the 5 or 10 lowest and highest values (the value extremes) on a key field may seem boring because only one record for each value is obtained, some interesting data anomalies are occasionally encountered. In a claims file, we discovered that one key field had a leading blank. This probably created in some legitimate data entry mode by a user (see Exhibit III-4-10). The irony is, that the user will never find that record again, because they probably didn't realize they had keyed in a leading space, and when they try to retrieve it, they most likely will not key in the leading space. The user may assume that the record didn't "take" for some reason, and reenter the same key. One questionable design decision that led to this problem is allowing trailing blanks in a key field.

The list of most common values shown in Exhibit III-4-11 reveals a pattern of two distinct formats of bill-of-lading numbers. This strongly suggests there are two kinds of bills-of-lading. Perhaps they come from different sources. Or, the field is used for a second purpose or meaning under some circumstances. This should be investigated, especially because most of the observed values fall so neatly into the two formats.

Foreign keys are sometimes rigorous, and sometimes optional. In the order file shown in Exhibit III-4-12, some anomalies are encountered. We seen that 235 orders have not specified the customers. Why? Some appear to be generated because of the consistency of the value encountered. But there, buried among legitimate-looking customer numbers, is the term **SAMPLE**. Orders may be allowed so that sales representatives can get some samples for themselves. How should that be modeled in the as-is model? How should that be handled in terms of business policy or practice in the new environment? Reading only the old documentation might not have revealed this.

TWENTY MOST COMMON
VALUES

BL_NUMBER	RECCNT
DEF40285A	41
DEF29571C	34
DEG15223H	25
C12-5298	22
DED15242P	21
C12-5693	19
C13-5223	17
DED13822R	16
DED14239H	16
F14-5234	16
FEF42352G	16
C13-2523	15
C17-4253	15
C42-1523	14
C43-3824	14
C52-4235	14

Exhibit III-4-11. Sample List of Most Common Values

LOOKING AT EXTREMES IN NUMERIC FIELDS

As mentioned, examining the five highest and five lowest values often reveals data anomalies, data errors, or new subject entities. In the product master file, one field (shown in Exhibit III-4-13) provided the unit weight (in pounds) for each product. The 34,000 pounds is so significantly higher than all the other

TWENTY MOST COMMON
VALUES

CUST_CODE	RECCNT
	235
. . .	112
295033	109
293841	104
284235	103
134234	101
425632	98
142522	97
SAMPLE	92
252342	91
252883	89
252342	87
968332	86
258329	86
938427	85
592883	82

Exhibit III-4-12. Sample Order File with Anomalies

FIVE HIGHEST VALUES

PROD__WT	RECCNT
34,000	1
410	1
381	1
362	2
340	3

Exhibit III-4-13. Sample Product Master File

---

values in the column, that we must wonder if it is an error, especially because there are three records with 340 pounds. If this is not an error, it represents a significantly different kind of product and perhaps should be studied more with the possibility of developing a new subtype of the product entity.

In a delivery history file, we may want to look at units sold. In approximately 6,000 records, we see 429 discrete values. This is not a problem because customers often purchase in 10s and 100s of units. But when we look at the extremes in the values (shown in Exhibit III-4-14) we discover that the **UNITS__SOLD** column can have negative values. These are probably not errors. Again, by asking around, we discovered that when products are returned, or credits provided to the customer for damaged shipments, records are posted with negative values.

TEXT FIELDS

Domain studies applied to text fields may provide some interesting—perhaps humorous—but not always crucial discoveries. Exhibit III-4-15 shows the prob-

---

FIVE HIGHEST VALUES

UNITS__SOLD	RECCNT
521	1
410	1
381	1
362	2
340	3

FIVE LOWEST VALUES

UNITS__SOLD	RECCNT
−25	2
−50	1
−100	1
−120	1
−140	1

Exhibit III-4-14. Sample Delivery History File with Extremes in Values

FIVE LOWEST VALUES

CITY	RECCNT
	316
NEW YORK	1
ABILENE	1
ALAMEDA	3
ALHAMBRA	2

a. Leading Space Anomalies

FIVE LOWEST VALUES

CITY	RECCNT
	114
@@RTGI	1
@FRESNO	1
AKRON	1
AZUSA	2

b. Other Anomalies

FIVE LOWEST VALUES

CITY	RECCNT
XENIA	1
ZANZIBAR	4
ZION	2
Z@	1
ZZZZZ	1

c. High-End Anomalies

Exhibit III-4-15. Sample Text Field Anomalies

---

lem of leading spaces and other similar anomalies. It also shows an example of anomalies at the high end of some text fields.

The ZZZZZ deserves some examination. It could be a different kind of record on the file. This happens often when a master file is used for verification of a field in some other application or process. If some of the transactions being verified have (because of the design of the application) some value other than a valid city name (in Exhibit III-4-15) something unusual is placed on the master file to enable the unusual transaction or process. These will often appear in the extremes of the domain range, but not always.

DATA HORROR STORIES

Looking at date fields can yield many interesting situations. Our query language allowed us to display dates with slashes between the subfields, even though they were not actually stored on the file. Using that, we discovered the data shown in Exhibit III-4-16.

FIVE LOWEST VALUES

RECEIVE_DT	RECCNT
/ /	452
01/02/87	3
01/02/89	9
01/02/90	4
01/03/91	16

FIVE HIGHEST VALUES

RECEIVE_DT	RECCNT
93/06/22	14
93/06/21	8
93/06/20	22
93/06/16	9
93/06/14	17

Exhibit III-4-16. Sample Date Field

This was a date field whose format was not clearly defined. Some of the old batch systems were inserting a date in the YY/MM/DD format, while other programs were inserting it as MM/DD/YY. Some records had no date whatsoever, which is another example of the need for a consistent policy on handling missing or unknown data.

There may be another benefit from running such a thorough analysis of the file (i.e., from reading every field in every record with your query language). It tests for some fundamental data exceptions, such as blanks in a numeric field. These would cause a different kind of error which is not technically a part of domain studies.

Some date fields located as part of a domain study have other text in them; Exhibit III-4-17 shows an example. (With this query language, the slashes between the components of the date are in the presentation, not in the raw data.) A simple sort by some text fields will reveal a variety of spellings of common names. This is not seen in the basic domain study format, but it can be done with a query language quite easily.

FIVE LOWEST VALUES

RECEIVE_DT	RECCNT
/ /	452
UN/KN/OW	4
01/02/87	3
01/02/89	9
01/02/90	4

Exhibit III-4-17. Sample Date Field with Text

THE MEANING OF BLANKS AND NULLS

Modern data bases provide us with the NULL value in a column, but for many years, this feature was not available. Programmers were allowed great latitude in how they dealt with this issue.

A zero in most numeric fields mean zero or null. Even when a reliable convention for indicating null exists, the null can mean:

- Not applicable.
- Unknown.
- To be supplied later.

In a historical file, the "to be supplied later" and "unknown" are probably not good interpretations of a zero value. Then, they must be "not applicable." For example, in an invoice history file, the line-item amount field might have the most common values—shown in Exhibit III-4-18.

Having 152 records on an *invoice history* file with a zero value suggests that not all line items are created equal. There may be line items that do not represent product movement, but perhaps other kinds of conditions or charges. In addition, the relatively high occurrence (18 count) of records with exactly $100.00 suggests that this is a fee rather than the cost of some item sold. It might be useful to take only the records with these amounts and cross-tabulate them against some other code, such as a record type.

Several illustrations in this chapter show blanks in some code fields, such as foreign keys. A data analyst should clarify just what these blanks mean—that is, is the data missing, not applicable, or to be supplied later?

TESTING NORMALIZATION AND DATA INTEGRITY

With a flexible query language, a variety of tests about data quality can be performed. Some of these have been shown in the previous examples. Another

---

TEN MOST COMMON
VALUES

LINEAMT	RECCNT
0.00	152
100.00	18
1050.00	7
26.49	6
156.24	6
245.42	4
88.02	3
52.97	3
79.42	2
25.42	1

III-4-18. Sample Invoice History File

set of tests is useful when evaluating the normalization of production flat files. Many older production files contain data about more than one subject entity. When there is a supertypesubtype relationship, it is easy to test for the presence or absence of data that applies only to the subtype.

Other unnormalized flat files contain redundant data about subordinate entities that, if properly normalized, would get their own, separate table. An example of this is the product file. A can of soup is a very common item to the consumer. Yet, it may be sold to the retailer in a variety of case sizes. For the rural store, soup may be sold in a small case containing only 24 cans. For the major chain, it may be sold in a larger case containing 72 cans. A 48-can case size may exist for other retailers (e.g., a caterer).

Although the characteristics of the case (e.g., dimension or weight) may be different, the characteristics of the consumer unit—the can of soup—(e.g., radius or height) should be the same.

Because the product file is a flat, unnormalized file and contains one record per case, and some cases may have the same can inside, some of the can data is assumed to be redundant. If it is, it should depend on a key field (the can code), and the redundant data should be consistent.

A query tool can be used to test that hypothesis ("all redundant data is consistent"). In the following query, CASECODE is the key for the product file, CANCODE is the logical key for consumer unit, and RADIUS is an attribute of the consumer unit. The steps in the query language code to eliminate consumer units occurring only in a single case is not shown.

```
TABLE FILE PRODMAST
PRINT RADIUS
BY CANCODE BY CASECODE
END
        *
```

The result is a table, which can be checked to see that the radius is the same for a particular can of soup (see Exhibit III-4-19). If the file has many unnormalized fields, a more general routine can be easily written to high-light data anomalies such as the fifth line in the report shown in Exhibit III-4-19.

CANCODE	CASECODE	RADIUS
52425	42552	4.525
	42553	4.525
	42553	4.525
65002	89001	2.125
	89002	2.120
	89002	2.125

Exhibit III-4-19. Sample Table Showing Consistent Redundant Data

CONCLUSION

Employing a convenient query language to apply the domain study technique can be an important source of knowledge about existing business policy and practice. It can reveal much that conventional documentation may omit.

Section IV
Models and Methodologies

This handbook covers many of the strategic concerns in getting an organization to endorse and adopt data management principles; however, it is impossible to ignore the tactical issues, the nitty-gritty, of getting the work done. This section (and the next) deals with several issues relating to data modeling—specifically, methodologies, deliverables, and approaches.

Chapter IV-1, "Data, Processes, and Events: Keys to Comprehensive Analysis," discusses the use of EERD—entity-event-relationship diagramming—as a tool that adds rigor to the modeling of both data and functions. "Comparison of Three Systems Modeling Techniques," Chapter IV-2, describes entity-relationship modeling, Shlaer and Mellor's Information Modeling, and Rumbaugh's Object Modeling Technique.

The object-oriented (OO) approach is supposed to deliver productivity improvements. Chapter IV-3, "Object-Oriented Modeling of MRP," describes how within the manufacturing environment, OO modeling works quite effectively with computer-aided design systems.

IV-1

Data, Processes, and Events: Keys to Comprehensive Analysis

PHILIP FRIEDLANDER

E vent-driven analysis can add an extra degree of rigor to both data and functional modeling as well as to the process of systems analysis. Event-driven analysis expands both the requirements-gathering and requirements-validation processes and introduces additional levels of depth and rigor to data, process, and event modeling techniques. This chapter introduces modeling tools that combine process, data, and event techniques.

ENTITY-LIFE HISTORIES AND DATA MODELING

Entity-life history (ELH) diagrams show all the events in the life of an entity; that is, all the states in which the entity can exist during its life. Each major data entity in the data model should have an ELH diagram that shows the major stages of its existence. However, more information than the stages of an entity's life are needed for a thorough understanding of the entity.

Most entities have certain required states (e.g., creation or instantiation, updating, and deletion). Exhibit IV-1-1 shows an ELH diagram for an entity called INSTRUCTOR. It has the required create, update, and delete stages. These stages are called the *entity support* stages, because these stages are required to support the entity's existence.

Exhibit IV-1-1 also shows an additional life stage, ASSIGN INSTRUCTOR TO CLASS. If this life stage does not support the entity, what is its purpose? The partial entity-relationship diagram (ERD) in Exhibit IV-1-2 shows that INSTRUCTOR teaches COURSE. The life stage of ASSIGN INSTRUCTOR TO COURSE supports the relationship that INSTRUCTOR has with COURSE. This type of entity-life stage is called a *relationship support stage*.

Therefore, each stage in an ELH must either support the entity or a relationship that the entity has with another entity. By understanding the differences between entity-support and relationship-support stages, a systems

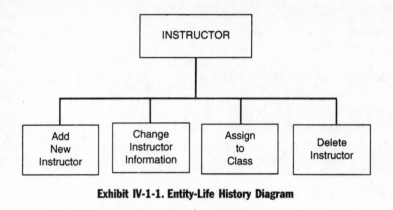

Exhibit IV-1-1. Entity-Life History Diagram

analyst can better understand the nature of relationships in data models. For example, a stage is an entity-support stage only if its event does not involve another entity; if another entity is involved, the stage is a relationship-support stage.

ELH AND PROCESS MODELING

Each stage of life of an entity is represented by one or more functions in a process model. A function may not equal a single process in the process model. The correspondence of functions to processes in the process model depends on the degree of abstraction with which the process model was developed. The degree to which there is one-to-one correspondence, however, is not critical during early analysis.

An important practice in analyzing life stages is that in addition to identifying the specific functionality required, analysts must also identify the events required to change the entity's state. A number of different analytical tools are available for the analysis of events. The most popular is the state-transition diagram (STD). Although they effectively model events and states. STDs have little connection to data flow and entity relationship diagrams.

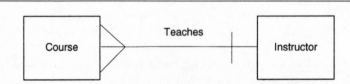

Exhibit IV-1-2. Sample of a Partial Entity-Relationship Diagram

EXISTENCE CRITERIA AND COUPLING

When examining a relationship between two entities, analysts must consider the relationship's cardinality and whether the relationship is required or optional for each entity. Exhibit IV-1-3 depicts existence criteria. The O symbol indicates that the relationship is optional, and the I symbol indicates that the relationship is required. Because all relationships are bidirectional, the analyst must show the existence criteria for each direction (i.e., entity). Exhibit IV-1-3 models the fact that a course must have an instructor. The two bars in the diagram indicate that a maximum of one instructor can teach a course. The O next to the COURSE entity indicates that an instructor does not have to teach any course.

In addition to existence criteria, the coupling of a relationship must also be examined. Coupling measures how much an action (i.e., change in stage) in one entity affects actions in a related entity. When assessing the coupling and existence criteria of a relationship, analysts must also determine whether the relationship is full or sparse. A relationship is considered *full* if the new occurrence of an entity immediately establishes a relationship with at least one occurrence of another entity. A full relationship is a form of moderate coupling, but this view of a relationship does not completely depict the nature of relationships.

In tightly coupled relationships, actions in one entity cause actions in another. There are nine possible combinations of a tightly coupled relationship. These nine possibilities are the product of combining create, update, and delete states in two entities (see Exhibit IV-1-4). The nine types of tightly coupled relationships are examined in the next section.

Types of Tightly Coupled Relationships

The following sections illustrate cases where action in one entity causes an action in another.

Create-Create. Exhibit IV-1-5 models an order-entity and billing system. A relationship exists between ORDER and LINE ITEMS. The ERD in Exhibit IV-1-5 shows that the relationship is required on both sides; that is, an order must have at least one line item and a line item must be associated with an order.

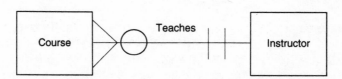

Exhibit IV-1-3. Existence Criteria in an Entity-Relationship Diagram

Effected Entity

	Create	Update	Delete
Create	Create Create	Create Update	Create Delete
Update	Update Create	Update Update	Update Delete
Delete	Delete Create	Delete Update	Delete Delete

Casual Entity (row axis label)

Exhibit IV-1-4. The Nine Combinations of Tight Coupling

The relationship between these two entities has another dimension. The creation of an ORDER immediately establishes a relationship with a LINE ITEM. Not only is this a full relationship but, more specific, the creation of an occurrence of one entity causes the creation of an occurrence of another entity. The creation of an ORDER does not just establish a relationship with an existing occurrence of LINE ITEM, it creates a new occurrence of LINE ITEM. In this tightly coupled relationship, the create state in one entity causes a create state in another entity.

Create-Update. Exhibit IV-1-5 shows that CUSTOMER has many IN-VOICES. The CUSTOMER entity has a data element called Date of Last Invoice. Thus, a new occurrence (i.e., creation) of INVOICE causes Date of Last Invoice to be updated.

Create-Delete. In the order-entry system, a customer who fails to pay after a certain period is placed in a bad customer file, which is used by the collections department. Such a customer is no longer allowed to conduct business with the supplier. The ERD in Exhibit IV-1-5 illustrates that the creation of an occurrence of a BAD CUSTOMER entity causes an instance of the CUSTOMER entity to be deleted.

Update-Create. The order-entry system must handle price changes, which can be volatile. The PRODUCT entity has a data element that stores the latest price, and for each price change a new instance of the PRICE CHANGE JOURNAL entity records the date, time, person changing, and old and new prices. In other words, an update in the PRODUCT entity causes the creation of a new occurrence of PRODUCT CHANGE JOURNAL.

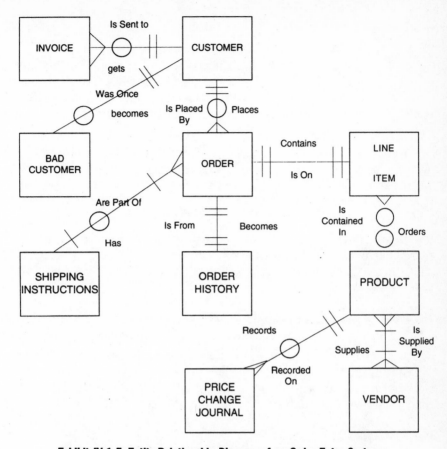

Exhibit IV-1-5. Entity-Relationship Diagram of an Order-Entry System

Update-Update. The system must store the price and availability of all products from every vendor. The **PRODUCT** entity must always reflect the best price of a product and its vendor. When the availability of a product is updated in the **VENDOR** entity, the summary of product availability is also updated in the **PRODUCT** entity.

Update-Delete. The system must record special handling and shipping instructions for a small percentage of orders. Often, special shipping instructions are canceled by the customer after the order has been taken. In such a case, an update to one entity causes the deletion of an occurrence of another. When special shipping instruction information is removed from the **ORDER** entity, the relationship with the **SHIPPING INSTRUCTIONS** entity changes, and that instance of the **SHIPPING INSTRUCTIONS** entity involved in the old relationship is deleted. An update to **ORDER** causes a deletion of **SHIPPING INSTRUCTIONS**.

Delete-Create. The ERD in Exhibit IV-1-5 shows that when an order is closed, information about the order is recorded in the **ORDER HISTORY** entity. Thus, the deletion of an instance of **ORDER** creates a new occurrence of **ORDER HISTORY**. Obviously, the rules concerning the timing of the delete-create event can vary by application.

Delete-Update. The system also tracks customers who have outstanding invoices. When an invoice is paid in full, the occurrence of that invoice is deleted from the **INVOICE** entity, and the **CUSTOMER** entity is updated to reflect the invoice-number date, and the amount of the last invoice paid in full. Deletion in **INVOICE** causes an update to **CUSTOMER**.

Delete-Delete. There are cases, of course, when the deletion of an occurrence of an entity causes the deletion of one or more occurrences of another entity. For example, if an instance of **ORDER** is deleted, all related **LINE ITEM** instances must also be deleted.

The Basis of the Event-Driven Approach

The nine types of slightly coupled relationships are the basis of the event-driven approach. This approach makes use of the ELH diagram. Unfortunately, the ELH diagram as it has been defined does not provide the richness and vigor required of an effective analysis tool. Although it can show changes, it cannot show what causes the change and how the change affects other entities.

The Four Types of Events

An event triggers a change in life stage of one or more entities. Based on this definition, there are only four categories of events.

Outside Influence. Exhibit IV-1-6 shows a simple ELH diagram for the **ORDER** entity of the example order entry system. The **ORDER** entity's first stage of life is the creation or addition of a new occurrence of the entity. This first stage is triggered by an outside influence. A new occurrence of **ORDER** would not have been created without the outside influence of the customer placing an order; this is modeled by **Is Placed By** relationship in the ERD in Exhibit IV-1-5. Outside influence is the most easily identified type of event.

Time. Time is another common trigger of state changes. Often, there are daily, weekly, monthly and end-of-year processing triggers. Such temporal triggers are obvious. Some time-based events are less obvious. For example, in Exhibit IV-1-5 there is a relationship between **CUSTOMER** and **BAD CUSTOMER** (see Exhibit IV-1-7). The creation of a new **BAD CUSTOMER** instance is triggered by time. A customer who does not pay a bill in a certain amount of time is classified a bad customer—a time triggered event.

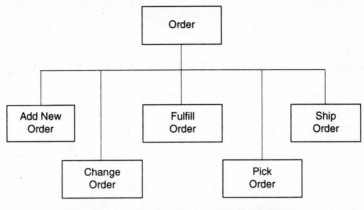

Exhibit IV-1-6. Entity-Life History of the ORDER Entity

Stage Change in Another Entity. Often, a stage change in one entity is a direct result of a stage change in another entity. The nine examples of tight coupling illustrate the ways in which this can happen.

Stage Change in the Same Entity. One change of stage in an entity can trigger another in the same entity. In Exhibit IV-1-6, the creation of a new instance of ORDER can trigger the stage Fulfill Order. The fulfilling of the order can trigger the picking of the inventory for the order. The picking stage cannot be triggered by only fulfilling an order but also by outside influences (i.e., someone writing the picking tickets). Often, an event occurs because of a combination of triggers.

TOWARD A MORE POWERFUL TOOL SET

The nine types of tight coupling and four types of events are used to formulate a new approach to requirements gathering and analysis. Analysis can be divided

---

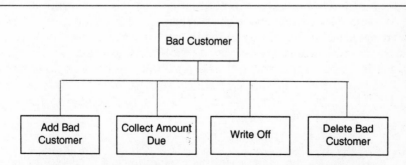

Exhibit IV-1-7. Entity-Life History Diagram of the BAD CUSTOMER Entity

into two major steps: requirements gathering and requirements validation. There has been much progress in the past few years in the validation of requirements. Requirements validation includes such steps as refinement and normalization of the data model, horizontal and vertical balancing of the process model, and rigorous synchronization of both models.

The requirements-gathering phase, however, has experienced less progress. Certainly, joint application design (JAD) and joint requirements definition (JRD) techniques have improved efficiency. These behavioral approaches, however, have two drawbacks. The first is that they depend on the skills of the facilitator; skills that are difficult to develop. The second drawback is that they are not highly structured and, moreover, cannot be readily replicated. The next objective, therefore, is to provide a framework for a more structured approach to requirements gathering, which can be repeated.

This framework specifies how to analyze the relationships between entities and each stage in the ELH. The first step in this technique requires that the major data entities be identified. Each pair of entities is analyzed for the nine potential combinations of tight coupling to derive the first-cut data relationships.

APPLYING THE APPROACH

The example used to illustrate this event-based approach is the order-entry system modeled in Exhibit IV-1-5. The four major entities—CUSTOMER, ORDER, LINE ITEM, and PRODUCT—have already been identified. Each pair of entities is examined for the nine combinations of tight coupling (see Exhibit IV-1-4).

The first entity pair is ORDER and LINE ITEM. One of the two is selected to be the causal entity and the other to be the affected entity. At this stage it does not matter which entity assumes which role because this exercise is repeated for the same pair in the other direction. This duality reflects the accepted concept that all data relationships are bidirectional. It is important to note that, the ORDER entity represents the header portion of an order and each occurrence of LINE ITEM reflects each line of an order.

The analyst compares each pair of entities to all nine types of tight coupling (see Exhibit IV-1-4) and examines each pair for relevance in the context of causal and affected entities. For example, starting with the upper left box, the analyst asks the client such a question as: Is there any case where the creation of an order (the causal entity) causes the creation of a line item (the affected entity)? The answer to this question is yes. When the system creates an order, the order must have at least one line item. The analyst checks the box to indicate the identification of an event.

These identified events are the building blocks of the requirements-gathering process. At first, it is not necessary to explore these events in detail. The fact that these events require further exploration and decomposition must be recorded.

Is there any case where the creation of an **ORDER** would cause the system to update a **LINE ITEM**? Probably not, because at the time an **ORDER** is created there would not have been an existing line item to which the order relates. Is there any case where the creation of an **ORDER** is cause to delete a **LINE ITEM**? Again, probably not.

Next considered is the update row of the causal entity. Is there any case where the update of the **ORDER** would cause the system to create a **LINE ITEM**? Once again, probably not. Is there any case where the update of **ORDER** would cause the system to update a line item? This would be a possibility if the **ORDER** contained an indication of customer type or order type that perhaps affects the pricing of each line item. If this is the case, it would once again be recorded as an event requiring further analysis. Is there any case where the update of an **ORDER** would cause the system to delete a **LINE ITEM**? Once again, probably not.

Proceeding to the final row (i.e., delete events), the practitioner asks the same set of questions. Is there any case where the deletion of an **ORDER** would cause the system to create a **LINE ITEM**? Probably not. Is there any case where the deletion of an **ORDER** would cause the system to update a **LINE ITEM**? Once again, probably not. Is there any case where the deletion of an **ORDER** would cause the system to delete an **LINE ITEM**? Definitely yes. When the system deletes an order it should delete all the line items attached to it. Once again, the practitioner records this as another event requiring further decomposition.

At least two and possibly three major events requiring further exploration have been identified. Exhibit IV-1-8 shows how an analyst would illustrate this

LINE ITEM Entity

		Create	Update	Delete
	Create	1 New Order		
ORDER Entity	Update		2 Change Customer Type	
	Delete			3 Delete or Cancel Order

Exhibit IV-1-8. Matrix for Identifying Events in a Pair of Entities

in the matrix. Because all relationships are bidirectional, the practitioner must look at causes and effects in both directions.

Looking from the Other Direction

Now the practitioner must go through the same procedure using the LINE ITEM as the causal entity and ORDER as the affected entity. There would be no case where the creation of a LINE ITEM causes the system to create an ORDER because the opposite is true; the creation of the ORDER causes the system to create a LINE ITEM. The creation of a LINE ITEM would, however, cause the system to update an ORDER; if the system adds a new line item to the order, it must reflect that in the order by updating the total cost, quantity, and number of line items.

The update of a LINE ITEM may also require the system to update the order to reflect changes in quantity or cost. The same thing would be true for the deletion of a line item. Deleting a line item would cause the system to reduce the total order cost, quantity, and number of line items.

THE DOCUMENTATION OF EVENTS

Once all the events associated with every entity pair have been identified, they must be documented. What information must analysts know about an event? They must know which entities are affected by the event. These entities were identified when the events were identified. Analysts must also know the event's trigger. Four basic types of event triggers have been identified:

- Time.
- Input.
- Stage change in another entity.
- Stage change in the same entity.

The latter two types are not really end-source event types because they are always ultimately triggered by one of the first two.

For example, the creation of a new ORDER causes the creation of at least one new LINE ITEM. In other words, this event is triggered by a stage change in the causal entity. However, this stage change in the causal entity is caused by the input of a new order. It is useful to review what has been discovered. There is an event that is caused by the input of a new order. This input-type of event in ORDER causes the creation stage of ORDER. In addition, it triggers the creation stage of LINE ITEM.

The business event or input that causes this event should be recorded as part of the event documentation. For example, the analyst should describe the various ways in which a customer can place an order, the type of order, and other such information. The analyst can also record the activities the system performs to process an order as well as the required interactions with the users.

This information about events has implications for the process model. Each stage in the ELH becomes one or more processes in the process model. Because an event can be triggered by input, the analyst has to account for the input in the process model as an input user-view (i.e., a data flow from an external entity to a process).

ITEMS TO BE RECORDED ABOUT AN EVENT

Exhibit IV-1-9 shows a sample of event documentation. This shows the documentation of an event called **Ship Order**. In Exhibit IV-1-9 the event's triggers have been listed; an order is shipped if it has already been picked and it is the end of the day. This is an example of a compound trigger: time (i.e., end of day) and another event (i.e., the picking of the order).

The event documentation also identifies the primary entity (i.e., **ORDER** and what happens to it as a result of this event (i.e., order is marked as shipped). The documentation also indicates the other events that are triggered by this event. Each of these triggered events has its own specific event documentation. This documentation can be used as process specifications for the process model.

EVENT NETWORKS

It is difficult to review each event document, its triggers, and resulting events and subsequently judge its correctness. It is difficult to visualize the trigger-to-trigger relationships of events. This difficulty can be overcome with aid of a graphic tool. This tool is an adaptation of the traditional Project Evaluation Review Technique/Critical Path Management (PERT/CPM) chart. Exhibit

---

Description:	Ship order
Primary entity:	Order
Trigger:	Order has been picked and end of the day
Action Required:	Mark order as shipped
Other Events Triggered:	Quanity added to shipped quantity
	History is added
	Update year-to-date amounts
	Order is deleted

Exhibit IV-1-9. Sample Event Documentation

IV-1-10 shows how event objects are placed into a PERT/CPM-like network to show relationships and dependencies.

Exhibit IV-1-10 also shows that additional triggers can be added to the event network to visually illustrate the trigger dependencies of certain events. For example, the **Ship Order** event in the network depends on two events—the picking of the order and the time trigger of **End-of-Day**. In the chart, parallelograms indicate an input trigger and squares indicate a time trigger.

An additional degree of structure can be added to the network by arranging the event network by primary entities (see Exhibit IV-1-11). Exhibit IV-1-11 is so arranged that it traces the ELH of each entity. Exhibit IV-1-12 shows how the ELH for the **ORDER** entity can be derived from the structured event network.

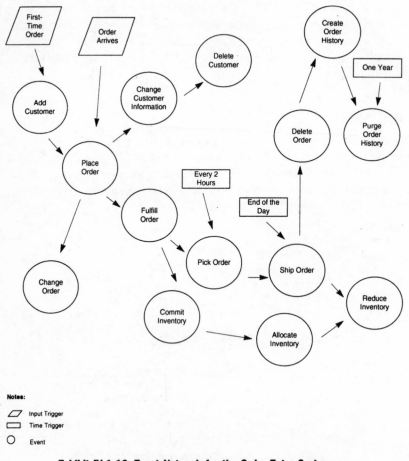

Notes:

⬦ Input Trigger
▭ Time Trigger
○ Event

Exhibit IV-1-10. Event Network for the Order-Entry System

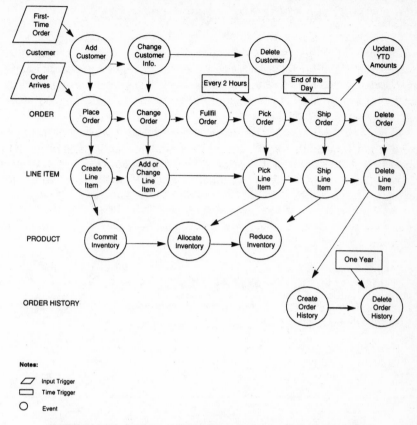

Notes:

⬭ Input Trigger

▭ Time Trigger

◯ Event

Exhibit IV-1-11. Structured Event Network for the Order-Entry System

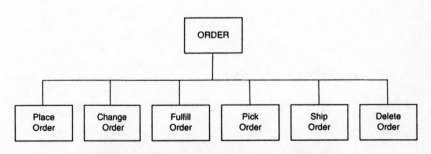

Exhibit IV-1-12. Entity-Life History for the ORDER Entity

WEAKNESSES IN THE EXISTING TOOLS AND TECHNIQUES

The event network shown in Exhibit IV-1-12 has many similarities to a STD that has been decomposed by entity. However, traditional STDs cannot relate events to data entities or processes. The event network takes into account the relationship between events and data. The entity-relationship model can effectively illustrate data and its relationships to other data. However, it cannot show events or transformations.

The data flow diagram (DFD) and other process models show both the movement and transformation of data. The DFD cannot explicitly show relationship among data entities and data dependencies. The ELH diagrams shows the life stages of the data entities and indirectly shows the transformations that take place. The ELH shows neither the triggers of events nor data dependencies.

Exhibit IV-1-13 illustrates how effectively DFDs, ERDs, ELHs and STDs model data, processes, and events. Obviously, the effectiveness of each type of diagram must be extended.

ANALYTICAL VALIDATION OF ANALYSIS DIAGRAMS

Following are rules for cross-checking and validating the different types of modeling tools discussed in previous sections:

1. *Each event should be identified as a stage in the ELH of every data entity it affects.* An event causes one or more entities to change stage.

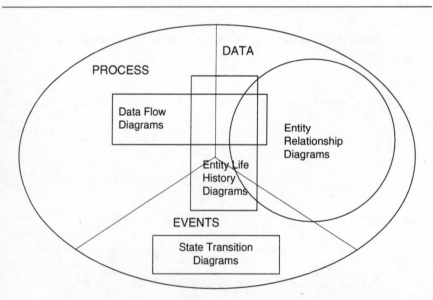

Exhibit IV-1-13. Areas of Effectiveness for Common Analysis Diagrams

For each event documented, the entity or entities affected by that event are identified. Therefore, each event should be represented as a stage in the ELH of each entity it affects.

2. *Each stage in the ELH represents a function on the corresponding DFD.* A stage in the life of an entity maps to a function in the process model. A function may or may not map one-to-one to a process on the process model at this stage. However, a function can be considered a fundamental unit of processing or task that must be performed.

3. *Each of those derived functions in a DFD should have the appropriate data stores attached to it.* A corollary to the second rule, this rule is related to the principle known as *horizontal process balancing* or *data conservation.* Once the processes in the process model that represent a stage of the entity have been identified, the data stores in the DFD that represents that data entity should be attached to the identified processes. If the model refers back to the event that represents that stage in the ELH, other entities may be associated with that event. The data stores that represent those entities should also be attached to the process.

4. *Each ELH stage triggered by input should have an input-user view associated with the corresponding processes.* For each stage triggered by input, an analyst should review that stage's corresponding processes in the DFD. One or more of the processes should be associated with an input-user view, which is a data flow going from a process to an external entity. If the stage is triggered by input, its process should indicate that it is receiving input from the appropriate external entity.

5. *Each stage change triggered by a stage change in another entity should be represented in the ERD as a relationship between the two entities.* A stage change caused by another stage change is a type of tight coupling, which is a unique kind of relationship. Thus, one entity cannot affect another entity unless the two are related.

6. *In the ELH diagram, each entity must have at least one create stage and at least one delete stage.* An occurrence of any entity must first be created if it is to be used in a meaningful way. For most practical business purposes, information is not kept indefinitely. Even information that is archived is usually deleted at one point. Thus, all ELH diagrams, except those for historical or archival data entities, should end in a delete stage.

EXPANDING THE COVERAGE OF THE DIAGRAMS

The ELH Diagram. The ELH diagrams—the one in Exhibit IV-1-12 for example—are effective at showing the events affecting a single entity. However, it does not show graphically the triggers for a given event. It can be enhanced (see Exhibit IV-1-14) by using the trigger symbols used in event network diagrams.

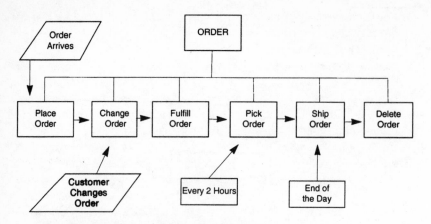

Exhibit IV-1-14. Entity-Life History Diagram Enhanced with Trigger Symbols

---

The Structured Event Network. This type of diagram (see Exhibit IV-1-11) effectively shows events and relates them to major data entities. However, it does not show the relationships among data entities other than through the perspective of events.

The DFD. The coverage of the DFD can easily be expanded by simply adding the event to the process legend, as shown in Exhibit IV-1-15. Various kinds of events can be illustrated in this manner. For example, the process-to-process data flow shown between processes 1 and 2 in Exhibit IV-1-15 illustrates a stage change triggered by a change in state in the same entity. In other words, as the ELH in Exhibit IV-1-14 illustrates, as soon as an order is edited, it goes immediately to the fulfillment stage. Because there is a data store between processes 2 and 4 in Exhibit IV-1-15, the diagram implies that a waiting time or delay exists. The legend in process 4 confirms that it is triggered every two hours; process 2 is triggered by input that starts with process 1. Process 6 illustrates a stage change in one entity triggered by a stage change in another entity; process 6 deletes the order and creates order history.

The Entity-Event-Relationship Diagram

Although the techniques discussed in the previous section enhance the capabilities of the analysis tools discussed in this article, an event-driven diagram that significantly bonds events to data and stage changes in entities is still needed. The structured event network shows the relationship of events but is an unsatisfactory link to other diagrams.

Object-oriented analysis (OOA) has many useful diagrams. OOA notations can be used to show the relationships of events to data and other events in

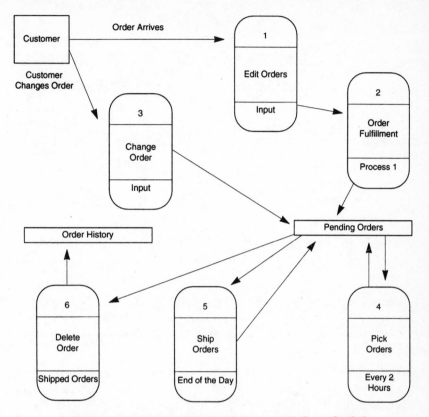

Exhibit IV-1-15. Data Flow Diagram Enhanced with Event Symbols

the entity-event-relationship diagram (EERD), which resembles an ERD. The boxes in the EERD still represent data entities, and the lines represent relationships. However, each data entity shows the stages it can enter.

Each entity can be thought of as a machine and each stage box as a button. Exhibit IV-1-16 is a partial EERD of the order entry system. It shows how one entity's event can push another entity's button. The direction of the arrows are important because it shows cause and effect. In addition, the standard symbols to show triggers from input (i.e., a parallelogram) and time (i.e., a box) have been added.

The diagram shows that the **Pick** event in **ORDER** triggers the **Pick** event in **LINE ITEM**. In turn, the **Pick** event in **LINE ITEM** causes the **Allocate** event in **INVENTORY**. A backwards trace from causal events reveals the original causal event (e.g., input or time). For example, to find the event that causes the inventory level to be reduced (i.e., the **Reduce** event in **INVENTORY**), a backward trace reveals that it is triggered by the **Ship** event in **LINE ITEM**.

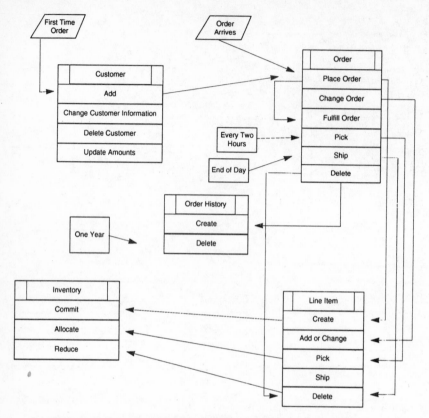

Exhibit IV-1-16. Entity-Event-Relationship Diagram for the Order-Entry System

This is in turn triggered by the Ship event in **ORDER**. This event is ultimately triggered by time (i.e., the **End-of-the-Day** event) as is indicated in the EERD.

CONCLUSION

Analysis of the relationships between entities and the events that trigger processes are keys to better understanding a system. There are also keys to developing more effective tools for analysis based on events. This article has illustrated how analysts can document the types of coupling in an entity's relationships to other entities as well as the types of events experienced by the entity. More important, this article has demonstrated the use of EERDs. This tool can be used to relate events, data, and processes and adds rigor to the modeling of both data and functions.

IV-2
A Comparison of Three Systems Modeling Methodologies

MICHAEL P. KUSHNER • II-YEOL SONG • KYU-YOUNG WHANG

O bject modeling methodologies are becoming increasingly popular. Many different methodologies are available to model a problem. The question is, how do these techniques differ? This chapter compares three object methodologies: entity-relationship (ER) modeling, Shlaer and Mellor's Information Modeling, and Rumbaugh's Object Modeling Technique (OMT). Two scenarios are used to illustrate the methodology's syntax and aid in the analysis of the techniques.

DESCRIPTION OF THE METHODOLOGIES

Entity-Relationship Modeling

The ER model was first proposed by Peter Chen in 1976 and has been expanded to include the concepts of participation constraints, generalization-specialization, and aggregation. The ER model is primarily used to design data bases. It emphasizes that the data model closely map to the real-world scenario being modeled.

Many variations of notations for an ER diagram exist. In this article, Elmasri and Navathe's definitions and notations are used except for the notation for total-partial participation. The basic components of this model are the entity, its attributes, and the relationships between entities. An entity is a thing that independently exists in the real world; it is usually a noun. It is modeled as a rectangle with the entity name inside the rectangle (see Exhibit IV-2-1). Entities also require more than one attribute and more than one instance to be a meaningful entity type in an application domain.

An attribute is a property of an entity or a relationship; however, some models do not permit an attribute to a relationship. It is depicted as an ellipse that is attached to an entity. The name of the attribute is placed in the middle of the ellipse (see Exhibit IV-2-1).

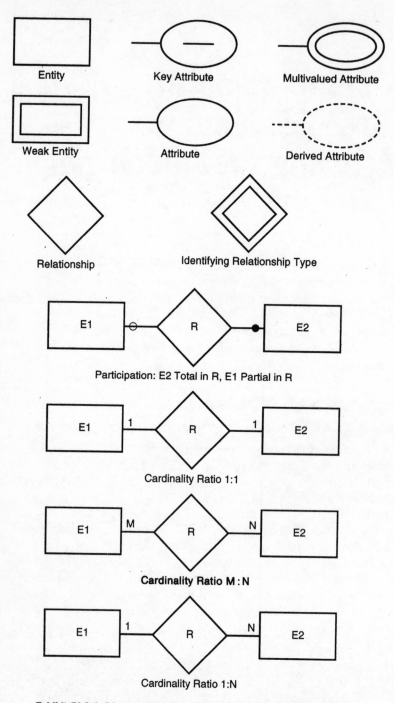

Exhibit IV-2-1. Diagram Notation for the Entity-Relationship Model

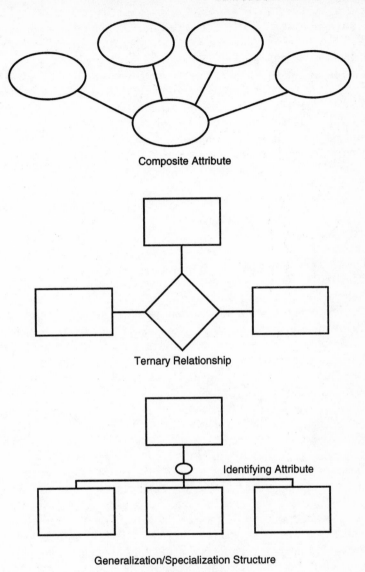

Composite Attribute

Ternary Relationship

Identifying Attribute

Generalization/Specialization Structure

Exhibit IV-2-1. (*Cont*)

Attributes can have many different roles. They can identify or describe. When an attribute identifies an entity, it distinguishes that entity from the other entity of the same type. An example of this is a person's Social Security number. If it is assumed that all Social Security numbers are unique, this attribute can be considered a primary key for this entity. A primary key uniquely identifies an entity. This attribute should not be null (this property is called entity constraint) or be changed often. It is represented as an attribute with the name underlined.

Attributes can be atomic, multivalued, composite, or derived. An atomic attribute has a single value. The age of a person is an atomic attribute. A multivalued attribute can have several values. If a person speaks many languages, the languages spoken by a person can be multivalued. An address is an example of a composite attribute, because it is composed of several more basic attributes. A derived attribute is one whose value can be calculated through the use of other attributes.

Entities that share the same attributes are grouped into entity types and are distinguished by the values of their attributes. For example, a company's employees would be grouped into an employee entity type.

The other basic component of an ER diagram is the relationship. A relationship is the association between entity types. It is represented by a diamond with lines connecting it to each related entity. The name of the relationship is written in the middle of the diamond (see Exhibit IV-2-1).

Relationships have three important properties; degree, cardinality, and participation. The degree of a relationship is based on the number of entities that are involved in the association. When an association occurs with only one entity it is called unary or recursive. Exhibit IV-2-2 illustrates such a relationship. The most common type of relationship is the binary type. This relationship has two entities involved in the association. All relationships in Exhibits IV-2-3 and IV-2-4 are binary relationships.

The cardinality of a relationship pertains to the maximum number of relationship instances that an entity can be involved in. The different levels of cardinality are: one-to-one (1:1), one-to-many (1:N), or many-cardinality are: one-to-one (1:1), one-to-many (1:N), or many-to-many (M:N).

Relationships also use the concept of participation. Participation specifies the minimum cardinality. The minimum cardinality specifies whether any instance of one entity can exist without being associated with at least one member of another entity set. If it can, the participation is optional or partial; if it cannot, it is mandatory or total. In Exhibit IV-2-1, optional participation is represented by an open circle and mandatory by a closed circle.

Another important concept in the ER model is the weak entity type. It is an entity that does not have its own unique identifier. The weak entity is depicted as a rectangle with double lines (see Exhibit IV-2-1). The relationship that associates the weak entity to its parent entity is called an identifying relationship and is modeled as a diamond with double lines (see Exhibit IV-2-1). An example of a weak entity type is an employee's dependents; a dependent cannot be identified without knowing the associated employee.

If entities have additional subgroups with important characteristics that require modeling, a generalization-specialization structure is used. This structure is often known as an is-a relationship. An example of this structure is

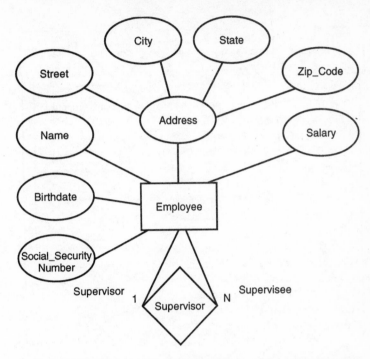

Exhibit IV-2-2. Entity-Relationship Model Showing a Unary Relationship

that an engineer entity is an employee entity. The employee entity is called a superclass and the other entities are subclasses. The subclasses have their own attributes plus they inherit all the attributes from their superclass.

The difference between generalization and specialization concerns how the structure is developed. Specialization is developed top-down whereas generalization is developed bottom-up. In specialization, an employee entity would be broken down into engineer, manager, and secretary entities. Using generalization, an analyst first develops engineer, manager, and secretary entities and then creates the employee entity. For ease of notation, the term generalization is used in this article to refer to both specialization and generalization.

A constraint on the generalization structure is whether the entities are disjoint or if they can overlap. If the structure is disjoint, an entity can only be a member of one subclass. If an entity can be a member of more than one subclass, the structure is overlapping. The employee structure is disjoint because an employee is exactly an engineer, manager, or secretary.

Exhibit 3 presents an ER diagram of an accounting system. The diagram shows a **Supplier, Account and Payment, Pay_Method, Check, Credit Card** and **Cash** entities. The **Account** has a single **Supplier** with total participation

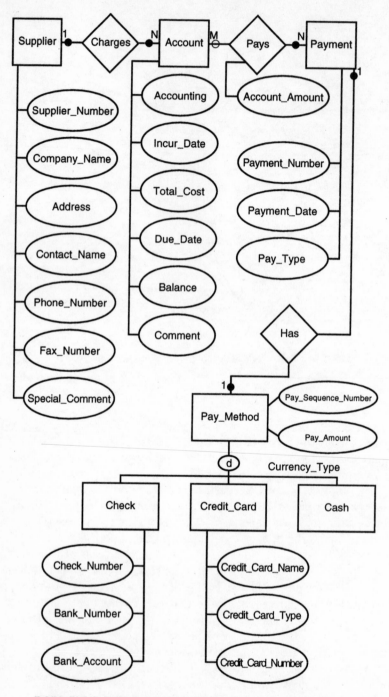

Exhibit IV-2-3. Entity-Relationship Model of an Accounting System

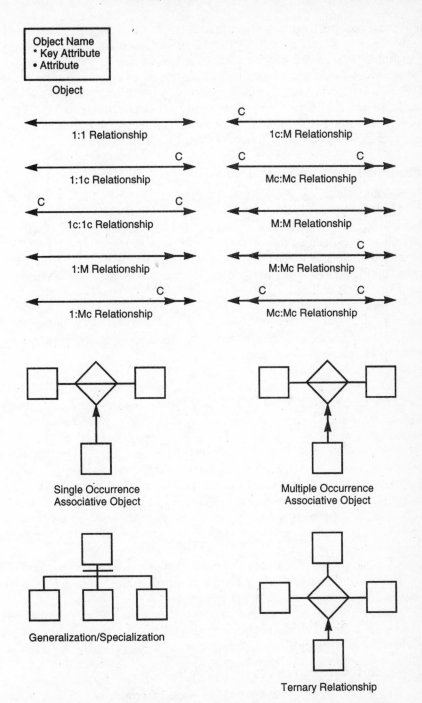

Exhibit IV-2-4. Diagram Notation for Shlaer and Mellor's Information Model

meaning that every account should have a responsible supplier. The **Supplier** entity charges many **Accounts,** with total participation. The **Account** has many **Payments** with partial participation. This means that an **Account** can exist without being paid at a certain time. The **Payment Pays** many **Accounts** and its participation is total. The **Pay** relationship has attributes because of the M:N relationship between **Payment** and **Account.** There is a total one to one relationship between **Pay_Method** and **Payment.** The **Pay_Method** is the superclass for the **Check, Cash,** and **Credit Card** subclasses.

Shlaer and Mellor's Information Model

Shlaer and Mellor developed the Information Model in 1988 to help solve problems associated with software systems development. The Information Model has been described as a thinking tool that uses graphical notation for describing and defining the vocabulary and conceptualization of a problem. It identifies what a problem is about and organizes these ideas into a format structure. This model can be regarded as a variation of the ER model discussed in the previous section.

The basic elements of this model are the object, its attributes, and the relationships between objects. The object is the basic part of the system. Shlaer and Mellor define an object as an abstraction of a set of real-world items such that all of the real-world items in the set—the instances—have the same characteristics and all instances are subject to and conform to the same rules.

An object is depicted as a rectangle. The name is placed at the top of the rectangle (see Exhibit IV-2-4). To identify objects, the Information Model uses five different categories—tangible things, roles, incidents, interactions, and specifications.

A role is the part played by a person or organization. Examples of role objects include a doctor, a patient, a nurse, a department, an employee, and a supervisor. Sometimes role objects distinguish between different roles played by the same person. An example of this is an employee who is also a supervisor.

Another type of object is an incident. They are used to represent an occurrence or event—something that happens at a specific time. Examples of incident objects are a flight, an accident, or a service call.

The fourth type of object is the interaction object. Interaction objects can be compared to transactions or contracts. An example is a purchase which relates a buyer, a seller, and the purchase item.

The last type of object is a specification object. Specification objects frequently show up in inventory or manufacturing applications. An example of this type of object is a radio specification. This object has the specifications of the specific model. There would most likely be another object that describes each instance of a specific model of a radio.

The Shlaer and Mellor method specifies an object description, naming conventions, and methods to test if objects are valid. An object description is a short, informative statement that allows an analyst to tell with certainty whether a particular item is an instance of the object conceptualized in the Information Model.

Attributes are another important part of the Information Model. An attribute is defined as the abstraction of a single characteristic possessed by all the entities that were, themselves, abstracted as an object. An attribute is represented by a line item inside the object rectangle. The objective is a collection of attributes that are complete, fully factored, and mutually independent.

Different categories of attributes include descriptive attributes, naming attributes, referential attributes, and identifier attributes. Descriptive attributes provide basic facts about each instance of an object. Examples are the salary and address of an employee object.

An identifier attribute is an attribute or combination of attributes that uniquely distinguishes one instance of an object from another. An identifier is sometimes called a candidate key. An example of identifier attributes are the state and title number for a car object. Neither attribute alone is sufficient to uniquely identify an instance of a car. Referential attributes are those that tie an instance of one object to an instance of another object. They are called foreign keys in a relational data base. Neither the ER model nor OMT capture the referential attribute at the diagram level.

To describe an attribute the Information Model uses an attribute description. This is a short description that explains the significance of the attribute. The method also formalizes the concept of object mapping to a relational data base table; the attributes of the object maps to the columns of the table.

The other important concept in this model is the relationship between objects. It is defined as the abstraction of a set of associations that holds systematically between different kinds of things in the real world. Examples include a person who borrows a book from the library or a research paper that has an author. Their relationships are similar to the ER model in that they include 1:1, 1:N and M:M cardinality. The Information Model is different from the ER model, however, because a diamond is used only when a relationship has its own attribute. When no attributes are in a relationship, the two related entities are simply connected by a line.

Another important concept is the conditionality of a relationship. This concept is similar to the ER model's participation constraint. Relationships that are unconditional include every instance of an object in the relationship with another object. Conditional relationships optionally allow objects to participate in a relationship.

Cardinality is called multiplicity and is represented by a single arrow representing one and a double arrow representing many. The conditional constraint is depicted with a C on the conditional side (see Exhibit IV-2-4). Whenever a relationship has its own attributes, an object symbol is created and linked to the diamond.

Shlaer and Mellor have specific methods for implementing different types of relationships in a relational data base. The implementation is based on the multiplicity and conditionality of a relationship.

Relationships can also show the association between subtypes and supertypes. This type of association is also known as generalization. This is a relationship in which distinct objects share common attributes. Exhibit IV-2-4 presents the notation for generalization and Exhibit IV-2-5 gives an example of generalization of the **Pay_Method** object.

Associative objects occur in many-to-many relationships where attributes are associated with a relationship. This type of object can be either a single or multiple occurrence. A single occurrence has one associative object instance associated with a single pairing of the two original relationship objects. A multiple occurrence form has many object instances per associated pair. If an associative object can be thought of as a distinct object with an identifier, it

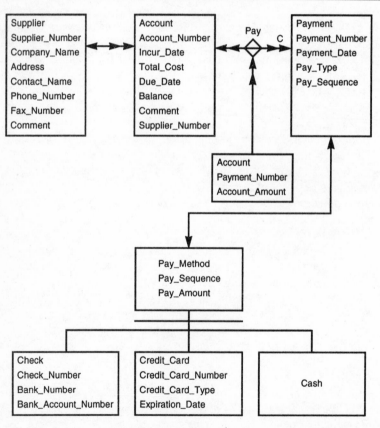

Exhibit IV-2-5. Information Model Diagram of an Accounting System

can be modeled as an object. Therefore, a ternary relationship would be created and it would still have the associative object that indicates the single or multiple occurrence form. Exhibit IV-2-4 gives an example of an associative relationship.

Exhibit IV-2-5 presents a Shlaer and Mellor information model of an accounting system. The diagram contains a Supplier, Account, Payment, Pay_Method, Check, Credit_Card, and Cash objects. The Account has a single Supplier with an unconditional relationship. The Supplier object charges many Accounts and the relationship is unconditional. The object Account has a conditional relationship with many Payments. The Payment object is related to many Accounts and its relationship with the Account object is unconditional. The Pay relationship has a single occurrence of an associative object because of the Account_Amount attribute associated with the M:N relationship between Payment and Account. There is a mandatory one-to-one relationship between Pay_Method and Payment. The Pay_Method is the superclass for the Check, Cash, and Credit_Card subclasses.

Rumbaugh's Object Modeling Technique

The Object Modeling Technique (OMT) is used to develop software objects that have both a data structure and behavior. The object model shows the structure of a system in terms of objects, their attributes, their operations, and the relationships between objects. The goal in constructing an object model is to capture those concepts from the real world that are important to an application.

The basic element of the model is the object, which is represented by a box. The name of the object is placed at the top of the box (see Exhibit IV-2-6). An object is an abstraction of a real-world entity that has definite boundaries and meaning. Objects that have similar attributes, operations, and relationships can be grouped together to form object classes. Each object in a class is distinguished by the value of its attributes.

In this model, an attribute is a value held by an object. These attributes can be given a data type and default value if desired. Unlike in the Shlaer and Mellor model, object identifiers that do not have a real-world meaning to the system are not used as attributes. An example is an identifier number that is generated to make a person object unique. If this number is not used by the outside world, the attribute should not be modeled. Such attributes as Social Security number and driver's license number can be modeled because they have meaning in the real world.

Attributes of an object are listed as line entries in the object box. They are written beneath the line drawn below the object name (see Exhibit IV-2-6).

An operation is a behavior associated with an object. This behavior can be an action performed by an object on another object. This behavior can be an action performed by an object on another object or it can be a transformation

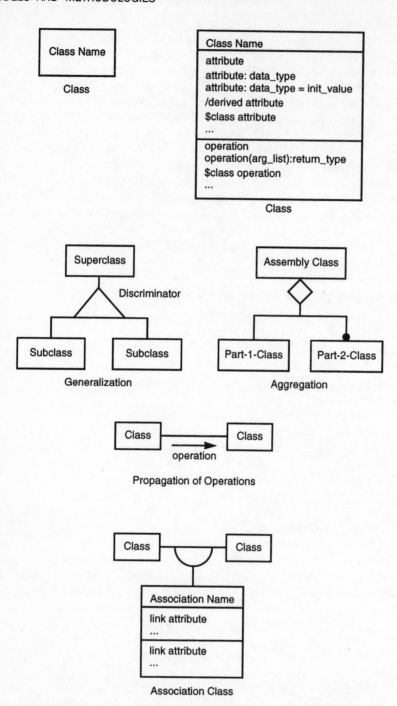

Exhibit IV-2-6. Rumbaugh's Object Model Technique Diagram Notation

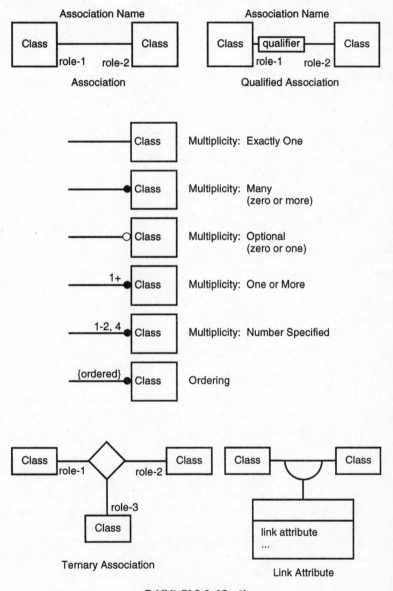

Exhibit IV-2-6. (*Cont*)

that an object undergoes. These operations are available to all instances of a class and can apply to different classes. When the same operation is applied to different classes it is called polymorphic. An operation is implemented by a method. An example of a polymorphic operation is the opening of a file or a window. They have the same name—open—but they are applied to different classes and implemented by different methods. An operation is also listed as a line item in an object box. It is written beneath the line drawn below the list of attributes. Each operation can optionally have an argument list and result type (see Exhibit IV-2-6).

In an object model, relationships are known as links or associations. A link relates object instances, and an association relates object classes. These relationships can be reflexive (i.e., unary), binary, ternary, or of a higher order. The multiplicity (i.e., cardinality) of an object is determined by how many instances of a class relate to a single instance of another class. Multiplicity can be one-to-one, one-to-many (including zero), one-to-zero-or-one (i.e., optional), one-to-one-or more, one to an exact number, or one to a specific range. Exhibit IV-2-6 illustrates the syntax of links, associations, and multiplicity.

When objects in many-to-many relationships have attributes that cannot be associated with only one object, a link attribute is used. An example is shown in Exhibit IV-2-7 where the **Account** and **Payment** objects have a link attribute for the amount of a payment associated with an account. If this attribute can have operations associated with it, it becomes a link object. Exhibit IV-2-7 show the link attribute and link object notation.

A special type of association that shows a whole-to-part relationship is called aggregation. Aggregation is also called a part-of relationship. This type of association is used when the elements are intrinsically part of a whole. These objects may or may not have an independent existence in a system. This relationship is both transitive and asymmetric. Transitive means if object A is part of object B and object B is part of object C, object A is part of object C. Asymmetric means that if object A is part of object B, object B is not part of object A.

Another important concept in the object model is generalization. In OMT, it is defined as the relationship between a class and one or more refined versions of the class. Generalization is also called an is-a relationship. An important property of generalization is inheritance. Inheritance is the sharing of attributes and operations among the classes in a generalization hierarchy. These features are inherited from a superclass by its subclasses.

Exhibit IV-2-7 illustrates these concepts in an OMT object diagram of an accounting system. The diagram contains a **Supplier, Account, Payment, Pay_Method, Check, Credit_Card,** and **Cash** objects. The **Account** must have a single **Supplier**. The **Supplier** object charges one or more **Accounts**. The **Account** object is associated with zero or more **Payment** objects. The **Payment** object pays one or more **Account**. A link attribute is associated with the **Account** and **Payment** objects. It occurs because of the amount attribute associated

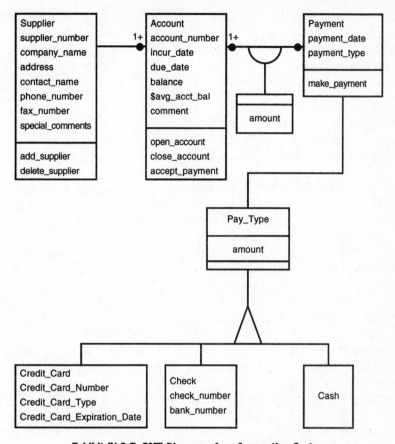

Exhibit IV-2-7. OMT Diagram of an Accounting System

with the many-to-many relationship between the **Payment** and **Account** objects. A one-to-one relationship exists between the **Pay_Method** and **Payment** objects. The **Pay_Method** object is the superclass for the **Check**, **Cash**, and **Credit_Card** subclasses.

COMPARISON OF THE MODELING METHODS

The three modeling techniques are somewhat similar—they all use the same basic elements: objects-entities, attributes, and relationships. When used to model the accounting system used as an example in this article, the three techniques produce essentially the same diagram; the only major difference is found in the notation. It is not true that this is the case for all applications, because there probably are certain scenarios where the models would look different.

The following sections compare the basic elements of these three modeling methodologies.

Entities and Objects

The most basic element of all three models is the object or entity. All three define this element in generally the same terms. To help analysts determine valid objects, the Information Model methodology lists five different categories of objects: tangible items, roles, incidents, interactions, and specifications. This methodology also provides tests to determine the validity of an object. These tests include a uniformity test, a more-than-a-name test, an or test, and a more-than-a-list test. All of these tests review the object definition or attributes to check the correctness and uniformity of an object.

OMT also provides guidelines for removing incorrect object classes. Invalid classes include those that are redundant, irrelevant, vague, attributes, operations, roles, and implementation constructs. In the ER model a rule governing entities states that a valid entity must have at least one attribute and one instance.

An entity in the ER model and an object in the Information Model are very similar. An object in OMT has a major difference. An OMT object has operations defined for it. Defining operations for an object in a system can give an analyst greater insight into the use of the object in the system. The other models are strictly concerned with the data associated with the object or entity.

One special type of entity in the ER model is the weak-entity type. This type is different from a normal entity in that it does not have an independent existence. The weak entity cannot exist without its parent entity. For example, an **Employee_Dependent** entity relies on an **Employee** entity for part of its unique identity. Although a unique attribute could be created for a weak entity, it should not be because of the strong bond between the entities. In the Information Model, there is no way to show the strength of an association in a diagram. In OMT, however, a qualified association can exist, which enhances the identification of an association by attaching an identifying attribute to a dependent class.

Attributes

All three models use similar definitions for object and entity attributes. In the ER model, primary keys are directly modeled, but foreign keys are implicitly hidden in relationships (i.e., they are not explicitly shown on ER diagrams). In the Information Model, both primary keys and foreign keys (called reference attributes) are directly modeled and explicitly represented. If a unique key does not exist for an object, one is created. A primary key is annotated in an ER model with an underline and with a star in the Information Model.

OMT does not use the concept of keys, because most object-oriented languages automatically generate implicit object identifiers. However, OMT does allow for these keys for relational data base management systems.

The use of keys is an important difference among these models. Both the ER and Information Models were developed on the assumption that a relational data base is used to store the system's data. OMT does not make this assumption and does not stipulate any model. This allows the development of a more flexible model that can be implemented by any system.

OMT notation can more thoroughly define an attribute because it uses data types, default values, and class attributes. An attribute can optionally have a data type and default value notated. This further definition of an attribute can give a quick understanding of an object and its attributes. When an OMT diagram is complicated by extra information, a simplified object diagram without the extra information can be shown.

Another special attribute only used in OMT is the class attribute. The class attribute is a value that only relates to the object class and not to any instance of that class. An example of a class attribute is the **Average_ Account_Balance** attribute of the **Account** object class in Exhibit IV-2-7. This attribute is simply the average value of account balances for all instances of the **Account** object class. Because it is an average of all account balances, this attribute can only apply to the class and not to any individual object instance.

Both OMT and the ER model have notation for derived attributes, but the Information Model does not. It is useful to know this type of information because derived attributes may affect final implementation of an attribute.

Another special type of attribute that differentiates OMT is the private attribute. A private attribute is one that can only be accessed by a class. This attribute type is not found in the other methodologies. Private attributes are used in the design phase of a project. They enforce a concept called information hiding. Information hiding is used to hide the details of the implementation of an object from the outside world. Information hiding also creates a clean interface that changes less frequently and is affected by changes to the internal processing of the object.

Relationships

All three models describe relationships with basically the same approach. One difference is in OMT where it specifies different terms for the relationships between object classes and object instances. The relationship between classes is called an association and the relationship between instances is called a link.

All three use different notation and terminology to define the number of objects in a relationship. The ER model uses the terms cardinality and participation. The Shlaer and Mellor method uses the terms multiplicity and conditionality to refer to the number of objects used in an association. The term multiplicity is equivalent to cardinality in Elmasri and Navathe's ER convention.

Conditionality in an information model is similar to participation in an ER model. The participation checks whether an entity can exist without being associated to another entity, but the conditionality concept checks whether all of the instances of one entity are mapped conditionally or unconditionally to another entity. The basic difference is in the notation that specifies participation and convention. Although the definition of conditionality is slightly different than that of participation the result is the same.

OMT uses the term multiplicity to represent both cardinality and participation as defined by the ER model. This is done by including zero in the cardinality (i.e., zero or one, zero or more, or one or more). Exhibit 6 presents all the OMT terms for multiplicity.

All three methodologies use different terminology and notation to describe the number of objects in a relationship. But the results of each notation is the same. Each method is successful at clearly displaying this information.

Each methodology also has special types of relationships. The ER model has relationship attributes, the Information Model has associative objects, and OMT has link attributes, link objects, ordering, qualifiers, and aggregation.

Relationship attributes, associative objects, and link attributes are all very similar. They occur in many-to-many relationships. An example of this is shown in the relationship between **Account** and **Payment** entities or objects in Exhibits IV-2-3, IV-2-5, and IV-2-7. The ER model and OMT notations are similar. The Information Model adds an extra dimension by indicating the number of occurrences of an attribute. A single arrow is used when there is only a single occurrence associated with a single relationship instance. A double arrow is used when multiple occurrences are associated with a single relationship instance. This gives added information that is not indicated by other models, but they can be simulated by ternary relationship in other models.

A qualifier and ordering constraint are used in OMT to further clarify an association. A qualifier can be used to reduce the multiplicity of an association. An ordering constraint that is shown at the many sides of an association shows that the object requires a specific order to be a valid relationship. An example is the relationship between a **Screen** object and a **Window** object. There can be many windows on a screen, but it is important to know which is the topmost window. To indicate this requirement, an ordered constraint is placed above the relationship line next to the **Window** object.

Another special type of relationship that can be used in OMT is aggregation. Neither the ER nor Information Models have this type of notation. This type of relationship shows the strength of a parts-whole relationship. An example is a **Lamp** object that is an aggregate of a **Base, Body, Shade,** and **Bulb** objects. Aggregation in a typical ER model is more limited, because it requires two entity types and one relationship to form a high-level entity.

To verify the relationship in ER and Information Models, a correlation table can be used. This is actually the implementation of a relationship. The table lists the instances involved in an association. By checking these instances the validity of an association can be confirmed. In OMT, the following criteria are used for determining unnecessary or incorrect associations:

- Associations between eliminated classes.
- Irrelevant or implementation associations.
- Actions.
- Derived associations.

It is also recommended to break ternary relationships into binary relationships.

The generalization structure and approach used by all three models is very similar. Both the ER model and OMT allow the use of an attribute to distinguish the type of generalization. In the ER model this attribute is called a classifying attribute. In OMT it is called a discriminator. An example of this concept is shown in the **Pay_Method** generalization structures in Exhibit IV-2-3 and IV-2-7.

All these models consider disjointness constraints. If generalization is disjoint, each entity can only be a member of one subclass. If it can be a member of more than one subclass, the generalization has overlap. Elmasri and Navathe's convention shows this constraint by placing a D for disjoint or an O for overlap in the circle of the generalization symbol. Exhibit IV-2-3 illustrates the disjoint structure of the **Pay_Method** generalization. The Information Model does not have any notation to indicate this constraint, but it is checked when producing an identifier for generalization.

CONCLUSION

Although the basic elements of the ER model, the Information Model, and OMT are similar, major differences exist. Both the ER and the Information models require the use of identifier attributes in the object or entity, but OMT does not. This identifier is only added during implementation if it is required. The ER and the Information models are created with intention that a relational data base will be used to implement the data. OMT does not force any implementation restrictions on the object model. This allows the model to be implemented by any type of system. Also, an OMT model is more complete because it shows not only the data associated with an object but also the processes that are performed on or by the object.

Another important difference concerns OMTs use of operations. OMT adds the extra dimension of operations for the objects, but the other models do not require them. The Information Model, however, captures operation information in later analysis phases by using the life cycle modeling technique. Also, both the Information Model and OMT do not use any symbol for relationships when they do not have any attributes.

The Information Model is also clearly different from the other two models because it directly models a foreign key at the diagram level. This requires more effort at the modeling level and less effort during implementation.

Topic	E-R	Information Model	OMT
Entity	Entity	Object	Object
Operations	No	No	Yes
Primary Key	Yes	Yes	No
Foreign Key	No	Yes	No
Participation Constraint	Yes	Yes	Yes
Participation Notation	Look Here[1] (LH)	Look Across[2] (LA)	LA
Ternary Relationships	Yes	Yes	Yes
Cardinality Notation	LA	LA	LA
Multiplicity to Association Object	No	Yes	No
Attributes on Relationships	Yes	Yes	Yes
Relationship Qualifiers:			
Role	Yes	Yes	Yes
Ordering	No	No	Yes
Qualifier	No	No	Yes
Attribute Data Type	No	No	Yes
Default Value	No	No	Yes
Generalization Hierarchy	Yes	Yes	Yes
Aggregation	Yes (limited)	No	Yes

Notes:
1. Look here (LH) notation is next to the primary entity in a relationship.
2. Look across (LA) notation is next to the secondary entity in a relationship.

Exhibit IV-2-8. Summary of Differences Among the E-R, Information Model, and OMT Systems Modeling Techniques

---

The only major difference between the ER and Information models is in the use of single and multiple occurrence forms of an associative object. The Information Model appears to be an updated version of the ER model and both are designed for implementation on a relational data base. OMT has, however, a design for object-oriented implementation. The differences between all three modeling techniques are summarized in Exhibit IV-2-8.

IV-3
Object-Oriented Modeling of MRP

FIKRI T. DWEIRI • HSIANG-HSI HUANG

Inventory control and maintenance are common problems for organizations in any sector of society. Inventories are part of manufacturing plants, wholesalers, hospitals, churches, universities, and governments. Because the total investment in inventory represents a large portion of any business, effective management is essential. Material requirements planning (MRP) is a useful method of production scheduling and purchasing of materials, and is normally implemented as a computer-based system. It is almost impossible to effectively plan, replan, and keep up-to-date records on hundreds of subassemblies with many levels of product structures without such a system. The rapid development of computer-aided design and computer-aided manufacturing (CAD/CAM) and computer integrated manufacturing systems (CIMS) in recent years creates a need for improved data base management systems (DBMSs) that can serve the automated manufacturing areas. Relational data base systems have been used in the past, but they have certain disadvantages (e.g., the need to write an application program to support the system). This approach adds to the complexity of developing the application and the interface time can slow down the system.

The decline in the number of manufacturing jobs over the last few years is a telling indicator of the need for an improved DBMS that can help revive the economy by creating more effective manufacturing organizations. There are four types of DBMSs: hierarchical, network, relational, and object-oriented. The first three types have been tried and applied in many fields, and have contributed significantly toward improving the manufacturing industry. This improvement has led many scientists to embrace the concept of the factory of the future. (Many authorities on this subject emphasize the need for a dynamic DBMS.)

Relational data bases are widely used in many manufacturing applications. Since the introduction of the relational model in 1970 by E.F. Codd, many vendors have adopted this technology. Relational modeling reached its maturity in the 1980s. Many vendors provide a support system written in an application programming language (e.g., the C language) to the DBMS. This approach has two disadvantages: first, the need to interface with DBMSs adds to the complexity of developing the application; and second, the interface time needed can slow down the system. Some object data bases provide integration between certain programming languages and the data base itself. LISP is an example of this procedure. Using object-oriented language coupled with an object data base can make the applications easier to develop, maintain, and revise more frequently. Many of the object data base vendors have focused on CAD workstations. Their effort is evident in the development of CAD systems that need to access information. Such information as process planning is located in the process-planning system, and is not part of the data base. The ease of accessibility among various subsystems is one of the primary goals of CIMS.

Research suggests that both relational and object-oriented data bases can play a significant role in the design of manufacturing systems. The use of object-oriented technology may not depend on only the technical advances, however, but also on the vendor size. The vendors' inability to target manufacturers with new initiatives made the developers of manufacturing systems overlook them. IBM Corp., a large relational vendor, controls many of the manufacturing aspects of the relational data base market, including MRP. Research also suggests that the relational model is best suited for such report-intensive applications as MRP.

The study discussed in this chapter shows that the object-oriented approach to MRP can improve productivity. This is especially true with increased use of CAD systems in the manufacturing environment, regardless of the amount of reports generated during the product life-cycle. This article presents a general view of MRP inputs, logic, outputs, and benefits. It also presents basic object-oriented concepts and describes the backtracking and iterative method used to model MRP using an object-oriented approach.

MATERIAL REQUIREMENTS PLANNING

MRP is a computational technique that converts the master production schedule (MPS) into a detailed schedule for raw materials and components used in the end products. MRP requires a high volume of data to be processed, and determines the required quantities of dependent demand items. To complete an assembly or a manufacturing task on time, MRP must allow for purchasing or manufacturing lead time.

MRP Input Data

To operate properly, MRP must have three files—a master production schedule, a bill of materials, and inventory record files or item master files. A master production schedule (MPS) is a listing of what end products are to be produced, and when they are to be ready for shipment. The end item quantity required is developed from customer orders or forecasted demands. A bill of materials (BOM) is also known as product structure records. It contains information on all materials, components, or subassemblies needed to produce each end item. Inventory record files or item master files consist of three parts, including:

- Item master data (e.g., part number, description, lead time, safety stock, and order quantity).
- Inventory status, which gives a time-phased record of the inventory status, gross requirements, scheduled receipts, on-hand item, and planned order releases.
- Subsidiary data (e.g., purchased orders, scrap or rejects, and engineering changes).

MRP Logic

The requirements for each item (e.g., end item, assembly, subassembly, or component) are computed using the following logic:

- Finding the net requirements for an item. This can be calculated using this formula:

$$\text{Net requirement} = \text{Gross requirement} - (\text{On-hand inventory} + \text{Scheduled receipts})$$

- Placing the planned order release for the requirements using the lead time as the offsetting factor.
- Using the BOM to find the quantity required of low level items to make the parent.

This process is repeated until the requirement plan for all items is generated.

MRP Output Data

MRP generates several reports that are useful to the daily operations of the plant. The most popular are: order release notices, planned order releases for future periods, reschedule notices, cancellation notices, inventory status reports, performance reports (e.g., cost or item use), and inventory forecasts for future periods. Exhibit IV-3-1 depicts the structure of an MRP system.

Benefits of MRP

A well-managed MRP system can benefit a manufacturing organization in many ways, including reducing inventory, responding quickly to changes in demand, reducing production and changeover costs, using machines effectively, and aiding in the development of MPSs.

CONCEPTS OF OBJECT-ORIENTED MODELING

Object-oriented programming was introduced during the mid-1960s—long before object-oriented system analysis methods became familiar in the late 1980s.

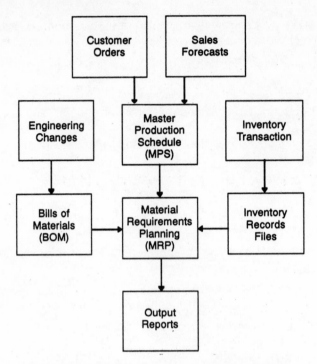

Exhibit IV-3-1. Material Requirements Planning Structure

The object-oriented approach promises to improve systems developers' ability to model complex systems. It will help develop less expensive and higher quality software. Object-oriented programs can reduce the number of lines of codes by 80% of the traditionally developed systems.

There are four basic elements of object-oriented systems, including:

- *Objects.* An object encapsulates the data (i.e., attributes of the object) and methods used to process the data. Information system modeling consists of four fundamental object classes:
  —*Physiomorphic objects* (i.e., *physical entities*). A customer and employee are physiomorphic objects—they can be structured as subclasses within a superclass.
  —*Events.* Events are time-dependent aspects, and usually involve a trigger that takes the form of: timing (e.g., once a month), attribute states (e.g., stock level reaches the reorder point), or information exchange (e.g., customer order).
  —*Output objects.* These typically take the form of a report (e.g., order release notices).

—*Input objects.* These are information entities that enter the system (e.g., BOM).

- *Classes.* A class describes similar objects with similar data structures and methods.
- *Inheritance.* A class inherits structure and methods from its superclass (i.e., parent), or it can have its own attributes and methods.
- *Messages.* Messages are communication procedures among objects.

Exhibit IV-3-2 depicts the object-oriented analysis diagram symbols.

MODELING MRP USING AN OBJECT-ORIENTED APPROACH

Analysts begin modeling MRP with an object-oriented approach by first identifying the output object classes, which are the output reports of the MRP

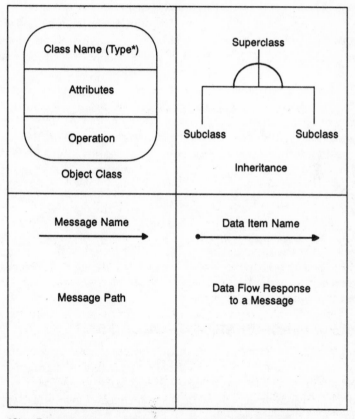

*Class Types are: i, input; o, output; e, event; and phys., physiomorphic.

Exhibit IV-3-2. Object-Oriented Analysis Diagram Symbols

system. Then, the analyst tracks backward from the output object classes to other classes. The output objects of MRP are triggered by an event called **Report Date**. This event retrieves information from the **Inventory Record File** (i.e., input object).

The **Report Date** event is triggered by another event called **System Clock** that indicates when reports are required. **Order Release Notices** (i.e., output object) are not only triggered by **Report Date**, but also by an event called **Reorder Point**. The **Reorder Point** is activated when the safety stock of a part reaches a predetermined level. This level is present and can be retrieved from the **Inventory Record File**.

The **Inventory Record File** is updated when a transaction takes place. The on-hand inventory is reduced when a shipment is delivered to a customer, and increased when a shipment is received from a supplier. The **Inventory Transaction** (i.e., input object) is triggered by an event called **Transaction**.

There are two physiomorphic objects—employee and customer. The employee objects are divided into three subclasses: engineer, sales, and marketing. The customer objects are divided into two subclasses; supplier and consumer. The BOM input object contains two subclasses; manufactured products and purchased parts. The MPS also contains two subclasses—ordered and forecasted end items.

The system receives an order from a customer or a sales forecast from an employee. An order can also be placed through a sales employee. A customer order for an end item or a marketing employee forecast for future sales are events that trigger the order to be processed. The MPS (i.e., input object) gets information about the item from the **Inventory Record File**. It then compares the quantity needed with the quantity on-hand, plus the scheduled receipts, to find the net requirements. Next, the MPS consults BOM (i.e., input object) to find the product structure of the item. The BOM can be changed by engineers modifying the product (i.e., process or assembly changes). When the BOM change occurs, an event called **Engineering Change** triggers the **Change** (input object) that includes the new information about the product Exhibits IV-3-3 and IV-3-4 depict the object-oriented analysis diagram of MRP.

BENEFITS OF OBJECT-ORIENTED DATA BASE SYSTEMS

Relational data base systems have many advantages and disadvantages. The disadvantages include high cost of DBMSs, high cost of hardware, difficult recovery after a system failure, failure of any component can bring the system to a standstill, and complexity and additional time needed to interface application programs with the data base.

ORION, an object-oriented data base support for CAD systems, was developed by Microelectronics and Computer Technology Corp. in the mid-1980s.

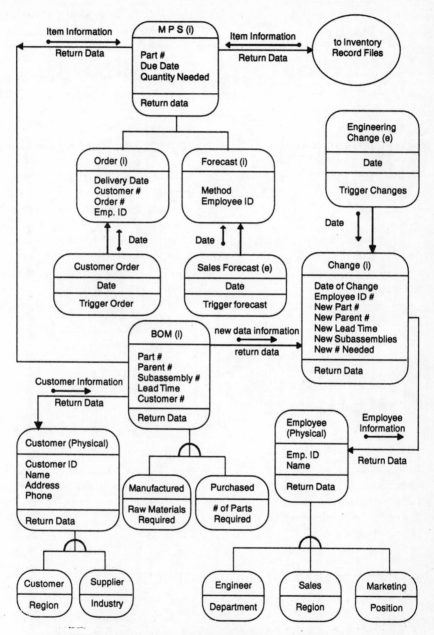

Exhibit IV-3-3. Object-Oriented Analysis Diagram of Material Requirements Planning System

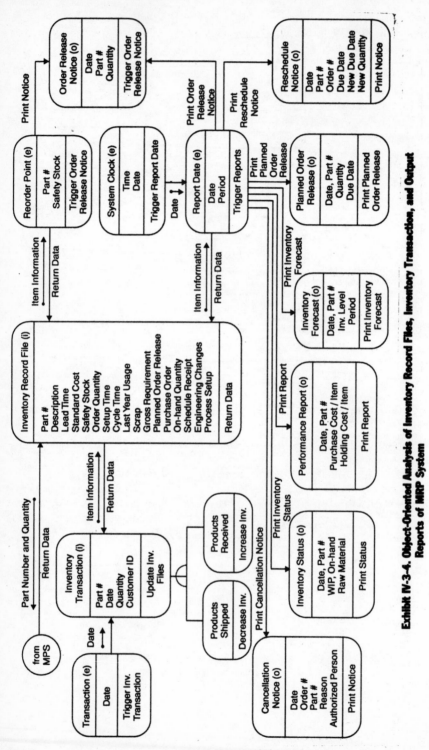

Exhibit IV-3-4. Object-Oriented Analysis of Inventory Record Files, Inventory Transaction, and Output Reports of MRP System

Application of ORION showed some of the benefits of object-oriented data base systems, including:

- Higher productivity and quality through reusability.
- Easy maintenance.
- Increased modeling power of the analyst.
- Reduced memory space needed to develop the application programs. The subclasses inherit attributes and methods from superclasses.
- Faster and easier changes using the trigger operations of the events. ORION uses this method as a change notification option.
- Protection of the data base integrity using transaction management. ORION has two types of transactions: session transaction, which is a sequence of transactions that can coexist simultaneously in multiple windows; and hypothetical transaction, which always deals with what-if changes to the data base. ORION also protects the integrity of the data base using concurrency control.

CONCLUSION

The fact that MRP is an important part of the manufacturing process stresses the need for a new versatile DBMS to aid in the proper application of MRP. This article showed that this goal can be reached using object-oriented system analysis. The method used to model the MRP system (i.e., backward tracking and iterative procedure) is practical and can help develop many applications in the manufacturing area (e.g., process planning, material handling, and group technology).

The goal of developing the sought-after DBMS can be reached faster with the contribution of large vendors. These vendors must invest, participate, and commit to developing design tools, styles, and techniques for modeling object-oriented systems. Data managers should prepare for the future by gaining an understanding of the object-oriented modeling, and evaluating existing systems and alternative approaches to existing problems. Finally, managers should be prepared to jump on the bandwagon of the object-oriented era.

Section V
Defining the Data

D is for data—if only it were that simple. This section looks at ways to handle the subtle, complex problems of describing business information in ways that all the people who deal with it can understand and in ways that can maximize its value as an asset.

The hazards of developing sloppy data elements can be avoided if data administrators follow the "One Concept Equals One Data Element" rule, as set out in Chapter V-1.

In Chapter VI-2, "Data Classification Concepts" underscore the explanation and understanding of the entity-relationship technique of data modeling.

To model data meaningfully, with the intent that users can make sense of it, data can be broken into four general categories. Chapter V-3, "A Framework for Classifying Data," describes these categories: internal administrative data, external administrative data, internal directional data, and external directional data.

Business rules capture the true business meaning behind business information, and as such are the foundation of data sharing. The task of the designer is to translate textual business rules—the plain-English expression of a rule's business intent, and the only part of the rule that is important to the user—into formal, precise, and implementable rules. A method for "Modeling Business Rules" is offered in Chapter V-4.

V-1
One Concept Equals One Data Element

JENNIFER LITTLE

D ata administrators' main products are standard data elements. Although data administrators agree that data elements are most useful when they follow the one-concept-equals-one-data-element rule, few standardization procedures and policies provide explicit methods for avoiding sloppy data elements. This chapter examines the hazards of developing data elements. It looks at the definitions involved and the benefits that can be gained from following the rule, presents how the development of data element valid values and the data element name often leads to data elements that violate the rule, and concludes with some guiding recommendations.

ESTABLISHING RULES

Data represents separate facts about objects. A data element is the smallest unit used to collect and document these facts. Data elements specify the rules to which data must conform, thereby establishing the structure of the data. For example, the data element in Exhibit V-1-1 establishes the structure in which people's last names are stored in a particular information system.

Because data elements provide structure for the data, poorly designed data elements lead to poor quality data. The most fundamental data element design principle is that a data element should encompass only one concept. Following the one-concept-equals-one-data-element rule when developing data elements can help ensure quality data elements. The rule can also help revise data elements during reengineering efforts to identify and improve problem data structures.

A data element has several parts (e.g., data element name, length, definition, format, and valid values), which are called data element attributes. When new data elements are developed, each attribute should be created to abide by the one-concept-equals-one-data-element rule. Also, when existing data elements are revised, the attributes can be examined to ensure that they conform to the rule. It is particularly critical to apply the one-concept-equals-one-data-element rule to two data element attributes—name and valid values.

Data Element Name:	PERSON LAST NAME
Data Element Definition:	The full unabbreviated last name of a person
Data Element Length:	65
Data Element Format:	Alphabetic
Data Element Edit Rules:	Only alphabetic characters are allowed. Spaces and special characters are not allowed.

Exhibit V-1-1. Sample Data Element Structure

This chapter examines these two data element attributes and suggests ways to ensure compliance with the rule.

PURPOSE OF THE RULE

A concept is a single directly conceived or intuited object of thought. Therefore, following the one-concept-equals-one-data-element rule ensures that data elements represent the smallest unit of meaningful intelligence. When a data element complies with the one-concept-equals-one-data-element rule, it is correct to call it a data element. Violations of the rule, however, should not be called data elements; they are referred to as melded data chunks throughout the remainder of this article. All organizations have melded data chunks; Exhibit V-1-2 represents a melded data chunk.

THE BENEFITS OF FLEXIBILITY

Data can be viewed as building blocks of information. Data that is collected using data elements is more flexible than data collected using melded data chunks. For example, a manager may want to know whether the training that a specific division received had any effect on its productivity. The division attended seven weeks of training during a one-year period, and the training was conducted in variable length segments with different people attending different segments at different times. The manager retrieves the productivity data from the personnel system that was created in the late 1960s to replace the manual monthly personnel productivity reports.

The productivity information is stored in the manner depicted in Exhibit V-1-3, because the employees' pay rate for each month is based on their average monthly output. The manager would have difficulty determining what effect the training had. At the most, he or she may be able to see whether total productivity increased after one year. On the other hand, if the data elements in Exhibit V-1-4 had been used in each personnel record, the manager would be able to make several comparisons of productivity and training to determine the effect of each training segment.

The issues of normalization notwithstanding and conceding the need to

Name: NEW AND IMPROVED INSURANCE ELIGIBILITY

Description: Indicates a person's eligibility for the new and improved insurance coverage.

Valid Values:

Position 1

0 = Full-time Employee started at the company before 1949.

1 = Full-time Employee started at the company between 1950 and 1954.

2 = Full-time Employee started at the company between 1955 and 1959.

3 = Full-time Employee started at the company between 1960 and 1964.

4 = Full-time Employee started at the company between 1965 and 1969.

5 = Full-time Employee started at the company between 1970 and 1974.

6 = Full-time Employee started at the company between 1975 and 1979.

7 = Full-time Employee started at the company between 1980 and 1984.

8 = Full-time Employee started at the company between 1985 and 1989.

9 = Full-time Employee started at the company between 1990 and 1992.

A = Full-time Employee started at the company between 1930 and 1970 and left for a period of longer than six months.

B = Full-time Employee started at the company between 1970 and the present, and tested positive for a communicable disease or refused the test.

C = Part-time Employee who is a relative of the owners of the company.

Positions 2–4

ABC = Employee currently has elected the ABC coverage plan for self only.

LNM = Employee currently has elected the LNM coverage plan for self only.

WIN = Employee currently has elected the WIN coverage plan for self only.

KJW = Employee currently has elected the KJW coverage plan for self only.

PRD = Employee currently has elected the PRD coverage plan for self only.

ABX = Employee currently has elected the ABC coverage plan for family.

LNX = Employee currently has elected the LNM coverage plan for family.

Exhibit V-1-2. Melded Data Chunk

WIX = Employee currently has elected the WIN coverage plan for family.

KJX = Employee currently has elected the KJW coverage plan for family or had converted to KJW coverage (for self and/or family) after maintaining ABC coverage for self and family or WIN coverage for self or for self and family for at least 12 consecutive months anytime during the last ten years.

PRX = Employee currently has elected the PRD coverage plan for self OR family type coverage.

Positions 5–7

DEN = Denied optional coverage
MED = Failed physical
DIS = Disqualifying pre-existing condition
PRE = Pregnant

Exhibit V-1-2. (Cont)

---

have equally flexible data elements to collect the training data, the second set provides more flexibility than the first. When all data elements conform to the one-concept-equals-one-data-element rule, the flexibility benefits not just the manager who wants to look at the relationship between the training the division received and its productivity; it also benefits other managers in the organization with different information requirements. In other words, more questions can be answered with the data.

AN ANALOGY

An anecdote about building a house offers helpful analogies regarding the lack of flexibility caused by not following the one-concept-equals-one-data-element rule. After determining requirements for the house, it is decided that prefabricated house components will meet the needs in the easiest, cheapest, and fastest way. Prefabricated parts are melded components; and like melded data chunks, they contain more than one concept (i.e., component).

The house is built, and construction was cheap, fast, and easy. Two years

---

Name	Definition
MONTHLY AVERAGE OUTPUT	The average number of widgets produced per month. Twelve occurrences are allowed.
AVERAGE OUTPUT MONTH	The month for which the average number of widgets is recorded for the employee.

Exhibit V-1-3. Monthly Productivity Information

Name	Definition
WIDGETS PRODUCED COUNT	The number of widgets produced by an employee per day. There is an unlimited number of occurrences allowed of this data element.
WIDGETS PRODUCED DATE	The date (YYYYMMDD) on which the widgets were produced by an employee.

Exhibit V-1-4. Revised Productivity Report

---

later, however, it is decided to add an office with a separate entrance and a security system. Because the house was built with prefabricated parts, it is more complicated to make the addition. The prefabricated parts are melded components; consequently, an entire side of the house must be removed and rebuilt to accommodate the addition. Unfortunately, using the prefabricated components to begin with was faster, cheaper, and easier until changes needed to be made. The melded components' lack of flexibility caused the increased cost.

The Bottom Line

How can things (e.g., buildings or information) that have maximum flexibility for the future be created within today's budget? Large building components that have specific, narrowly defined purposes (e.g., prefabricated parts) cannot be made into as many end-products as the individual substances of which they are composed. For example, prefabricated components cannot be taken apart and have unaffected nails, screws, pipes, glue, lumber, and plaster. Each of these ingredients has been altered by the process of constructing the prefabricated part, and they cannot return to their original state. Similarly, melded data chunks that are created for specific narrow purposes cannot be used to create as many end-products as data elements can. In addition, the benefits of flexible data elements that comply with the one-concept-equals-one-data-element rule apply not only when using them but when maintaining them. It is easier to make modifications to data elements than it is to change melded data chunks.

THE DATA ELEMENT NAMING PROCESS

Data Element Names

Most data element naming standards agree on a basic data element name structure: one prime word (which represents the thing about which the data is being collected), one class word (which provides the category of information and some indication of the format and structure), and one or more modifiers (i.e., adjectives that modify the prime word or class word) to make the data

Prime Word	Modifier	Class Word
PERSON	BIRTH	DATE

Exhibit V-1-5. Data Element Name Structure

element name unique and meaningful. Exhibit V-1-5 contains an example of this structure.

Existing naming standards, however, fail to produce data elements that comply with the one-concept-equals-one-data-element rule for at least two reasons: they do not provide guidelines for choosing appropriate modifiers, and they imply that developing data element names is the correct first step.

Modifiers

One of the deficiencies in data element standardization procedures is that they focus on naming data elements while other important data element development aspects are underrepresented. Some data element naming standard designers claim that using entity names from a data model as prime words ensures that the data element includes only one concept. Using entity names from a data model for the prime words is insufficient to ensure that a data element complies with the one-concept-equals-one-data-element rule. A naming convention of this type unnecessarily relies on the accuracy and completeness of the data model. Data element development rules should have the capability to be applied effectively outside any specific data modeling effort. They should also support data modeling efforts by providing a quality check of the content of the data model. In other words, if the data elements developed during modeling do not comply with the data element standards or if some of the standard data elements developed do not fit with the model, a closer look at the model would be prudent.

Data element naming standards must provide guidelines in selecting modifiers to ensure that the data element complies with the one-concept-equals-one-data-element rule. The following example illustrates how uncontrolled use of modifiers violates the rule and results in melded data chunks instead of data elements.

The melded data chunks in Exhibit V-1-6 were created to meet the needs of an organization's personnel department. They may have been created over a period of 10 years as the personnel information system was modified to keep pace with the business requirements, or they may have been created all at one time to satisfy different divisions within the personnel department. Melded data chunks and redundant data elements are created inadvertently by carelessly inserting modifiers in data element names. If the previous examples were restricted to one prime word, one modifier, and one class word, the result—EMPLOYEE START DATE—makes it clear that the concept is the date

EMPLOYEE FULL-TIME START DATE
EMPLOYEE PART-TIME START DATE
EMPLOYEE COOP STUDENT FIRST DAY
EMPLOYEE EXECUTIVE INITIAL STATUS DATE
EMPLOYEE DATE REINSTATED
EMPLOYEE MALE START DATE
EMPLOYEE FEMALE START DATE
EMPLOYEE HANDICAPPED START DATE
EMPLOYEE VETERAN START DATE
EMPLOYEE POSITION BEGIN DATE

Exhibit V-1-6. Personnel Department's Melded Data Chunks

---

the employee started working for the organization. The more modifiers a melded data chunk name has, the stronger the warning should sound that several concepts are included.

Some of those additional concepts are easier to spot than others, but they can be uncovered during data element cleanup efforts by restricting data element names to one modifier. Then, as large groups of related melded data chunks are being analyzed and refined into data elements, modifiers can be kept to a minimum. Typically during this process it becomes obvious how the quality of the data elements is related to the quality of the data model and logical data base design. As many data elements are eliminated and some new data elements are created, new data base designs can be contemplated.

Here, the key benefit obtained from ensuring that data elements comply to the one-concept-equals-one-data-element rule is reducing redundancy. Redundant data elements not only require more computer storage space, they frequently lead to lower data quality when different sources are updated at different times, allowing the data to become inconsistent.

The First Step

The problems caused by naming data elements before defining them also must be addressed. People become attached to labels assigned to objects and are reluctant to change those labels. Functional users, programmers, data base administrators, and even data administrators usually rely on the data element name as the unique identifier of the data element (whether it is a full name or an abbreviated name). Therefore, the process of naming data elements should not be taken lightly. A suggested sequence of data element standardization involves the following steps:

- *Developing the data element definition.* This involves working with the proposed data element custodian, steward, sponsor, or responsible agent, ensuring that the data element definition includes only one concept.
- *Developing the valid values.* This involves ensuring that they include

only one concept and are completely consistent with the definition. Then the length, format, and edit criteria must be established.

- *Developing the name from the definition.* This involves selecting words from the definition. All the words in the name should come from the definition, but not all the words in the definition should be included in the name. The urge to name the data element first should be resisted and the definition from the name should be created. The processes are not the same.
- *Developing the remaining required attributes.* These attributes differ, depending on the organization.

Dependence on Names

An inverse relationship exists between the number of data element attributes documented for a data element and the degree to which users must depend on the data element name for meaning. As depicted in Exhibit V-1-7, as more attributes are documented for a data element, the user needs to depend on the name less and less to provide a complete understanding of the data element. The significance of this relationship is that organizations that are documenting (or intend to document) several attributes for their data elements need not rely on a rigidly structured naming standard.

On the other hand, organizations or projects that are documenting only the names of their data elements can benefit more from a stringent naming convention. For example, administrators working on high-level data modeling projects may find it unnecessary to document more than the name of the data elements in their models. Because the data element name is all that the readers of those models have on which to base their comprehension of the data elements, it is crucial that every word used in the names be chosen according to a well-thought-out naming standard and defined in the repository along with the model. Class words are usually limited to a small set of precisely defined terms, and prime words coming from a data model can rely on the definition of the entities. Modifiers also should be defined to avoid misunderstandings between business areas that use these common business terms differently.

Because dependence on the name for the data element's meaning decreases as more data element attributes are documented, data element naming

---

Homogeneous Valid Values? NO

PERSON HAIR COLOR: 1 = BROWN
2 = BLACK
3 = BLONDE
4 = RED
5 = GREY
6 = BALD

Exhibit V-1-7. Multiple Data Element Attributes

is less crucial for projects in which data elements are fully defined. Data administrators should keep this in mind when developing data element standardization programs. They must ask. Who is the target community? Is it new systems development teams, data modeling teams, or systems reengineering teams? Data element standardization rules that are appropriate for one organization often do not apply to others.

DATA ELEMENT ATTRIBUTES
Valid Values

Homogeneous and mutually exclusive valid values will not, by themselves, ensure a quality data element. Many other features of data element design must be considered. Starting with these two goals, however, makes other common data element design problems easier to identify and avoid. The main goal in developing quality data elements is to make data elements as self-evident and useful as possible.

Usefulness is maximized through flexibility. If a data element can be used by only one small group of users in one small system because its definition and valid values are restrictive, it is not as useful as one that serves many needs in the organization. An example of an extremely useful data element is a Social Security number. Any information system that stores personal data can use this data element as the key to its personnel records with confidence that innumerable other systems are using the same data element.

Making data elements self-evident is one of the data administrator's main responsibilities. By constructing their data repository schema, data administrators establish the attributes to be documented for each data element. These attributes must be comprehensive enough to ensure that the data elements can be understood completely and consistently. Sometimes, data elements that are poorly named and not defined create no problems for the long-time users of the system because they already have a complete understanding. When systems are redeployed in a distributed environment or are reengineered and enhanced, however, both the previous users and the new users are likely to assign their own meaning to the new and revised data elements that are poorly named and defined. This may lead to incorrect reports to management, poor decisions, misunderstandings, or delayed business functions. Data administrators assist in the creation of data elements by developing the set of attributes that provides the structure to facilitate comprehensive definitions.

Homogeneity. Homogeneous valid values represent a set of like items. The valid values are the representations, or instances, of the concept that the data element embodies. Blue, green, and brown are all instances of eye color. The way in which the valid values are like each other is the concept. For example, it is helpful to ask what do blue, green, and brown have in common? Because they all represent colors of people's eyes, the concept is person eye color.

The presence of valid values that are not homogeneous indicates that more than one concept is being included. The example in Exhibit V-1-8 contains valid values that are not homogeneous. These valid values represent more than one concept. The following phrases can be analyzed to determine the concepts they represent:

- The amount of hair a person has.
- The color of the hair that a person has.
- Whether or not a person has hair.

The phrases do not take into account whether the person wears a wig or whether the hair is more than one color (e.g., salt and pepper, has a white shock, or is dyed). If the amount of hair is concluded to be one of the concepts, the valid values for that concept must be determined.

Before continuing too far down this path, it would be wise to step back and look at the original concept. A data element may exist in personnel information systems because it is needed by the personnel business area to identify people. They may use it as one piece of data to visually observe someone's outward appearance to verify a person's identity. This instance is very different from a medical research laboratory that documents hair color by identifying and documenting the person's genetic structure responsible for hair color. It is important not to lose sight of the reason for collecting the data. Some data

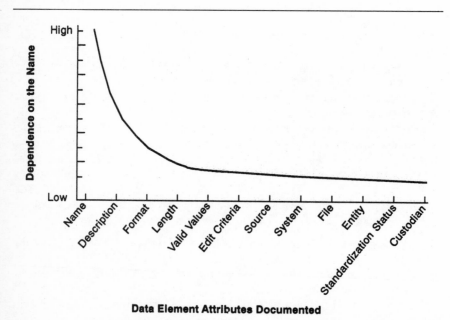

Data Element Attributes Documented

Exhibit V-1-8. Nonhomogeneous Valid Values

analysts have been accused of going off the deep end when it comes to developing data elements. A balance must be found between rigorous adherence to the one-concept-equals-one-data-element rule and the need for useful data elements.

Mutual Exclusivity. The other reason that abstracting to a higher level to combine concepts is risky is that the valid values themselves usually represent a combination of concepts. This results in valid values that are not mutually exclusive. The loss of flexibility in deriving meaningful information from values that are not mutually exclusive is the cost that must be paid.

A set of valid values are mutually exclusive when only one value applies to each instance. For example, the valid values in Exhibit V-1-9 are not mutually exclusive because the term single can apply to someone who is widowed or divorced or who has never married. Also, someone could be divorced and remarried and both D and M would apply. Many data elements have valid values like these, and the matter is usually dealt with by instructing the people who collect the data (e.g., customers, employees, or data entry clerks) to pick the choice that best fits. Relying on the data entry clerks or the people filling out the forms to pick the best choice indicates that someone knew that the choices were not mutually exclusive and that the quality of the data would probably suffer as a result.

Valid values that are not mutually exclusive often are developed for data elements that encompass more than one concept. In addition, data elements that include more than one concept are often developed to document the effect of implementing several related business rules on an instance of a business entity. The previous example implements the following implicit business rules:

- Only marriages that a US state recognizes as valid are recognized as valid by the organization.
- Marriages can be legally created and dissolved only by one of the US states.

Data Element Name:	EMPLOYEE MARITAL STATUS CODE
Data Element Definition:	An employee's status with regard to any US state's law concerning marriage
Valid Values:	M = Married
	S = Single
	D = Divorced
	W = Widowed
	L = Legally separated
	I = Interlocutory
	A = Annulled

Exhibit V-1-9. Nonmutually Exclusive Valid Values

- A person can be married to only one other person at a time.
- Once a valid marriage has been dissolved by the state, the persons can be legally married again.

Many laws define under what circumstances marriages can be dissolved by annulment or divorce. One data element, EMPLOYEE MARITAL STATUS CODE, attempts to document the relationship between an employee and all these business rules. The fact that this data element violates the one-concept-equals-one-data-element rule is evidenced by its valid values. It combines the following concepts: whether or not a person is currently married, whether or not a person was previously married, and what event caused the most recent previous marriage to end if the person has not remarried.

To remedy this situation, data elements that comply with the one-concept-equals-one-data-element rule can be developed for the concepts presented. A person's job may require the person to determine and analyze trends in marital relationships from a legal perspective; the data collected using the previous data element would be inadequate. Such persons would benefit from modeling their data requirements and constructing more precise data elements that would conform to the one-concept-equals-one-data-element rule.

Indicators

Homogeneity and mutual exclusivity among valid values help ensure that the data element addresses only one concept. However, there are other pitfalls to watch out for in developing valid values. Data elements with yes or no values are easy to create. They can be easily named and their valid values are mutually exclusive. But they often mask more meaningful data that may be more useful, and it is easy to end up with several yes or no data elements when a more comprehensive concept is more appropriate. The example in Exhibit V-1-10 demonstrates this. The higher-level concept in the example in Exhibit V-1-11 may be less obvious. These data elements could be assigned to the entity PERSON. A way to develop one meaningful data element to replace these, however, would be to reassign them as the valid values for a data element, PERSON HEALTH RISK CODE. This data element could be assigned to an entity called PERSON HEALTH RISK, which would be an associative entity between PERSON and HEALTH RISK. This associative entity could have data

---

Person Blue Eye Color Indicator
Person Green Eye Color Indicator
Person Gray Eye Color Indicator
Person Brown Eye Color Indicator
Person Hazel Eye Color Indicator

Exhibit V-1-10. Nonmeaningful Indicators

Person Smoking Indicator
Person Drinking Indicator
Person Exercise Indicator
Person Family History Indicator
Person High Blood Pressure Indicator
Person High Dietary Fat Intake Indicator

Exhibit V-1-11. Higher-Level Indicators

---

elements to document such additional concepts as date of onset, duration, and severity.

CONCLUSION

Strict adherence to the one-concept-equals-one-data-element rule is not always recommended. Situations do occur in which it is neither practical nor cost-effective to collect and store that level of detail because it will never be needed. These situations, however, are difficult to foresee. In addition, the data element designer is often not in a position to predict future users' data requirements. Therefore, the rule is an excellent foundation on which to build. If all data elements were initially developed to comply with this rule, changes to the data elements could be made selectively afterwards to the few that need not comply. This would then be done with full knowledge of the costs incurred by doing so. The cost is measured by the loss of flexibility and the subsequent risk that this lack of flexibility can cause when unforeseen requirements emerge.

Although data element development standards must be independent of data modeling efforts, they should support and be easily embraced by data modeling efforts (i.e., the data element standardization rules should be capable of being used with different modeling techniques). Also, even when organizations are not involved in full-scale modeling efforts, rudimentary data modeling during data element development often helps answer important questions. Data element development is often easier when done as part of a well-planned data modeling effort. The value of standardizing data elements in legacy systems, however, should not be ignored. Slow-moving cleanup efforts often provide steady improvements in data quality while new systems or data bases are still in development.

Data element standardization, like data administration itself, will not yield significant benefits as a separate and disconnected activity. Developing flexible, long-lasting data elements must be an integral goal of all systems development activities, whether they are develpment or maintenance activities. The enforcement of the data element standardization policy also must be an integral component of the system development process. Monitoring data element development can provide necessary training to the developers in an informal setting and serve as an enforcement mechanism. The tools used by the developers place limits on the configuration and attributes allowed for data elements that frequently do not coincide with the requirements of the data element standardization policy of the organization. Therefore, the data administrator trying to monitor the data element development requires a powerful tool that can overcome these discrepancies.

Supporting Tools

Repositories to store complex relationships between nonstandard and standard data elements are needed to support the process of migrating from legacy data elements to standard data elements. Data element cleanup efforts can be accomplished without repositories that can do this, but they will take longer, cost more, and be more error prone. Few data repositories exist that can store these complex relationships; most must be modified in some way.

Unfortunately, the tasks needed to prepare for a data element analysis and cleanup efforts are often perceived as a delay in the actual work. The tasks of designing an appropriate repository structure, which requires knowledge of what problems are likely to be encountered and prediction of what aspects of those problems need to be documented, are additional pressures. The end result is often that very little forethought goes into designing the repository structure to support data element analysis and cleanup.

Data administrators should not standardize data elements for the sake of reporting growing numbers of standard data elements. The proponents, agents, users, custodians, and functional sponsors should understand the value of quality data elements and demand quality data elements. As is often the case with other information resource management concepts, data administrators take it on themselves to educate their proponents, agents, users, custodians, and functional sponsors. After these people see the light, the data administrator should not hide away with the data analysts pounding and pummeling melded data chunks into quality data elements. The information customers must remain involved in the analysis and creation of their data elements.

Well-designed data elements can provide many benefits to an organization. Information customers can confidently share data and discuss changes to the systems they use with the developers with confidence that they are speaking about the same things. Developers can forgo the inconvenience of inventing data element names or guessing about the meaning of names concocted by some other developer. However, standard data elements are not easy to develop. Using sloppy standardization policies may be worse than not having any standards because the developers and information customers may conclude that standardization has not helped them at all if they spent substantial resources complying with a poorly conceived standardization program. Large data element standardization programs in existence for several years have had varying degrees of success. Any organization just embarking on establishing a data element standardization program would be wise to thoroughly scrutinize those programs to identify what works, what does not, and why.

V-2
Data Classification Concepts

MARTIN E. MODELL

The most prevalent data modeling technique currently in use is the entity-relationship (ER) approach developed by Peter Chen in the mid-1970s. This approach uses three basic constructs: the entity, the attribute, and the relationship. This chapter assumes a basic knowledge of the ER model and focuses on applying the concepts from classification as an aid to a more comprehensive understanding of that modeling approach.

UNDERSTANDING ER MODELING LANGUAGE

The term *entity*, as used throughout this chapter, refers to any group of persons, places, things, or concepts about which an organization must collect and maintain records (in this case, business records). Most dictionaries define the term *entity* as the fact of being, or something that exists. The term is used as a surrogate, linguistic symbol, or linguistic convenience in place of a more specific reference. Entity does not refer to any kind of thing in specific, and is usually a surrogate until an analyst determines its true identity.

In the data model, the term entity refers to the central components of the model, as opposed to the supporting components of attributes and relationships. Any difficulty with the term entity, probably occurs because in data modeling the term has as much meaning and definition as the term X has in mathematics. X has meaning when used as part of an equation, but is meaningless by itself. X is almost always defined in terms of other symbols and numbers. *Entity* is the data modeling equivalent of X.

Because of the inherent vagueness of the term in unqualified form, the term *entity* is often used:

- As both a group and singular term, sometimes within the same context.
- To refer to the whole group and a portion of the same group, sometimes within the same context.
- As a general term when it is impractical or cumbersome to use the phrase person, place, thing, or concept.
- To refer to many levels of aggregation and conceptually different components at the various design levels (i.e., conceptual, logical, and physical).
- By physical designers and by CASE tool vendors who borrow the term to refer to the records in the data base structure models.

Because of the ambiguity of meaning, the term *entity* should always be qualified in some manner with an adjective or other noun to make clear the kind of entity or group of entities being referred to.

The term *attribute* represents a property, aspect, descriptor, data group, data element, identifier, qualifier, or characteristic of an entity or a relationship. This definition creates difficulties, however, because these terms are not synonymous and, therefore, the term *attribute* is used:

- As both a group and in singular form, sometimes within the same context.
- To refer to a group of data elements, a portion of a group of elements, or a single element, sometimes within the same context.
- To refer to many levels of aggregation and to conceptually different components at the various design levels (i.e., conceptual, logical, and physical).
- By physical designers and by CASE tool vendors, who borrow it to refer to the data elements in the data base structure models.
- To refer to the properties (i.e., descriptors) and the characteristics of entities and of data elements.

In addition, within some data models, attributes have been elevated to the status of entities. In general, however, many models and most CASE tools have only two constructs: the entity and the attribute. The attribute is a single data element and the entity is anything that has more than one attribute.

As a further complication, the classification of a model component as either an entity or an attribute is subjective and based on perception, organizational emphasis, and contextual use. Simply put, whether something is an attribute of an entity (or relationship) or whether it is an entity (or relationship) in its own right is in most cases a design choice. In the same manner, the treatment of many components as either an entity or a relationship is also a design choice.

DATA ORGANIZING TECHNIQUES

For all public, private, government, and commercial enterprises, the typical course of doing business generates numerous forms and other business records. These records reflect business transactions, the actions of personnel, and the information collected and stored for current and future reference. The collective data and information contained in these records constitute the organization's base.

If not properly and consistently organized and cross-referenced, the sheer number, complexity, and interrelated aspects of these business records, could easily inundate the organization. All organizations therefore have created systems that can organize, categorize, classify, and store business records for easy retrieval, later reference, and use. All of these systems began by segregating the records by major category or group. Data organization methods exist in all organizations, regardless of whether their business records are stored manually, electronically, or some combination of both. Unless the company was highly perceptive and very well organized, the systems used to organize business data use a personal or local perspective in some areas and a common, centralized, or partially centralized perspective in others. A given set of records may be used by a relatively small group of persons or a relatively large group of employees. Unless its record storage method is centralized and uses a corporate perspective, a given set of records is rarely used by all personnel within the organization.

Many organizations are currently attempting to reduce data acquisition and maintenance and storage costs, increase productivity, and improve information access by centralizing the storage of such commonly used records as those contained in central account files and those used for central reference. Centralization ensures that the same set of records can service the largest group of employees possible. This process must accommodate the many diverse business perspectives and data retrieval needs of large groups with differing needs for the same records. This process can be simplified with ER modeling, which facilitates the development of a categorization and classification scheme for data storage. The data model is developed using an analysis of an organization's data requirements, the characteristics of its data, and the integration of the various views and perspectives of the functional areas of the organization that collect, maintain, or rely on this data.

All processing, whether automated or manual, can be divided into two categories: processing of every record and processing of selected records. In most procedural systems, the selection of records for conditional processing (i.e., each kind of record is processed differently) is based on tests that are performed on the values of the data contained within the records. Usually, each discrete value tested corresponds to a specific type of processing. Based on the results of these tests, certain records are selected, others discarded, and specific processing performed. Records can be sequenced by the contents of a data element, and specific processing takes place when the contents of the data element change: this is another variation on value testing. The values of certain data elements can be used to indicate the presence or absence of other (i.e., dependent) data elements. All of these procedures represent uses of classification.

CLASSIFICATION DEFINED

Things or entities are distinguished from one another to form groups to facilitate management or understanding. To classify is to organize, arrange, or group things according to family, class, or category. These are biological terms that refer to various levels of specificity or generality when discussing sets, groups, or collections that contain members with common characteristics. These terms are used in taxonomic charts for biology—the origin of modern classification—to categorize flora and fauna and each imples a group that ranges from the general to the specific. The level of specificity of a group is determined by the number of characteristics the members of the group have in common.

Because the term *entity* must always be qualified by some adjective or noun, because a data model must distinguish between groups of entities in the same general-to-specific manner, and because it is necessary to distinguish between a whole group and a portion of that group, the following terms will be used in the remainder of this discussion:

- Entity family—The largest, most general group.
- Entity group—A subdivision of the entity family.
- Entity occurrence—A single entity.

Such taxonomic terms as *type* are unsuitable as a qualifier, because although it means a group, it has been so widely used with so many definitions that it has become meaningless. Data classification is not just a general-to-specific decomposition; therefore, it might be misleading to use terms that imply that it is. Although many taxonomic terms refer to level of specificity and commonality of characteristic and have specific meanings when used in relation to each other, the simple term *entity group* conveys sufficient meaning.

The use of the terms *family, group,* and *occurrence* is more significant than the use of *class, type,* and *subtype* because the latter group of terms implies a hierarchic decomposition of an entity in much the same context as the hierarchic decomposition of function and process. The term *family,* in particular, has been chosen primarily because it has no specific usage within the current data modeling language. In addition, although the data model concentrates on the identification of groups within groups (i.e., decomposition), it must also account for overlapping groups and multiple groups that are decomposed from the same population and share some characteristics and not others.

ENTITY FAMILIES VERSUS ENTITY GROUPS

An entity family is composed of members with at least one characteristic in common. The fewer characteristics that the members of a group have in common, the more members the group can potentially have. Of all the components in a data model, an entity family has the largest possible membership. Entity families are identified in the first phase (i.e., the enterprise or conceptual phase) of data model construction and are the components of the conceptual or highest-level data model.

With few exceptions, each entity family becomes the subject of a data base. When there is a one-to-one correspondence between an entity family and a data base, the term *subject entity* may be used instead of entity family. The entity families of a data model are general groups of things that are often only loosely related. Organizational business processes usually deal with families and selected (i.e., specific) entity groups within those families and they need both general (i.e., family wide) data and specific (i.e., group) data. The identification of both family and group and the relationship between the two becomes critical to the effectiveness of the data model.

A data entity family represents a collection of records—each containing data that is common to all family members. For each distinct entity group within the family and each business user perspective, the data also includes:

- Characteristics that distinguish all entity groups from each other at every level of categorization.
- Details of the general-to-specific progression of the characteristic sequence or string for each characteristic of the entity group.
- Attributes of interest for the entity group that are beyond the characteristics used to form the group.

CHARACTERISTICS AND ATTRIBUTES

An attribute is some aspect or descriptor of an entity and many contain one or more highly interrelated data elements. Attributes have no meaning, existence, or interest to an organization, except in terms of the entity (or relationship) they describe. An attribute may be abstract or general information, a specific data element, or some piece of information in between these two extremes. In a data model, most attributes are clusters of highly interrelated data elements that together describe some aspect of the entity. The values of most data elements are not critical to the data model and in most cases are unique to an entity occurrence. A data model, however, must document the valid ranges of the values for each data element as well as its format.

A characteristic is a multipurpose, multivalued, attribute whose discrete values identify or describe entities, families, and entity groups or distinguish one entity group or family from another. Within the data model, all valid values of each characteristic must be identified and documented. These values then form the basis of entity classification, which controls processing, data grouping, and entity identification. Both the characteristic and its values are of interest to the data model. Characteristics are best diagrammed as a T-list. An example of the standard form of a T-list is illustrated in Exhibit V-2-1.

The most definitive characteristic within any model is the identifier, or key, whose values distinguish one member of a family or group from another.

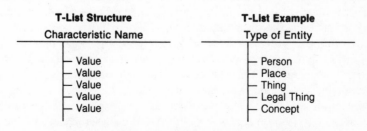

Exhibit V-2-1. Diagramming Characteristics Using T-Lists

In other words, the unique range of values of the identifier creates the smallest, most restrictive group—a group with only one member. All entity families and entity groups must have an associated characteristic. Each entity occurrence must have a specific set of characteristics for correct identification, processing, and data grouping.

THE USE OF CHARACTERISTICS IN DATA MODELING

The primary goal of data analysis is to identify the data requirements of the company (or a portion of it) and to identify the data elements needed to satisfy those requirements. The primary goal of data modeling is to assist the data analyst in the requirements definition, and to provide a means for determining the most effective method for organizing that data.

The ER approach states that companies require data about people, places, and things (and concepts) and that data should be organized around those entities. The ER approach also states that there is a difference between analyzing entities and determining requirements for data about them, and analyzing data to determine how best to organize that data into records for storage and processing. Data organization must be centered around entities. The concept of normalization as proposed by Codd organizes data around primary keys and into functional dependency groups. The same concept as incorporated into the ER approach organizes data around entities and into attribute groups. The success of both approaches depends on effectively determining how to group the required data. In effect, a data model attempts to organize and group data and each approach attempts to describe how to accomplish that task.

Classification is the science of organizing and grouping. Classification techniques, when properly applied, can be highly effective when used to organize and group data. Classification techniques can be most effective when first applied to the real world entity models and then translated to data models. Classification science uses characteristics to group like entities. Data modeling uses attributes to describe entities and uses characteristics to group both entities and attributes. Data modeling uses two kinds of characteristics: extensional and intensional.

Extensional characteristics are developed from organizational policies, business rules, and the organization's perception of the entities that it deals with. Extensional characteristics are largely fixed by policy and are subjective in that they are what the organization deems them to be. Extensional characteristics determine the criteria for entity family creation and membership. In other words, organizational policies determine what entity groups are to be treated the same and how these groups are to be identified. Extensional characteristics define the boundaries around a group, in this case an entity family. Extensional characteristics are multivalued, as are all other characteristics, but by definition, each member of the family must have the same value of a given extensional characteristic. If family membership is defined by multiple extensional characteristics, then each member must have the same value of each selected extensional characteristic. All members of a given entity family must have the same extensional characteristics because possession of those characteristics is the criterion for family membership.

Intensional characteristics are used to determine the differences between the members of an entity family, to determine how the members should be grouped, and as an aid in processing. Intensional characteristics also determine data grouping requirements, and data content. All members of a given group within an entity family have the same intensional characteristic values. Intensional characteristics define the various types of members, their identifiers, and their relationship to each other. Intensional characteristics make up the majority of the characteristics of interest for an organization and are used to construct the entity family model. Unless otherwise noted, all characteristics that are discussed in the remainder of this chapter are intensional characteristics. Characteristics are value dependent. The presence or absence of a characteristic is the presence or absence of a specific value. Group (and family) membership is specified in the form of a series of equations (e.g., something is a contract if there are at least two parties, and there is an agreement between the parties and there is consideration).

Dependent and Independent Characteristics

Intensional characteristics may in turn be dependent or independent. Independent characteristics do not depend on each other for definition and use. Characteristics may be together, or chained, to form sequences where characteristics qualify other characteristics. All characteristics between chains and at the first level (i.e., below the family) within a chain must be independent of each other. (Characteristic chains are discussed in detail in the latter part of this section.) Examples of independent characteristics include contract price terms (i.e., fixed price or variable price) and contract payment type (i.e., lump-sum or installment).

Dependent characteristics are those whose values qualify the values of another characteristic. The value of a dependent characteristic depends on another characteristic for its definition and use. At a specific level, however, dependent characteristics must be independent of each other. An example of a dependent characteristic is type of price variability (i.e., incentive, discount, or indexed), which depends on the variable price value of the characteristic contract price terms.

A characteristic chain is similar to the leg of a hierarchy. A chain is, however, a sequence of values, not data fields. More specifically, a chain is a sequence of characteristic values that is headed by the value of an independent characteristic and is followed by one value from each of its dependent characteristics. The extensional characteristics that identify an entity family and distinguish its members from other families' members are also, by definition,

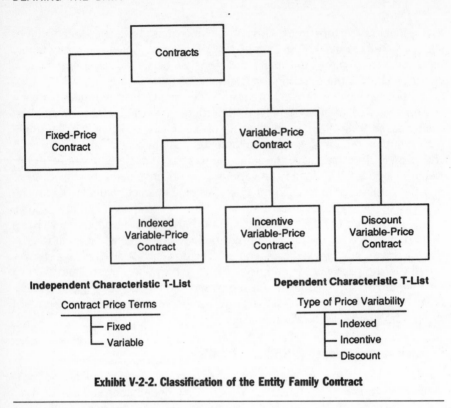

Exhibit V-2-2. Classification of the Entity Family Contract

intrinsic or intensional to the entity. Exhibit V-2-2 illustrates the classification of a contract entity family by the intensional characteristic price terms, further price term classification by type of price variability. Exhibit V-2-2 also illustrates a diagrammatic representation of this classification chain.

As a matter of diagrammatic convenience, characteristic chains are assembled from most specific to least specific, or bottom-up. The following is an example of characteristic chains:

> Contracts
> > fixed-price contracts
> > variable-price contracts
> > > incentive variable-price contracts
> > > discount variable-price contracts
> > > indexed variable-price contracts

Each chain consists of one or more characteristics, and the indentation level of each chain represents a specific type of contract. Each indentation level also represents a more restrictive group than that of the group at the preceding level.

A characteristic chain can include multiple dependent characteristics, each of which is independent of the other; however, they are still considered dependent characteristics. Each characteristic chain begins with an independent characteristic followed by one or more dependent characteristics.

Levels of Characteristics

A first-level, or base, characteristic must be capable of grouping all members of the entity family population independently of any other grouping of the same population. Second-level characteristics are dependent because they group only within a first-level characteristic. This representation of qualification levels (i.e., the length of qualifier chain) and the entity groups that are determined by these qualification levels give rise to the notion of entity decomposition—the idea that entities can be decomposed in the same manner as functional area activities.

Exhibit V-2-3 uses the concurrent classification of employee entities by both employee type and pay status to demonstrate two first-level entity family classifications. Within the exhibit, both *employee type* (full time, part time) and *pay status* (nonexempt, exempt) are considered independent first-level characteristics because all employees work full or part time and are either exempt or nonexempt. If, for example, all part-time employees were paid weekly, but full-time employees had a choice of pay cycle, the *pay cycle* (weekly, biweekly, semimonthly, monthly) would depend only on the full-time value.

Rules Governing Characteristics

The values of a characteristic must be exhaustive and mutually exclusive; that is, they must cover all possible conditions, and two values of the same characteristic cannot apply to the same entity. Each entity occurrence within a given entity group must have only one value from the values list used to identify the group; each entity must have the same value, and every entity in any other group must have some other valid value. For example, the *sex of employee* characteristic (male, female) is both mutually exclusive and exhaustive. The concept of mutual exclusivity can be further illustrated by the term *French language proficiency* (reading, writing, and speaking). This term is exhaustive, but its components are not mutually exclusive, because an individual can have proficiency in reading, writing, speaking, or any combination.

The values of *both, other, all others,* and *unknown* are not valid values for a characteristic. An individual characteristic value cannot include the connectors *and* or *or.* Characteristic values should, whenever possible, be a single word or, at most, a two-word phrase. The list of characteristic values should not have an explicit or implicit *and* between individual terms. A list of characteristic values must, however, always have an implicit *or* in the list of terms (male *or* female).

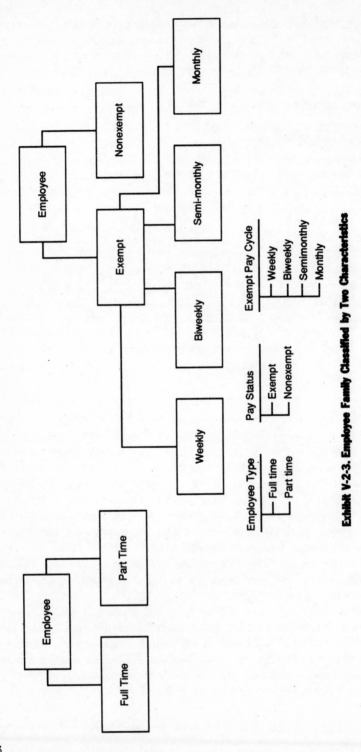

Employee

Full Time   Part Time

Employee

Nonexempt   Exempt

Monthly

Semi-monthly   Biweekly   Weekly

Employee Type
├─ Full time
└─ Part time

Pay Status
├─ Exempt
└─ Nonexempt

Exempt Pay Cycle
├─ Weekly
├─ Biweekly
├─ Semimonthly
└─ Monthly

Exhibit V-2-3. Employee Family Classified by Two Characteristics

Each first-level intensional characteristic must completely divide up the entire family population. Each value of every first-level intensional characteristic forms the name of one of the divisional groups and heads its own independent chain. The use of additional dependent intensional characteristics further groups the members of the value-dependent entity group represented by each chain.

Characteristics in Action

Characteristics serve three distinct purposes. First, their values distinguish one entity family from another (i.e., extensional characteristics) and, within an entity family, one entity group from another (i.e., intensional characteristics). Entities may be grouped for the following reasons:

- When each individual value represents a different kind of processing, a characteristic determines which entity occurrence should be processed and in what manner—For example, the characteristic *pay status* has two values: exempt and nonexempt. Employees who are coded exempt do not get paid for overtime, those coded nonexempt are paid for overtime.
- The entire family or a group within the family must be sequenced for reporting purposes, based on the values of one or more characteristics. Characteristics separate entities into groups and, as an extreme case, separate one entity from another.

Second, characteristics are used to name entity groups. Although characteristics are usually manifested as coded attributes, these codes represent some condition, state, or test result that has an English-language word or phrase associated with it. The word or phrase associated with each characteristic value, alone or together with the value name of one or more other characteristics, also provides the name of the entity group that contains the members with that particular set of characteristic values. For example, the two named groups from Exhibit V-2-3 are exempt employees and nonexempt employees.

Third, characteristics are surrogates for, and usually the keys or identifiers of, larger data groups that depend entirely on the presence of those characteristics. In many cases, each characteristic value implies the need for one set of attributes or group of data elements that is unique to it—one specific data group per characteristic value. These data groups are also known as records or functional dependency groups.

As illustrated in Exhibit V-2-4, the business data required for nonexempt employees must include data that determines how overtime is to be compensated (e.g., according to an agreed-on work week, agreed-on work hours per day, agreed-on work start and end times, rates per overtime hour, and rates per shift). Generally, these groups of data items (elements) are associated with the characteristic value itself or on a unique sequence of characteristic values.

```
┌─────────────────┐       • Pay status—nonexempt
│                 │       • Agreed-on work week
│                 │       • Agreed-on work hours per day
│   Nonexempt     │   =   • Agreed-on start time
│                 │       • Agreed-on end time
│                 │       • Rate per overtime hour
└─────────────────┘       • Rate per shift
```

Exhibit V-2-4. Characteristic Value Used to Identify Additional Data

Defining Characteristics

Data models group entities by characteristics to form families and groups within families. Each entity must have a set of distinguishing characteristics that determines its family and group membership. These characteristics form a data equation:

$$\text{entity} = f(\text{characteristic 1, characteristic 2, . . ., characteristic } n)$$

The definition of each characteristic describes its function, its role in identifying family or group membership, and the aspect of the entity it represents. The definition describes the reason for the characteristic and where its values originate. A suggested form for the definition of a characteristic follows:

The values of the characteristic (*name of characteristic*) delineate the (*item being delineated*) aspect of the entity (*name of entity*). The list of values of the characteristic (*name of characteristic*) are:

1. Code value—English equivalent.
2. Code value—English equivalent.
3. Code value—English equivalent.
4. Code value—English equivalent.

.
.
.

n. Code value—English equivalent.

The following statement should be added when the characteristic is dependent on another characteristic:

The characteristic (*name of characteristic*) further qualifies the characteristic (*name of characteristic*),

where

(*name of characteristic*) is the English name of the list of values.
(*item being delineated*) states the aspect of the entity that is being described, and
(*name of entity*) is the name of the entity family.

The following is an example of a characteristic definition:

> The values of the characteristic *pay cycle* delineate the frequency of the exempt employee paycheck issuance aspect of the entity employee. The list of values of the characteristic *pay cycle* are:
>
> > 1. w—weekly paycheck.
> > 2. b—biweekly paycheck.
> > 3. s—semimonthly paycheck.
> > 4. m—monthly paycheck.
>
> The characteristic *pay cycle* further qualifies the characteristic *pay status.*

CONCLUSION

Many techniques have been developed to organize data. Entity-relationship data modeling is such a technique for organizing and grouping data. To use this method effectively, however, familiarity with the concepts of classification, entities, and entity characteristics is essential. The terminology adapted from classification science, when used to define and apply these concepts, while highly specialized, can be clearly understood. By becoming thoroughly conversant with this terminology and these concepts and by using them when creating and discussing data models, an organization can begin to understand and take the necessary steps that are involved in classification and data modeling.

V-3
A Framework for Classifying Data

WILLIAM H. INMON

In its entirety, the organization, codification, and use of raw data constitute a vast and complex subject. The types of data are manifold and for users to make sense of raw data, it must be organized into subsets. Each subset can then be understood in terms of its properties, uses, and relations to other data subsets. Two of the more interesting ways to classify data are by its internal or external attributes, and by its administrative or directional attributes. Each of these classes of data has its own characteristics, implications, and properties. This chapter examines those classes and suggests a framework for understanding the relationship between classes of data.

DATA MODELS

A useful vehicle for the examination of the properties and characteristics of the different data types is the data model. A data model is the classical vehicle by which organizations begin to make sense of their data. The worth of a data model in the systems development process is seldom questioned in today's sophisticated world of data management and development.

A data model has the following characteristics:

- *It provides a paradigm for systematization.* The paradigm typically organizes data in subject areas, entities, and tables of data, all of which satisfy an organization's collective processing requirements.
- *It is a means of identifying commonality of data across applications.* Typically, subject areas such as customer, policy, account, and product apply across multiple applications.
- *It is a blueprint for the organization of details at all levels.* An orderly and rigorous transformation occurs in the structure of data from the subject area, the high level, to the low-level data model.
- *It is central to the relationship between primitive and derived data.* Knowing how to identify derived data, relate it back to its primitive source, and then eliminate it from the data model is crucial to the ability to build and implement a data model in a finite time period.

INTERNAL AND EXTERNAL DATA MODELS

In most cases the result of the data modeling exercise is a model of the customer (or external) interaction with the organization. Banks, insurance companies, retailers, and public utilities usually focus their data model on the organization as it interacts with its external environment. Such a data model is called an external data model because it is developed to facilitate understanding of the external forces acting on (and interacting with) the organization.

Another type of data model is an internal one; its focus is on the data reflecting the organization's internal components, dynamics, and relationships. The difference in focus between the internal and external data models is also evident in their content. Typical major subject areas found in the internal model are: mission, goal, strategy, objective, and problem. Typical major subject areas found in the external model are: product, customer, transaction, and account.

These areas are indicative of the great difference between the two types of models. From the external perspective, the customer is related to such concepts as products, accounts, and shipments. Although customers may be aware that the organization has underlying goals and objectives, as long as its products are of high quality and competitively priced, they do not need to know about the organization's internal issues and demographics. Similarly, for the manager focusing on the organization's internal relationships, such external factors as product, customer, and account (though still important) are a secondary consideration.

ADMINISTRATIVE AND DIRECTIONAL DATA MODELS

Another classification for data and data models is according to the organization's administrative and directional aspects. The focus of the administrative manager is on making short-term, frequently minor adjustments to the organization. The administrative decision maker typically is concerned with protecting existing market share and with attempts to minimize costs and maximize revenues. With an eye to the organization's continuity and stability, the administrative decision maker necessarily has a short-term horizon.

The counterpart of the administrative manager is the directional decision maker. This is the manager who handles longer-term issues (e.g., new markets, new uses of technology, and new investments). The directional decision maker makes decisions less frequently, but makes the ones that have broad consequences for the organization and that change the direction in which the organization is heading.

It is noteworthy that the decisions made by the administrative manager are often at odds with those made by the directional decision maker. This springs from a basic dichotomy between the administrative and operational management functions. Major subject areas that are typically relevant to the administrative manager include: employees, the organization chart, rate adjustment, the production quota, and late shipments. Subjects typically relevant to the directional manager include: competition, new technology, the economic forecast, and market share. A matrix (see Exhibit V-3-1) can be constructed to distinguish between the internal and external perspectives of data and the administrative or directional perspectives.

The focus in the internal administrative quadrant is an introspective look at the organization. Typical data found in this quadrant includes the organization chart, employee particulars, compensation, and office location. In the internal directional quadrant, the interest centers on such issues as the organization's strategy, policy, mission, and goals. The focus of the organization's external administrative quadrants is on the customers, accounts, transactions, and product. This quadrant is the most familiar to modelers because most data and most systems fit here. The focus of the external directional quadrant is the marketplace, technology, competition, and the economic forecast, these are broad subjects of interest to the organization as a whole.

An interesting feature of the matrix showing internal, external, administrative, and directional data is the tendency toward mutual exclusivity of data within the quadrant. Most data seems to fit naturally into one quadrant, and no others. This concept is discussed further in the next section.

Mutual Exclusivity

The tendency toward mutual exclusivity of data within the matrix is reflected in the data models that represent the data in each quadrant. In general, the data found in data models for each quadrant applies only to that quadrant—rarely does an organization's data model successfully include data from more than one quadrant. The most successful modeling efforts seem to be those that do not mix data from the different quadrants.

There is good reason for not mixing data from different quadrants in the

	Internal	External
Administrative	• Organization Chart • Employee Particulars • Compensation • Office Location	• Customer • Account • Transaction • Product
Directional	• Strategy • Policy • Mission • Goals	• Marketplace • Technology • Competition • Economic Forecast

Exhibit V-3-1. Representative Data in the Four Quadrants

data model. The goal of most modeling efforts is some form of systematization. From systematization there results payback to the organization, either through the leveraging of technology, or through the economies of consolidation that can be achieved through integration of common data and processing. Without some payback, however it is measured and realized, systematization makes no sense. A method of measuring payback is described in the next section.

Rating the Quadrants

Each quadrant can be assigned a payback and systematization rating. On a scale of 1 to 10, a payback rating of 10 means that, historically, major payback is (or has been) possible from systematization in the quadrant. A payback rating of 1 indicates that very little payback has ever been achieved. A systematization rating of 10 indicates that the data represented in the quadrant has been methodically systematized in the past. A systematization rating of 1 indicates the data has resisted attempts at systematization. Exhibit V-3-2 shows the matrix with the payback and systematization ratings for each of the quadrants. An explanation of the ratings that have been assigned follows.

The Internal Administrative Quadrant. In this quadrant the payback of administrative internal systems is low. Typical systems would be those for employee payroll and employee education. Although an organization may run efficiently as far as its internal administrative systems are concerned, this efficiency does little toward winning new market share, lowering costs, and raising revenues. Because this quadrant does not directly affect profitability, there is only a small payback for systematization. Systematization in this quadrant is rated highly, however, because the data is fairly easy to systematize.

The Internal Directional Quadrant. This quadrant contains such data as mission, goal, and objective. There is a fairly high payback to the systematization of such data, but the track record of systematization here is very low. It is neither easy nor even appropriate in many cases to attempt to systematize strategy and objectives. The data in this quadrant is so ambiguous and amorphous as to be almost impervious to systematization.

	Internal	External
Administrative	• Payback *2* • Systematization *9*	• Payback *9* • Systematization *9*
Directional	• Payback *6* • Systematization *1*	• Payback *10* • Systematization *1*

Exhibit V-3-2. Payback and Systematization Ratings for the Four Quadrants

The External Administrative Quadrant. This quadrant contains the classical data (e.g., that relating to customer, account, product, and transaction). No other quadrant has benefited from data automation to the extent that this quadrant has, and for good reason. The data in this quadrant has a fairly high payback for systematization and is fairly easily systematized, making it the most popular for automation.

The External Directional Quadrant. This quadrant contains such data as new technology, competition, and economic conditions. Under any rules, there is a very high payback to the systematization of this data but there are also many problems. Some of these are:

- The irregularity of the availability of the data.
- The extreme diversity of media over which information is transmitted.
- The lack of uniformity of the data itself.

In short, the data in this quadrant, as important as it is, resists systematization at every turn.

Adding the Ratings

Another, somewhat arbitrary, way to assess the affinity of the quadrants for automation is simply to add together the payback and the systematization ratings, as illustrated in Exhibit V-3-3. The exhibit shows that the administrative external quadrant is easily the most favored target for automation, whereas the directional internal quadrant is the least amenable. An argument can be made that adding payback and systematization ratings further obscures an already obscure rating. But the rebuttal is that, whatever the payback, if systematization is very difficult, then the likelihood of automation is just as poor as if the systematization prospects were very high and the prospects for payback were poor.

The key for a customer is usually fairly clear, while the key for an objective is not. The attributes for a product are fairly clear, while the attributes for a goal are ambiguous. The specifics of, for instance, an insurance policy are clear and well defined, whereas the specifics for an organization's policy regarding

	Internal	External
Administrative	11	18
Directional	7	11

Exhibit V-3-3. Combined Payback and Systematization Ratings of Each Quadrant

overtime or employee absences are less clear. These reasons lead to the conclusion that internal data is difficult to automate and external data is not. If the purpose of a data model is to enhance or enable automation, it is questionable whether modeling the internal directional environment is even appropriate. Data from such areas as mission, strategy, and objective does not lend itself to automation in the same way that customer, product, and account data does. There may be real benefits to modeling the organization's internal workings, but these may not be easily realized by automation. Modeling the internal directional data of the organization can be useful in identifying and streamlining the organization's business practices. Some results of modeling this quadrant might be:

- Identification of conflicting goals.
- Recognition of a strategy misalignment.
- Recognition that no objectives are identified.
- Discovery of misalignments in an organizational chart.

The benefits of modeling in this quadrant are less tangible than those of modeling in other quadrants. Data models in this quadrant have the reputation of being blue-sky exercises that contribute little to the automation effort. As such, it is questionable whether they should be built in the first place.

Generic Data Models

Another interesting aspect of the internal directional quadrant is the potential for developing a generic internal directional (or even administrative) model. The models of most organizations are affected by their industry sector as a whole, at least insofar as the external model is concerned. But the internal model remains fairly constant regardless of the type of organization, the industry, and even the size of the organization. In other words, if there is any prospect at all for a generic data model, the model will most likely be of internal directional and administrative data. As with any data model, the more detailed it is, the less generic it is. A the high level, the model is likely to be highly generic, and at lower levels, successively less so.

An interesting phenomenon of modeling in the internal administrative and the internal directional quadrants is that the relationship between objects tends to be much more ambiguous than it is in other quadrants. In some cases, a relationship will apply so broadly as to be meaningless. An example of a broad relationship is that between strategy and mission. Such a relationship undoubtedly exists, but it is difficult to quantify and describe. In other cases, a relationship between data at the internal quadrants may be so specific and narrow as to be equally meaningless. The relationship of office location to compensation is valid, but it is of interest to so few people that its worth is questionable. The whole dimension of relationships in the internal quadrants, particularly the internal directional quadrant, needs to be thoroughly analyzed and established before the modeling process for this quadrant begins. Using standard techniques here for representation of relationships may prove to be more misleading than useful.

Overlapping Data

The mutual exclusivity of data from one quadrant to the next is not absolute; there is some overlap of data, particularly at the higher modeling levels. For example, for many environments the major subject (i.e., customer) fits into the external administrative and the external directional quadrants. However, what is meant by the term customer is not necessarily constant; and the more detailed the data attributes applied to it, the less commonality of data exists across quadrants.

For example, in the external administrative quadrant, the interest in customer focuses on current customers and on servicing their immediate needs to keep them. But in the external directional quadrant, the focus is more on potential customers and on demographics that are useful in helping the organization to attract new customers. In the external directional quadrant, there may be an interest in the existing customer base, but only insofar as the existing customer is also a potential candidate for new services or products.

The essential difference in the interest and focus of the data model or data administration in each of the quadrants shows up in at least two ways: the number of attributes in each quadrant, and the stability of the model in each quadrant.

In the external administrative quadrant, data in a data model typically has many attributes. For example, the major subjects and their subtypes in account would have such attributes as:

- Date opened.
- Domicile.
- Current balance.
- Type.
- Fund assignment.
- Statement date.
- Statement cycle.
- Social security number.

The major subjects and their subtypes of loan have such attributes as:

- Interest rate.
- Collateral.
- Late payment penalty.
- Balloon payment.
- Renegotiation date.

The major subjects and their subtypes of savings have such attributes as:

- Interest rate.
- Christmas club.
- Minimum balance.
- Minimum deposit.
- Withdrawal date.

The data attributes found in the external administrative quadrant are relatively stable and numerous. But this is not so with regard to major categories in the external directional quadrant—customer, competition, and new technology. The major subjects and their subtypes of customer have such attributes as:

- Address.
- Age.
- Salary.
- Occupation.
- Number of dependents.

The major subjects and their subtypes of competition have such attributes as:

- Market share.
- Product line.
- Length of time in business.

The major subjects and their subtypes of new technology have such attributes as:

- Description.
- Developer.
- Potential uses.

Not only are the attributes fewer and less stable, but the major subject areas in this quadrant are constantly changing. The gathering, use, and content of data in this quadrant are very different from those of data in other quadrants.

Other Dissimilarities

The dissimilarities of data from one quadrant to the next are not limited to the differences between the external administrative and the external directional quadrants. They extend to the representation of data from the external administrative and the internal directional quadrants. The data in the external administrative quadrant represents such tangible objects as shipments, products, parts, and customers. In addition, there are less eligible entities that have a legal and logical form, if not a physically tangible form. These include bank accounts, insurance claims, and financial transactions. In short, the external directional quadrant contains data that measures tangible objects.

In contrast to this, the objects represented in the internal directional quadrant tend to be intangible. Such data as objectives, goals, and motivations are found in this quadrant. The amorphous nature of these objects is reflected in the difficulty of trying to assign significant keys, attributes, and relationships to the data model representing them.

The very different nature of data in the various quadrants can also be seen from the perspective of the audience served by them. Some overlap exists between the audiences served, but to a great extent senior management is interested in the external directional quadrant, middle management in the internal administrative quadrant, and clerical personnel in the external administrative quadrant. In addition, the audience served by each quadrant can be categorized by job function. The marketing function is interested in the external directional quadrant; the sales function is interested in the external administrative quadrant; and the personnel administration function in the internal administrative quadrant.

CONCLUSION

The task of data modeling is confused enormously if all data is treated as if it were equal. To model data meaningfully, it should be broken into four general categories: internal administrative data, external administrative data, internal directional data, and external directional data. Each of these quadrants of data contains essentially different data with different characteristics. Models of data within any quadrant can be meaningfully created. But when data from one quadrant is mixed with that from another, the modeling process is best served by the creation of indirect relationships from one model to the next, rather than by mixing data models from different quadrants into a single integrated model.

V-4
Modeling Business Rules

RONALD G. ROSS

Business rules traditionally have been implemented in procedural logic buried deep in application programs—in a form that is virtually unrecognizable, and far removed from original business intent. Such strategies not only produce highly inconsistent enforcement of the business rules, but make rapid changes in them virtually impossible. Sadly, this has been true even for information engineering, and other data-driven approaches. Process-oriented approaches have proven much worse.

A rule may be defined as a constraint, or a test, exercised for the purpose of maintaining the integrity (i.e., correctness) of persistent data. Every rule defined for a data base should have a specific type, which should be selected from a standard set. The purpose of a rule generally is to control the updating of persistent data—in other words, the results that the execution of actions are permitted to leave behind.

Such control reflects desired patterns for business behavior. A rule therefore embodies a formal, implementable expression of some user requirement, or business rule, usually stated in textual form using a natural language (e.g., English). Business rules indicate a discrete, operational practice or policy in running the business, without reference to any particular implementation strategy or specific technology. Users, of course, generally should not be concerned with how business rules actually are enforced.

The textual statement of business rules is extremely important. Every rule should be accompanied by an English-language expression of the rule's business intent. Unfortunately, textual statements often are ambiguous, and cannot be translated directly into an actual implementation (i.e., into running code). The task of the designer therefore is to translate textual business rules into formal, precise (and implementable) rules.

Some business rules translate directly to corresponding rules. Most, however, are more involved, and may require multiple rules to express fully. Often such rules can be interconnected in building-block fashion, enabling the data base designer to work from standard rule components. This simplifies the task of translation significantly.

EXTENDING DATA (AND OBJECT) MODELS

A successful approach to modeling business rules requires careful attention to several crucial objectives, as follows.

- Rules depend on specification of underlying data types; these data types must be defined comprehensively and uniquely.
- To achieve maximum consistency and adaptability, rules themselves should be specified in discrete and nonredundant fashion.
- Users generally are not concerned with how business rules are implemented; therefore nonprocedural specification of rules is preferred.
- Communication of business intent usually is served best by pictures.

The framework that satisfies all these objectives most fully is provided by data models. Object models also may satisfy these objectives. This is discussed briefly in the following sections. Ross Method therefore uses data models as a given in specifying rules.

This preference is grounded in fundamental beliefs about the nature of production-level business operations. The computing problem this environment represents is the extreme opposite of single-user systems (even highly complex ones). The defining characteristic of the operational level of a business is extensive, multipurpose concurrency. It includes significant ad hoc access to persistent data by query languages. The processing requirements of different concurrent users often are significantly different—and not infrequently, at odds with one another.

In environments of this type, ensuring consistency on the process side (by embedding support for business rules in all the processes) ultimately is futile. The only feasible solution is viewing specification of rules as an extension of the data base problem, and using data models (or possibly object models) as the specification vehicle to achieve it.

Ross Method does not address data (or object) modeling per se. Rather, it assumes a robust, state-of-the-art technique already is familiar. Such technique must include complete, unencumbered support for type hierarchies. Any data modeling technique that satisfies these criteria may be used. The rule-modeling approach of Ross Method therefore is intended as a self-contained set of extensions to general modeling practices.

This includes many object-oriented (OO) approaches, assuming the following: the given approach permits properties of objects to be viewed publicly. (Certain OO approaches might be described as featuring hardcore encapsulation. These permit no access to the properties of an object except through messages to its operations. How declarative rules might be specified under these approaches is unclear.)

RULE TYPES

The power of the rule-based design approach prescribed by Ross Method arises in part from selection of standard, high-level rule types. These indicate the types of test a rule may perform. Recognized rule types can be organized into families sharing common purpose and mechanics, as follows:

- *Instance verifiers.* Rule types that test for possession of instances, present, or past.
- *Type verifiers.* Rule types that test for co-existence of instances of different types.
- *Sequence verifiers.* Rule types that test for patterns of aging (sequence of states).
- *Position selectors.* Rule types that test for rank or position by value or age.
- *Functional evaluators.* Rule types that test for patterns of values.
- *Comparative evaluators.* Rule types that compare values.
- *Calculators.* Rule types that compute values.
- *Update controllers.* Rule types that provide direct control over updating.
- *Timing controllers.* Rule types that test how long instances have existed.

The basic rule types in these families are atomic (i.e., they cannot be derived from combinations of other rule types). The rule families and their individual rule types therefore represent a fundamental classification scheme for business rules.

Rule types can be viewed as an alphabet for a business-rule language (or more precisely, for a sublanguage for integrity). Words are formed from this alphabet by selecting the rule type appropriate for a rule, then combining these rules in building-block fashion. The syntax presented in the remainder of this article indicates how this is accomplished.

Rule types also can be viewed as equivalent to the atomic elements in the Periodic Table used in chemistry. To form various chemical compounds (of which millions exist), the atomic elements (of which slightly more than a hundred exist) are combined (bonded) in appropriate fashion. The properties of a compound depend on which elements have been combined, and in what fashion. The same also is true for rule types, which similarly exist in atomic types. These can be combined in building-block fashion to form compound business rules.

INTEGRITY CONSTRAINTS VERSUS CONDITIONS

Rules are of two, and only two, varieties—those that possess built-in enforcement power, and those that do not. A rule with built-in enforcement power is called an integrity constraint; a rule without such power is called a condition.

More precisely, a rule can be viewed as a logical expression yielding either true or false (or null, if it is switched off).

- An integrity constraint is a rule that always must yield true (or null). It has enforcement power because it never is permitted to yield false. Business rules for which integrity constraints are appropriate generally indicate the sense of "must."

- A condition is a rule that may yield either true or false (or null). Because it is permitted to yield false, it lacks direct enforcement power. Its usefulness arises in providing a test for the enforcement (or testing) of one or more other rules. Specifically, these other rules are enforced (or tested) only while the condition yields true. (Conditions therefore provide one important means for connecting rules in building-block fashion.) Business rules for which conditions are appropriate generally indicate the sense of "if."

Integrity constraints and conditions must be distinguished in modeling business rules. Each is given a distinct graphic symbol, as illustrated in Exhibit V-4-1. These symbols may be rotated to any position in 360.

Each of the two graphic symbols is directional in an important sense—each symbol has a back, a front, and two sides. The back and front are essential in modeling every individual rule; the sides provide points for connecting different rules in building-block fashion. Recognizing this directionality is a key element of the rule syntax.

MODELING RULES

Selection of rule type is crucial for rules. All rules must have a rule type. Generally, these rule types are selected from a standard set such as the set offered by Ross Method. Other rule types are possible, however, including derivatives. These are discussed later.

With practice, selection of rule types for most business rules becomes relatively straightforward. Each rule type has a particular sense, which always is applied in its interpretation. Exhibits V-4-2 and V-4-3 provide simple examples. It is important to note that all rule types can be used either for integrity constraints or for conditions.

In Exhibit V-4-2, the rule type has been indicated as **MANDATORY** (abbreviated X) within the integrity constraint symbol for rule #16. This selection of rule type was based on the sense of the business rule, which suggested possession of a property (must have).

Integrity
Constraint

Condition

11. Enforce a rule, or merely test it?

Exhibit V-4-1. Integrity Constraint Versus Condition

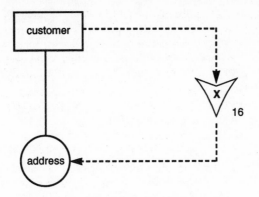

16. A customer must have an address.

Exhibit V-4-2. A Simple Integrity Constraint

Exhibit V-4-2 also illustrates that every rule must have special connections (the dashed lines) with the data types it affects.

- The dashed line coming into the back of the integrity constraint symbol connects from the rule's constrained object (i.e., Customer). Instances of customer therefore provide reference points for interpretation of this rule (i.e., an instance may exist only if the rule is satisfied). Every rule is considered to be a property of its constrained object.
- The dashed line coming out the front of the integrity constraint symbol

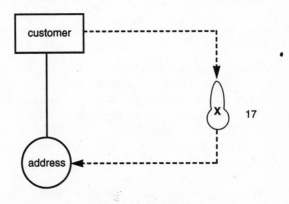

17. If a customer has an address, then . . .

Exhibit V-4-3. A Simple Condition

connects to the rule's constraining object (i.e., address). Instances of this type are referenced to determine whether the rule is satisfied.

Very simple business rules (e.g., the example in Exhibit V-4-2) often can be abbreviated. Typical business rules, however, are much more complicated and require full specification.

Exhibit V-4-3 presents a modification of the previous examples. The rule type again has been specified as **MANDATORY** (abbreviated X), but now within a condition symbol, as appropriate for rule #17. As before, this selection of rule type was based on the sense of the business rule, which suggests (a test for) possession of a property (has). Specification of the condition itself now is complete. Without specification of what rule is to fire while the condition yields true (the "then. . ." portion of the business rule), however, rule #17 remains without effect. This is illustrated later.

Enablers and Timers

Most rule types, when used as integrity constraints, have enforcement power, but are not capable of updates on their own. There are two notable exceptions, which are crucial in modeling more complex business rules. These two exceptions, enablers and timers, are discussed briefly in the following paragraphs.

An enabler is an integrity constraint of rule type **ENABLED** (abbreviated **EA**), or **ENABLED-WITH-REVERSAL** (abbreviated **REA**), with a lower or fixed enumeration type (which may be implicit). An enabler actually creates (i.e., enables, or switches on) instances of the constraining object when an instance of the constrained object exists.

- If the constraining object is a valued object, the enabler creates actual instances in the data base. (This represents a simple form of inference).
- If the constraining object is another rule, the enabler switches on (i.e., enables) this other rule. (Otherwise the rule remains disabled, in other words, off.)
- If the constraining object is an action, the enabler makes execution possible. (Otherwise, the action may not be executed.)

In Exhibit V-4-4, rule #20.1 is indicated as an integrity constraint of type **ENABLED-WITH-REVERSAL** (with an implicit lower enumeration type). This indicates its being an enabler, capable of update actions on its own. Specifically, if an instance of its constrained object (address) exists, rule #20.1 enables instances of action #20.2, its constraining object. (This action has not been specified fully in the rule diagram.) Consequently, the action may be executed. The enabler disables (switches off) instances of action #20.2 for an instance of address when deleted. This renders them incapable of execution.

A timer is an integrity constraint of rule type **TIMED** (abbreviated **TI**) with an upper or fixed enumeration type. A timer actually deletes (i.e., disables, or switches off) instances of the constraining object for an instance of the constrained object after a specified amount of time:

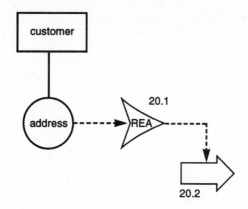

20. Enable execution of action #20.2 for a customer that has an address

Exhibit V-4-4. An Enabler

- If the constraining object is a valued object, the timer deletes actual instances in the data base.
- If the constraining object is another rule, the timer switches off (i.e., disables) this other rule. (Otherwise the rule is enabled, in other words, on.)
- If the constraining object is an action, the enabler makes execution impossible. (Otherwise, the action is ready to execute.)

In Exhibit V-4-5, rule #21.1 is indicated as an integrity constraint of type **TIMED** with a fixed enumeration type. This indicates its being a timer, capable of update actions on its own. Specifically, for an instance of the rule's constrained object, address, once exactly five days have accumulated in which instances of action #21.2 are enabled (i.e., capable of being executed), the enabler will disable them automatically. (The action has not been specified fully in the rule diagram.) Once disabled, the instances of the action no longer may be executed.

Yield Rules

As mentioned, rules may be interconnected in building-block fashion to model more complex business rules. The first manner in which this may be accomplished is by indicating one rule as the constrained object of another rule. This makes the latter rule, called a yield rule, dependent on the yield of the former rule. Usually, this former rule is a condition and therefore may yield either true or false. An example can illustrate this concept.

In Exhibit V-4-6, rule #22.1, a condition of type **MANDATORY**, is indicated as the constrained object of rule #22.2, an integrity constraint. This indicates that rule #22.2 (not specified in full) is a yield rule, and therefore is dependent

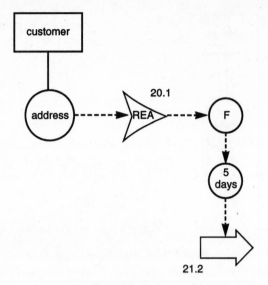

21. Disable execution of action #21.2 after 5 days

Exhibit V-4-5. A Timer

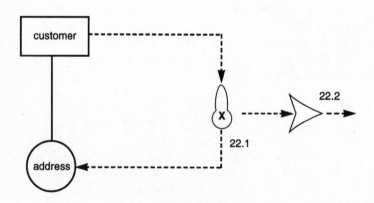

22. If a customer has an address, then enforce rule #22.2.

Exhibit V-4-6. A Yield Rule

on the truth value of rule #22.1. If this condition yields true, rule #22.2 must be enforced; if the condition yields false (or null), rule #22.2 is not enforced (i.e., must yield null). Rule #22.2 may be an enabler for some other rule (not shown), which now also will be dependent (indirectly) on the yield of condition #22.1.

Inclusion Rules

The second manner in which rules may be interconnected in building-block fashion to model more complex business rules is for one rule to be indicated as the constraining object of another rule. This other rule, called an inclusion rule, often (but not always) is an enabler or timer. (Very sophisticated rules may be modeled using rule types other than enablers or timers as inclusion rules.)

All inclusion rules always effect the interpretation of scope for the constraining rule (i.e., for which instances, and in what manner, the rule will be applied). If the inclusion rule is an enabler or timer, it also may reduce the of the scope of the constraining rule by enabling only certain instances, or disabling others. An example illustrates this.

In Exhibit V-4-7, rule #23.1, an enabler, indicates another rule (#23.2) as its constraining object. This indicates the enabler as being an inclusion rule. Typically, rule #23.2, an integrity constraint type **MANDATORY,** would be enforced for every instance of its constrained object, Order. The inclusion rule, however, changes this usual interpretation. Specifically, the enabler switches on (i.e., enables) rule #23.2 for only those orders contained on express shipments.

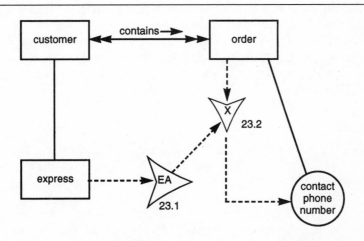

23. Orders contained on an express shipment must have a contact phone number.

Exhibit V-4-7. An Inclusion Rule

Those orders on shipments not indicated as express, or contained on no shipment whatsoever, are not subject to rule #23.2 (i.e., rule #23.2 remains disabled for such orders). The inclusion rule acts to reduce the scope of rule #23.2 (i.e., to reduce the enforcement of rule #23.2 to only selected instances of Order).

Yield Value

Every rule performs some test for instances of the constrained object and constraining object(s), as indicated by its rule type. This test always requires these instances to be reflected, evaluated, tallied or computed in some manner unique to that rule type. For each instance of the rule's constrained object, this always produces a single-valued result at any point in time.

Usually, this result, called the yield value (abbreviated yv), is transparent. It is used internally by the rule to apply some test, or to enforce some constraint (i.e., to achieve the appropriate truth value for the rule). The yield value of every rule type is discrete and unique, and always is separate from truth value.

Sometimes, business rules require testing the yield value of a rule directly. Often, but not always this occurs for condition-type rules, rather than for integrity constraints.

To satisfy this need, the yield value of a rule may be externalized. When externalized in this fashion, the yield value appears as an attribute type for the rule itself. As such it may appear as the constrained object or the constraining object for other rules. This is another way in which rules may be combined in building-block fashion to satisfy more complex business rules. The following example illustrates.

In Exhibit V-4-8, rule #26, a condition of type **LIMITED**, indicates its yield value externalized as an attribute type. The yield value of a **LIMITED**-type rule counts the current number of instances of the rule's constraining object for each instance of its constrained object. Therefore, the yield value of condition #26 provides a current count of the number of line items for each instance of Order. This yield value may be tested by other rules.

Derivatives

A derivative is any rule type that may also be expressed by specification of other rules. Such a rule type therefore is not a basic or atomic rule type—that is, one that cannot be derived from expression of other rules.

Sometimes the specification of the other rules for a derivative can become quite complex, involving many rules of basic types (or other derivatives) interconnected in building-block fashion. (Such specification is called the derivative's template.) If the derivative were not predefined, this template would have to be specified (correctly) for every business rule to which it applies.

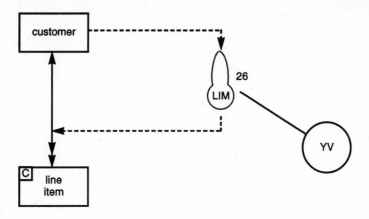

26. The number of line items on an order is ...

Exhibit V-4-8. Yield Value

Derivatives are similar to all other rule types in the following ways:

- They must follow rigorous specification conventions, which must be deline-ated beforehand. These conventions must be consistent with the general prescriptions for expressing rules described earlier.
- The must produce a yield value specific to their type. This yield value may be externalized for use by other rules. (The yield value for a derivative, of course, can be produced from the other rules that comprise its template. In this sense, the yield value of a derivative also is not basic like that of atomic rule types.)

In summary, derivative represents a convenient short-hand (i.e., a single utility rule type) for some test that appears frequently in business rules, or that is highly complex, or both. Derivatives represent an important means by which the set of standard atomic rule types may be extended.

CONCLUSION

Traditional business rule strategies have been inconsistent at best—making change almost impossible. Turning this trend around requires a new attitude toward building information systems. To that end, this article described a method for modeling business rules directly, using extensions to existing data and object models.

Section VI
Designing and Managing Data Bases

After working through the strategic and tactical issues of data management, it comes time to actually implement data bases that serve the enterprise. Chapter VI-1, "Distributed Data Base Design," examines the interconnection of already-existing data base management applications as well as the development of a distributed data base environment using a bottom-up approach. Chapter VI-2, "A Framework for Relational DBMS Client/Server Applications," covers the essential groundwork involved in using a relational DBMS in general, as well as specific issues of relational DBMS support in distributed environments.

In client/server environments with distributed data bases, additional procedures have to be established to restore, validate, and return the system to normal in the event of a system crash or portions of the data become unusable. Chapter VI-3 reviews practical "DBMS Recovery Procedures."

A PC-based geographic information system (GIS) can be an integral part of any decision support system, and if business users think of the G as standing for graphical rather than geographic, they will be able to appreciate the GIS's applicability to small business needs, parts of large enterprises, and specific tasks in any organization. Chapter VI-4, "Geographic Information Systems as a Business Tool: A Case Study," describes one implementation of such a system.

VI-1
Distributed Data Base Design

ELIZABETH N. FONG • CHARLES L. SHEPPARD •
KATHRYN A. HARVILL

A distributed data base environment enables a user to access data residing anywhere in a corporation's computer network without regard to differences among computers, operating systems, data manipulation languages, or file structures. Data that is actually distributed across multiple remote computers will appear to the user as if it resided on the user's own computer. This scenario is functionally limited with today's distributed data base technology; true distributed data base technology is still a research consideration. The functional limitations are generally in the following areas:

- Transaction management.
- Standard protocols for establishing a remote connection.
- Independence of network technology.

Transaction management capabilities are essential to maintaining reliable and accurate data bases. In some cases, today's distributed data base software places responsibility of managing transactions on the application program. In other cases, transactions are committed or rolled back at each location independently, which means that it is not possible to create a single distributed transaction. For example, multiple-site updates require multiple transations.

CURRENT DBMS TECHNOLOGY

In today's distributed data base technology, different gateway software must be used and installed to connect nodes using different distributed data base management system (DBMS) software. Therefore, connectivity among heterogeneous distributed DBMS nodes is not readily available (i.e., available only through selected vendor markets).

In some instances, distributed DBMS software is tied to a single network operating system. This limits the design alternatives for the distributed DBMS environment to the products of a single vendor.

It is advisable to select a product that supports more than one network operating system. This will increase the possibility of successfully integrating the distributed DBMS software into existing computer environments.

In reality, distributed data bases encompass a wide spectrum of possibilities, including the following:

- Remote terminal access to centralized DBMS (e.g., an airline reservation system).
- Remote terminal access to different DBMSs, but one at a time (e.g., Prodigy, CompuServe, and Dow Jones).
- Simple pairwise interconnection with data sharing that requires users to know the data location, data access language, and the log-on procedure to the remote DBMS.
- Distributed data base management with a generic data definition language and a data manipulation language at all nodes.
- Distributed update and transaction management.
- Distributed data bases with replication that support vertical and horizontal fragmentation.
- "True" distributed DBMSs with heterogeneous hardware, software, and communications.

The definition of distributed DBMSs lies anywhere along this spectrum. For the purpose of this chapter, the remote terminal access to data as discussed in the preceding list is not considered a distributed DBMS because a node in the distributed DBMS must have its own hardware, central processor, and software.

Limitations of Commercial Products

Some of the problems that currently frustrate managers and technicians who might otherwise be interested in exploring distributed data solutions include the following:

- A distributed data base environment has all the problems associated with the single centralized data base environment but at a more complex level.
- There are no basic, step-by-step guidelines covering the analysis, design, and implementation of a distributed data base environment.

A distributed DBMS offers many benefits. However, there are also many architectural choices that make the applications design for distributed data bases very complex.

To ensure an effective and productive distributed data base environment, it is essential that the distributed environment be properly designed to support the expected distributed data base applications. In addition, an effective design will depend on the limitations of the distributed DBMS software. Therefore, implementing today's distributed data base technology requires identifying the functional limitations of a selected commercial product. Identification of these limitations is critical to the successful operation of an application in a distributed data base environment.

DISTRIBUTED DATA BASE DEVELOPMENT PHASES

Effective corporationwide distributed data base processing is not going to happen overnight. It requires a carefully planned infrastructure within which an orderly evolution can occur. The four major development phases are planning, design, installation and implementation, and support and maintenance.

The Planning Phase. The planning phase consists of high-level management strategy planning. During the planning phase, an organization must consider whether it is advantageous to migrate to a distributed environment. This chapter assumes that migration to a distributed environment is desirable and feasible and that the corporate strategy planning issues and tasks have been identified. The results of this phase is the total management commitment for cost, resources, and a careful migration path toward a distributed data base environment.

The Design Phase. The design phase is concerned with the overall design of the distributed data base strategy. The overall design task involves the selection of a distributed DBMS environment in terms of the hardware, software, and communications network for each node and how these elements are to be interconnected. The design of the distributed data base environment must incorporate the requirements for the actual distributed data base application. The overall design divides into two main tasks: the detailed design of the distributed data base environment and the detailed design of the initial distributed data base application. In certain cases, the initial application may be a prototype that is intended to pave the way for the full-production distributed data base application.

The Installation and Implementation Phase. This phase consists of the installation and implementation of the environment that provides basic software support for the distributed DBMS application. The task of developing the distributed data base application could occur in parallel with the installation of the environment.

The Support and Maintenance Phase. The support and maintenance phase consists of support for the distributed DBMS environment and the support and maintenance of the application. Although these support and maintenance tasks can be performed by the same people, the nature of the tasks and responsibilities are quite distinct. For example, the distributed application may require modification of report formats, whereas the distributed environment may require modification to add more memory.

CORPORATION STRATEGY PLANNING

The main task during the strategic planning phase is to obtain the commitment of senior management. The measure of this commitment is the amount of resources—both personnel and equipment—necessary for the development of a distributed DBMS. The factors that must be considered during the strategy planning phase are as follows:

- What are the objectives of the organization's next five-year plan?
- How will technological changes affect the organization's way of doing business?
- What resources are needed to plan for the development of, and migration to, a distributed DBMS?
- How will outcomes be measured relative to the impact on the organization's competitive position?

The corporate strategy plan must include detailed specifications of the total system life cycle. It must also include a realistic timetable of schedules and milestones. Important consideration must be paid to the allocation of cost for new acquisitions, training personnel, physical space requirements, and other tangible items.

During the strategic planning phase, information must be gathered on the organization's business functions and goals, related constraints and problem areas, and the organization's user groups. Only after the need information has been gathered is it possible to develop high-level information categories and their interrelationships.

The process of developing the distributed data base plan is iterative. The activities involved are performed by IS managers. Although these individuals often have the vision to recognize the long-term benefits of a distributed DBMS environment to an organization, they must rely on the participation and input of those in the organization who are directly involved with the business functions and use information to make decisions and manage operations. There must be considerable interaction among many different people in the organization, each of whom provides feedback to validate and refine the plans.

Strategic planning must first provide a sufficient justification for the expenditure of resources necessary to migrate to a distributed environment. Only after this justification has been accepted and fully approved by senior management can the task of initiating projects to design, develop, and implement a distributed DBMS environment and application start.

OVERALL DESIGN OF DISTRIBUTED DATA BASE STRATEGY

A distributed data base environment consists of a collection of sites or nodes connected by a communications network. Each node has its own hardware, central processor, and software, which may or may not include a DBMS. The primary objective of a distributed DBMS is to give interactive query and application programs access to remote data as well as local data.

Individual nodes within the distributed environment can have different computing requirements. Accordingly, these nodes may have different hardware and different software, and they may be connected in many different

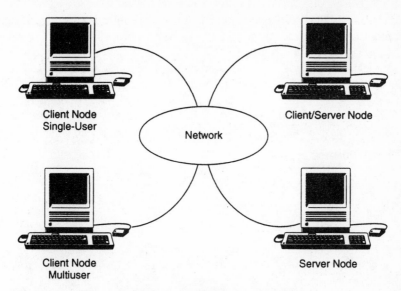

Exhibit VI-1-1. Client/Server Computing

ways. Some of the variations possible in the distributed data base environment are discussed in the following sections.

Client/Server Computing

The most basic distributed capability is remote data base access from single users at a node. A node may be a mainframe, a minicomputer, or a microcomputer (personal computer). The node that makes the data base access request is referred to as a client node, and the node that responds to the request and provides data base services is referred to as the server node. The association is limited to the two parties involved—the client and the server. Exhibit VI-1-1 represents several different configurations available under a client/server computing environment. The following are descriptions of the different configurations shown in the exhibit.

Client Single-User Node. The operating environment of an individual node can be single user or multiuser, depending on the operating system of that node. In a single-user operating environment, a node can be only a client. Such a node may or may not have data bases. For non-data base client nodes, the software typically consists of front-end application programs used to access remote data base server nodes. This front-end software is generally in the form of end-user interface tools (e.g., a query language processor, a form processor, or some other application-specific program written in a third-generation language).

The front-end software formulates and issues user requests. It processes user requests through its established links with appropriate communications software. The front-end software only captures a user's request and uses communications software to send that request to a remote data base node requesting its DBMS to process the request. In addition to the capabilities outlined, single-user nodes with data bases allow local data to be included in the same query operations specified for remote data. Therefore, operationally, the query results will appear as if all data is coming from a single central data base.

Client Multiuser Node. The functional capabilities outlined for the client single-user node are expanded in the client multiuser node because of the presence of a multiuser operating system at the user node. Such a configuration generally has several user processes running at the same time. At peak use time, the presence of several user processes can cause slower response time than is experienced in a client single-user node. The client multiuser node is more cost-effective, however, because it can allow multiple remote data base access at different sites by different users at the same time. This is made possible through an identifiable list of remote server node locations. In addition, as with the client single-user node, the client multiuser node can include local data base access in conjunction with access to remote data bases.

Server Node. The server node is capable of providing data base services to other client requests as well as to itself. It is a special multiuser node that is dedicated to servicing remote data base requests and any local processes. This means that incoming requests are serviced, but it does not originate requests to other server nodes. The functional capabilities of a server node are as follows: this node must be included in the server list of some remote client node, there must be an operating DBMS, and there must be a continuously running process that listens for incoming data base requests.

Client/Server Node. A node with a data base can be a client as well as a server. This means that this node can service remote data base requests as well as originate data base requests to other server nodes. Therefore, the client/server node can play a dual role.

Homogeneous Distributed DBMS Environment

A completely homogeneous distributed DBMS environment exists when all the nodes in the distributed environment have the same DBMS but not necessarily the same hardware and operating system. However, the communication software for each node must use the same protocol to send or receive requests and data.

Design and implementation of a homogeneous distributed DBMS environment need involve only a single vendor. Any data request issued at a client node does not require translation, because the data base language and data model are the same across all nodes in the network.

Heterogeneous Distributed DBMS Environment

In a truly heterogeneous distributed DBMS environment, the hardware, operating systems, communication systems, and DBMSs can all be different. Different DBMSs may mean different data models along with different data base languages for definition and manipulation. Any data base request issued at a client node would have to be translated so that the server node responding to the request would understand how to execute the request.

Various degrees of heterogeneity can exist. For example, within the distributed environment, different DBMSs can still be compatible if they all support the relational data model and understand SQL, a relational query language that is an ANSI and ISO standard. Presently, however, even among SQL conforming systems, there is no general communications software that will accept generic SQL statements from any other SQL conforming DBMS. This is an area in which the pending remote data access standards are needed.

DISTRIBUTED ENVIRONMENT ARCHITECTURE

The design of a distributed data base environment can be evolutionary—by incremental interconnection of existing systems, or by developing a totally new distributed DBMS environment using the bottom-up approach. Some of the design issues in adopting either approach are described in the following sections.

Interconnection of Existing Systems

Not all organizations have the luxury of developing the distributed data base environment from scratch. Already-existing data base management applications are costly investments that are not likely to be replaced all at once by new distributed systems. The existing environment, including hardware, software, and data bases, can be preserved by providing a mechanism for producing federated systems (i.e., systems composed of autonomous software components).

The federated approach is a practical, first-step solution toward a distributed data base environment. It accommodates a legacy of existing systems while extending to incorporate new nodes. Therefore, it is important to select distributed DBMS software that supports existing computing hardware and allows for expansion. Within a federated system, pairs of nodes can be coupled in ways that range from very loose (i.e., each node is autonomous) to very tight (i.e., each node interacts directly with the other). The various forms of coupling affect the design, execution, and capability of the distributed applications.

The mode of coupling affects the number of translations required to exchange information between each site. Zero translations are needed when both components use the same representations. Some systems may choose to translate the data produced by one site directly to the format required by the other site. A more common method is to translate the data into a neutral format first, and then translate into the target format.

Loose Coupling. Loosely coupled systems are the most modular and in some ways are easier to maintain. This is because changes to the implementation of a site's system characteristics and its DBMS are not as likely to affect other sites. The disadvantage of loosely coupled systems is that users must have some knowledge of each site's characteristics to execute requests. Because very little central authority to control consistency exists, correctness cannot be guaranteed. In addition, loosely coupled systems typically involve more translations that may cause performance problems.

Tight Coupling. Tightly coupled systems behave more like a single, integrated system. Users need not be aware of the characteristics of the sites fulfilling a request. With centralized control, the tightly coupled systems are more consistent in their use of resources and in their management of shared data. The disadvantage of tight coupling is that because sites are independent, changes to one site are likely to affect other sites. Also, users at some sites may object to the loss of freedom to the central control mechanisms necessary to maintain the tight coupling of all the systems.

Cooperation Between Sites

For a truly distributed DBMS environment, a variety of methods are available to specify cooperation between sites. One way of classifying the distributed environment is to define the amount of transparency offered to the users. Another way is to define the amount of site autonomy available to each site, and the way sites interact cooperatively.

Degrees of Transparency. Transparency is the degree to which a service is offered by the distributed DBMS so that the user does not need to be aware of it. One example of transparency is location transparency, which means users can retrieve data from any site without having to know where the data is located.

Types of Site Autonomy. Site autonomy refers to the amount of independence that a site has in making policy decisions. Some examples of policy decisions include ownership of data, policies for accessing the data, policies for hours and days of operation, and human support. In addtion, all modifications to the site's data structures must be approved by the cooperating federation of data administrators.

Interconnection of Newly Purchased Systems

An organization will have much more freedom if it decides to establish a distributed data base environment from scratch. Currently, vendors are offering homogeneous distributed DBMSs with a compatible family of software. This approach, however, can lock the organization into a single vendor's proprietary products.

Other distributed architecture choices are as follows:

- Identical DBMS products at each node, with possibly different hardware environments but a single proprietary communications network to interconnect all sites.
- Standard conforming DBMS products at each node that rely on standard communications protocols.
- Different DBMSs, using the same data model (e.g., relational), interconnected by a single or standard communications protocol.
- Different DBMSs, using different data models (e.g., relational or object-oriented), interconnected by a single or standard communications protocol.

Some distributed DBMS vendors offer a bridge (gateway) mechanism from their distributed data base software to any foreign distributed data base software. This bridge (gateway) may be obtained at additional development cost if it has not already been included in the vendor's library of available software.

In the design of a totally new distributed DBMS product, it is advisable to consider a mixture of standard conforming DBMSs and communications protocols. Because the technology and products are changing quickly, the designed architecture must be continuously reviewed to prevent it from being locked into an inflexible mode.

CONSIDERATION FOR STANDARDS

As the trend toward distributed computing accelerates, the need for standards, guidance, and support will increase. Application distribution and use will be chaotic unless there is an architectural vision and some degree of uniformity in information technology platforms. This is particularly true in client/server and workstation environments. To achieve this goal a systems architecture incorporating standards to meet the users' needs must be established. This architecture must isolate the application software from the lower levels of machine architecture and systems service implementation. The systems architecture serves as the context for user requirements, technology integration, and standards specifications.

The benefits of standardization for both the user and the vendor are many. The number and variety of distributed DBMS products are increasing. By insisting that purchased products conform to standards, users may be able to choose the best product for each function without being locked into a specific vendor. Therefore, small to misdsize vendors may effectively compete in the open marketplace. For effective planning and designing of a distributed DBMS environment, it is important for the designers to consider what standards already exist and what standards will be emerging to be able to incorporate standardized products.

There are many areas of distributed DBMS environment in which standards should be applied. Some of the standards relevant to the design of a distributed DBMS include communications protocols, application programming interfaces, data languages for DBMSs, data representation and interchange formats, and remote data access.

Communications protocol standards are necessary so that systems from different products can connect to a communications network and understand the information being transmitted. An example of a communications protocol standard is the Government Open Systems Interconnection Profile (GOSIP).

The application programming interface (API) standard is directed toward the goal of having portable applications. This enables software applications developed in one computing environment to run almost unchanged in any other environment. An example of an application programming interface standard is the Portable Operating System Interface for Computer Environments (POSIX).

The data languages commonly supported by a DBMS are the data definition language, the data manipulation language, and the data control language. An example of a standard data language for the relational DBMS model is SQL.

To exchange data among open systems, a standard interchange format is necessary. The interchange format consists of a language for defining general data structures and the encoding rules. An example of a standard data interchange language is Abstract Syntax Notation One (ASN.1).

An important standard for the distributed processing environment is the remote access of data from a client site to a data base server site. A specialized remote data access protocol based on the SQL standard is currently under development.

CONCLUSION

To start the overall design process, a review of the organization's existing facilities should be conducted. This review is done to determine whether the new distributed data base environment can use some or all of the existing facilities. In the decision to move into a distributed environment, requirements for additional functionalities must be identified. Such organizational issues as setting up regional offices may also be involved. The distributed architecture must take into consideration the actual application operating, the characteristics of the user population, and the work loads to be placed on the system. Such an architecture must also incorporate standardized components.

VI-2
A Framework for Relational DBMS Client/Server Applications

STEVEN D. RABIN

M any IS organizations are in the process of or planning to reengineer their host-based applications to take advantage of distributed client/server architectures. Making the transition across distributed computing media permits solutions to a variety of complex business problems in the platforms best suited to each individual organization.

These software solutions are focused on the heart of the enterprise—in other words, mission-critical, legacy systems that drive much of the organization's business computing. Environments include DOS, Windows, OS/2 PM, and UNIX Motif operating systems, often running on local area networks (LANs), wide area networks (WANs), and transparent interfaces to traditional services and host machines.

To successfully architect and develop applications in these newer environments, organizations must develop a model or framework around which application transitioning can occur. This framework must specify the individual components required to move from the current business processing environment to the future one. In addition, it should also specify the business professional (IS or other) best suited to perform the tasks identified by each component.

At the highest level of business modeling, business process redesign, architecture, and development-implementation issues must be identified. This includes policies, processes, technical considerations, and, of course, software elements. Whenever possible, plans are implemented to reengineer existing facilities to maximize the benefit gained from current asset use—both business policies and processes, application codes and services, and the professionals who understand them. Ultimately, reusable components or objects must be identified and catalogued for use throughout the enterprise (see Exhibit VI-2-1).

A sophisticated model defines an architecture that encompasses the entire enterprise. This architecture includes the use and deployment of computing resources (e.g., hardware, software, and data) throughout the organization. The key components of this architecture are application-specific business logic,

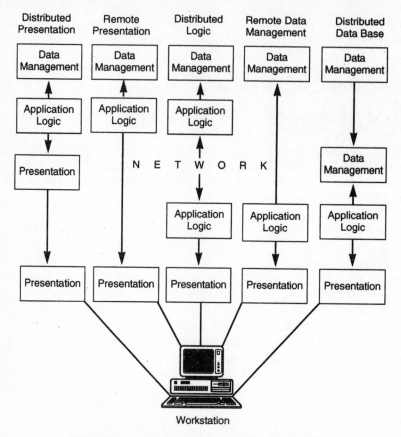

Exhibit VI-2-1. Business Process Redesign Architecture

presentation services, data services (both local and remote), and control services that tie the distributed and local processing characteristics of the architecture together.

RESOURCE MANAGEMENT

Current business realities dictate that an organization must efficiently use available resources if it is to achieve the benefits defined in the model. Competitive advantage through information technology comes at a price that no organization can afford to squander. Use of existing assets is one way to increase the return on investment of previous development projects while moving forward. Two key IS resources are current production application code and the professionals who developed and are maintaining the code.

Distributed applications can be created by combining code that currently exists—possibly from a host system or even simpler workstation application-tion—with new code. This combination makes the best use of existing and still valuable application code while allowing new code and its underlying technology to be efficiently integrated. The resulting new application code should therefore meet the organization's framework in a most productive and cost-efficient way.

The blending together of old and new code involves the redevelopment of current application code. It must be determined which portions of the code are still relevant and what, if anything, must be done to this code. This analysis process also lends itself to the creation of reusable modules; in other words, source code sets that can be used on a variety of platforms and environments with little more than a recompilation.

This is a critical concept because no one has a crystal ball capable of foreseeing future production and development environments. As new users and groups are introduced to this software, it is quite likely that the code will be required to operate on platforms that were not originally envisioned. It is important that these distributed applications be as portable as possible to maximize the investment, both long and short term, being made to the application and its underlying technology.

The idea of reengineering applications rather than starting development from scratch provides several additional benefits. The most important of these is that existing software solutions have been refined through the years to analyze and solve real business issues. These refinements have come from two sources: End-user business experts who use the software on a daily basis and the professionals responsible for architecting the software. It is this collective experience that must be taken advantage of during and after the transformation process.

Client/Server Models

Alternative client/server models used by most organizations as the basis for distributed client/server design are illustrated in Exhibit VI-2-2. The distributed logic model is well suited to true distributed processing because it is especially efficient for critical, high-volume applications. To ensure that each segment of the application operates as efficiently as possible, the model breaks each application segment into layers, so that each portion of the application is isolated from everything but the adjacent layers.

Isolation of functions as well as application segments helps ensure that a true distributed client/server model is implemented. System services are requested and used without any additional application overhead. In this way, each application segment does not unnecessarily interfere with the operation of the environment as a whole.

Distributed client/server applications must be designed to work in unison with other applications and processes—both locally and distributed—and to behave in a controlled, nonintrusive manner. On a scale of good, bad, and ugly,

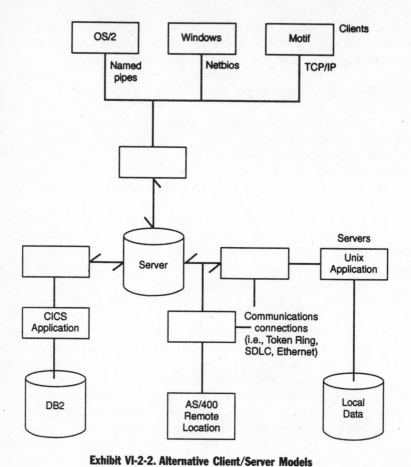

Exhibit VI-2-2. Alternative Client/Server Models

the distributed logic model is good especially with regard to its relationship to the use of system services. Applications must be designed to take advantage—not control—of the central processing unit, operating system presentation manager, relational data base management systems (DBMSs), and other associated facilities (i.e., network and communication services).

Components

Four key components are part of distributed client/server software:

- Graphical user interface (GUI).
- Relational DBMSs.
- Application-specific business logic.
- Control and communication functions.

The relational DBMS may be the most critical of these components because the data base system provides much of the system's distributed processing capabilities.

Client/server computing is facilitated by both system and application architectures combined with distributed processing facilities. For the purposes of this discussion, client/server is viewed as a data base engine residing on a server which is tied to multiple client workstations each containing a GUI. The application-specific code and processes may reside on the server, the client, or both. Finally, both clients and servers can be split among different hardware platforms and systems requiring distributed processing facilities. Distributed systems must be logically designed to isolate application-specific code, including graphical presentation from server-specific code. This maximizes the benefits of the client/server environment.

OPERATING ENVIRONMENT

The environments used and supported by the client/server distributed application include both operating systems, their underlying interface mechanism (e.g., GUI), and system services. The operating systems include DOS, DOS Windows, OS/2, UNIX, and Windows NT. The GUIs include Windows, Presentation Manager, and Motif. System services are varied and include communication interfaces. Clients can be attached to servers locally by a LAN or remotely by a WAN. In addition, transparent access to a mainframe or midframe can be used as a data repository or for application-specific processing.

Communications environments need careful planning. It is important to consider all the platforms that will be accessed and select a scheme that is supported in as open a manner as possible. Open communications offer the means of adding new, potentially unplanned for, platforms in a relatively seamless manner. Although many interface combinations are possible, the following are, in general, mostly supported across heterogeneous platforms: TCP/IP, named pipes, APPC, IPX, NFS, and Netbios.

The communications backbone, which comprises one of the key components of the applications infrastructure, must be designed by professionals. Familiarity with all the environments to be supported, along with an understanding of the required facilities and available tools, is also a prerequisite. Exhibit VI-2-3 is an example of the type of distributed environment likely requiring support and potential communication methods used to interface the enterprise together.

Definitions of Key Terms

Before looking at the specific issues of relational DBMS support in a distributed environment, several terms must be defined. "Distributed client/server computing" are four words that are constantly used to describe a variety of things.

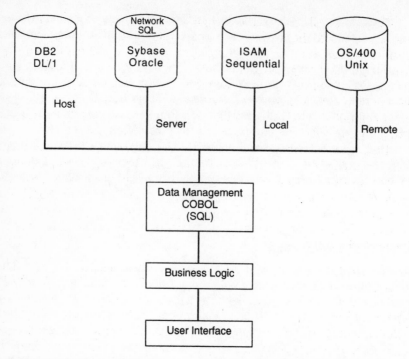

Exhibit VI-2-3. Distributed Data Access Platforms to File Structures and Relational Data Bases

These terms mean different things to different people and thus often cause unnecessary confusion. The following definitions should be used as the basis for the remainder of this chapter and are described in relation to the relational DBMS.

Server. A server is one or more logically connected pieces of hardware providing services to requesting clients. Because the physical composition of a server can be quite complex, it is easier to think of a server as a process. In this way, client/server environments hide this complexity from the application. The nature and capabilities of the relational DBMS often determine how well the server is hidden.

The server can process individual or multiple requests. In addition, these requests may all originate locally from a single source or be distributed, cross platform, among many sources. Ideally, the server is responsible for managing all requests received from other processes (i.e., both servers and clients) through request queue management, buffer management, service execution, results notification, and a variety of delivery functions. Most important, it is the server's responsibility to synchronize all services and appropriately handle the communication issues once a request has been initiated.

Two additional points should be considered. In general, a server does not send any results to the requesters until asked to do so. This is important when considering specific relational DBMS features and their ability to interact with client/server application programs. Also, a server should not be confused with any one specific piece of hardware. Although the server may be an individual piece of hardware, a client/server system is always designed from the logical server point of view. In other words, the server processes requests regardless of the physical environment.

The remainder of this chapter uses the terms *server* and *data base server* interchangeably. Although there is a difference between the functions and services provided by a server as compared to a data base server or engine, the point of this chapter is to analyze the requirements of the relational DBMS in conjunction with the distributed model. Therefore, the functions of a server are considered synonymous with the functions of the relational data base engine on the server.

Client. A client is anything requesting services from a server. These requests may come from individual workstations or other servers. One characteristic that differentiates a client from its server is that the client always initiates the request by some type of communications transaction. The server seldom initiates the transaction with its client. The only exception is event notification, where the server is able to notify a client of some server-detectable event (e.g., a message resulting from a background task process not available).

It is always the client's task to initiate communications, request services, acknowledge completion of services, and process the results. Clients request services interactively, and these requests are either processed immediately or placed in a queue for later processing. Regardless of the type of service requested, the client does not manage the synchronization or communication of those services. In a distributed application, many clients can share a single server—even if it is a logical server distributed among several systems.

Distributed Client/Server Communications. The interface among clients and servers may involve a variety of communication facilities including communications around a LAN or across a WAN, task-to-task services (i.e., APPC), or shared memory (i.e., named pipes). Client/server applications are generally designed to be independent of these methods and the physical communication among them and to have no knowledge of these environmental issues. Many support tools available to the application are designed to handle all the low-level communications, including API-related calls. This includes cross-platform operating system extension tools, application-to-application interface tools, client-to-server file-sharing tools, distributed file support tools, API translation tools, and a variety of communications-related services provided by the related DBMS. Architectural considerations allow for additional transparency provided by run-time facilities for dynamic reconfiguration and replacement of individual pieces of the client/server interface without user impact. This includes changing client GUIs, operating systems, and associated network server services.

Client/Server Data Base Connectivity. The relational DBMS must support both the client and the server. Based on other definitions, the data base requirements of these two segments are distinct. The data base engine that resides on the server must have the capability of managing multiple client requests, each having the same or different environment, operating system, or GUI.

It is strongly recommended that distributed applications use SQL as the common data acquisition language. SQL is platform independent, so the key issue is the variant of SQL that the relational DBMS supports. Many organizations develop applications requiring support of several relational data base products. This is normally because of standards and products already in use at specific locations that are either unwilling or unable to change or support a different relational data base. Because of this, it is critical that the features, communication facilities, and basic relational data base requirements of the application be understood and matched to the facilities.

Whenever appropriate, specific features of each relational DBMS should be used to full advantage. This is rather difficult to plan for and even more difficult to develop. In addition, some basic differences must be accounted for, including differences in data interpretation, messages/codes, referential integrity triggers, and even the SQL language itself.

Once it understands the fundamental advantages of resource management and the blending of codes that is necessary to make a transition to a distributed client/server environment succeed, a company can begin to lay the groundwork for the development of relational DBMS codes.

APPLICATION CODING FOR RELATIONAL DBMS CLIENT/SERVER COMPUTING

Applications must be specifically designed and coded to achieve the benefits of distributed client/server computing. One significant benefit is the possibility of redeploying application code in varying environments. This is true regardless of the nature of the client to server physical environment. For example, if within an organization a client changed the computing environment from OS/2 to Windows NT, only the run-time environment would change without changes to the application code.

Client/server relational DBMS processing assumes that the client and server have no knowledge of the state of the other. A request is issued to the engine in the form of a communications transaction, and the server processes the request and ships the results or notification of the results back to the requester. If the client is unavailable (i.e., logged off the network), the results should be queued so that the conversation can take place at another time.

Requests from the client and responses from the server are most efficiently processed when the client and server are synchronized. In other words, the functions being performed by the server can satisfy the requests of any one client in the most efficient means possible. Although this sounds appropriate from a single client's point of view, it is much more difficult when the server is responding to multiple client requests. The processing solution from one request may not be the optimal solution from another client's request.

No individual client should be able to hold the resources of the server to satisfy its specific request, nor should any client require specific or special synchronization. That is exclusively the job of the server because it alone has a view of the entire work load. The server schedules and optimizes its data management chores based on all the functions being requested. It is the only component in the distributed environment with the ability to do this because it is the only process that has a view of the entire application playing field; each client has knowledge only of the requests it made.

When the relational data base application resides on the same physical platform as the data base engine, the data services can be synchronized through shared memory, resulting in more efficiency. Record locking or commit-rollback logic are more easily implemented and synchronized by the services performing those specific functions. For example, an application operating alone in a UNIX environment (i.e., UNIX server attached to UNIX clients) will provide significantly better performance than if either of these elements was disbursed (i.e., distributed across non-UNIX platforms).

When a distributed platform is involved, synchronization is not as easy to accomplish. Whatever communications exist between the client and data base server, it is not as fast as those involving shared memory environments. Although the required functions do not change, additional processing cycles are required as transactions are communicated to and processed by the server. When the data is truly distributed or multiple data bases (or servers) are involved, performance becomes the key consideration. The server must distinguish between data base-related requests and other server services. Such functions as record locking and commit-rollback must now be synchronized across the network.

BENEFITS OF SQL

The use of SQL provides a variety of benefits. These benefits include improved request handling when accessing data base servers and a common approach to data acquisition. When remote communications are involved, the distributed model must consider the optimization of all SQL calls. This is normally provided by the precompiler process facilities of the language or the data base vendor. Part of this optimization involves returning only that portion of the data that actually satisfies the request.

Because many host applications are written in COBOL, it is natural to consider the reuse of as much of this code as possible. This is true of the business logic as well as the embedded SQL data access logic. Micro Focus, Inc provides a variety of COBOL-related tools, including SQL optimization and precompiler functions for several relational DBMSs. This multivendor support approach is very important because it does not lock the organization into a specific product. The model can be designed solely based on processing requirements and the data base selected on its ability to meet the needs of the application.

SQL processing allows the client application to retrieve or modify a set of data base server records with a single instruction. This set level processing significantly improves application performance because, as compared to standard input/output (I/O), it is not necessary to issue separate sequential transactions for each request. In addition, the model must allow SQL transactions to be grouped together and optimized. This grouping allows the server to schedule and respond to client requests faster, resulting in reduced network traffic.

Grouping frequently performed SQL transactions is a technique called *stored procedures.* This mechanism permits SQL code sharing across clients and servers. Several relational DBMSs (e.g., Oracle and Sybase) permit these stored procedures to reside with the engine. The client need only notify the data base to execute them. This is a particularly attractive mechanism from a processing efficiency point of view. Messages between the client and server are reduced to the bare minimum and processing occurs on the platform best suited to handle the data request.

One issue to consider is that stored procedures are not always implemented in the same fashion by relational data base vendors. Therefore, the stored procedures feature must be carefully implemented to ensure that all supported relational data base packages efficiently use the developed code. This is another area in which multivendor standards and protocols can play an important factor. Facilities are being devised to allow transparent stored procedure implementation regardless of the data bases used.

REQUEST SERVICING CONSIDERATIONS

One of the major considerations when designing the relational DBMS application is how efficiently it handles servicing and requests. Although SQL and stored procedures significantly reduce network traffic on the inbound side of the data management equation, the results—usually in the form of a table with rows and columns—still must be communicated to the requester.

Most relational applications use a cursor to position and fetch data, one row at a time. This process involves considerable overhead, especially when the service requester and service provider are remote from each other. Blocking, synchronization, and the relational model type used by the relational data base are all critical factors. The types of data base I/O and processing rules used by the relational data base and how it physically accesses the data to satisfy a request have a direct effect on the applications' processing capabilities. Although the concepts and implementation of referential integrity will not be discussed here, this is another area that significantly impacts performance. The better the relational DBMS enforces integrity, the less communication is required between client and server and the more code that can reside on the server. When developing the model and overall requirements for the distributed client/server relational DBMS, all these factors must be carefully evaluated.

DISTRIBUTED CLIENT/SERVER ISSUES: STRENGTHS AND WEAKNESSES

The practical benefits of client/server technology often get lost in the hype surrounding that technology. The reality is that there are both strengths and weaknesses in client/server applications. Maximizing the strengths while minimizing the weaknesses is a key goal in the design of the model. This is not an easy task and is only accomplished once the specific requirements of the data base are known. In addition, the detailed functions and specifications of the relational data base product must also be carefully analyzed.

Some of the key strengths of this technology include the following:

- Savings in host processing resources.
- Independent, vertical scalability of client and server platforms.
- Interoperability and open system environments for application asset protection.
- Code modularity through shared services (run times handle issues of platform-specific APIs).
- Sophisticated development environment.
- Availability of end-user tools.

Some the key weaknesses of this technology include the following:

- Performance and performance tuning issues.
- Communication bottlenecks and related processing overhead data management problems (including synchronization and integrity).
- Potentially more complex systems/network management.

How these strengths and weaknesses are handled depends heavily on the design of the application software and the characteristics of the relational DBMS. In simple environments, the programs, data, and data definitions are stored in one place. Distributed environments are not as straightforward and, without care, application and data integrity can be compromised.

The model should be designed to handle appropriately local, centralized, and distributed environments to realize the following benefits:

- Efficient coordination and communication among distributed application components.
- Management of client and server resources.

- Backup and recovery including rollback recovery in the event of remote services interruptions.

RELATIONAL DBMS-RELATED ISSUES

As mentioned previously, the cursor is a key component of the relational DBMS. A cursor is positioned on a particular row of the result set—data provided in response to a query or request for service. The application must have knowledge of the cursor and a means of accessing the result set. The more sophisticated the interface provided by the relational DBMS, the easier it is for the application to access and manipulate the data. This is not a trivial issue when the data may be remote to the requester and possibly distributed across the network.

Related to cursor positioning are functions that the data base engine must provide. This includes maintaining the cursor position as other clients request similar services. A lock or similar hold mechanism maintains the cursor position for the requester. This becomes more involved as multiple locks are maintained across the clients requesting services. Across distributed environments, these locks become unwieldy and can affect the performance and viability of the application. Careful consideration must be given to these points during the modeling stage of the applications development.

Because the result set may be unordered (i.e., mixed among the entire data base), the relational data base must provide the application with the ability to request the results in an ordered fashion. The notion of positioning on the first, next, or last row must be supported and considered within the application model. Similar to the above, this must be carefully considered during the modeling stage of the applications development.

When applicable, client/server applications are designed to avoid traditional online transaction processing (OLTP) record-level processing and associated locking. It is more efficient to view data a set or page at a time rather than a row at a time. Applications using a relational data base are considerably more efficient when designed based on set processing (with associated locking) logic. When necessary, however, OLTP-like row-level locking should be incorporated into the design model.

DATA UPDATING AND SYNCHRONIZATION

The synchronization of information between the application and data base engine is critical if data integrity is to be maintained. Many applications are likely to share the same data. This means that data must be accessed efficiently and updated in logical segments. Logical segments can be designed to be many things. In the absence of application-specific requirements, page-level segments should be considered as the basic unit of work.

Many relational DBMSs perform inflight updates: in other words, interactively as records on the disk are physically accessed. Oracle is an example of this. This is basically a sequentially ordered approach that uses the concept of cursor positioning and orientation. To ensure success of the entire update, a unit of work must be established. For commit logic, this unit of work is assumed to commence at the end of the entire transaction. For rollback purposes, the unit is assumed to commence at the beginning of the transaction.

Another update mechanism is deferred updating. This is a technique that uses a copy of the original data for update purposes. This method simply transforms the original set of data into a new set based on the update set or transaction. Sybase is an example of this. Although advantages and disadvantages are associated with both inflight updating and deferred updating, they both provide the facilities necessary to ensure data integrity.

The lack of tightly coupled transaction logic is sometimes a weakness of the relational DBMS (and one of the primary reasons the facilities of an OLTP may need consideration). Applications should define transactions with tightly coupled transaction logic specifically for commit and rollback purposes. Updates occur across the enterprise in a distributed fashion with local and remote data equally sharing a transaction set. A high degree of synchronization must exist among clients and servers to ensure appropriate data manipulation. The tighter a transaction is defined, the better a data base engine is able to provide greater throughput and lower resource use.

MONITORING AND TUNING FACILITIES

Server monitoring, performance tuning, and resource use are generally within the domain of the relational DBMS. Although the application does not control how the data base engine operates, it certainly can have a positive or negative effect on it. As mentioned earlier, applications are architected to interact with the data base system as efficiently as possible. This was clearly illustrated in the discussion of transaction modeling.

Although the application can be designed to minimize its effect on the relational data base engine, it is still important for the relational DBMS to provide the ability to monitor what is going on. Without adequate information, the server cannot be managed intelligently, which could negatively affect performance. Most relational DBMS vendors offer built-in mechanisms for server monitoring. In addition, several network management packages (e.g., IBM's Netview) also provide monitoring facilities. Although these tools do not specifically capture data base statistics, they do an excellent job of surveying server use, including use of a disk array storage device.

Performance tuning is also important. Many vendors (e.g., Oracle and Sybase) offer a set of system options configurable at run time. These permit the tuning of memory, CPU disk space use, response time, throughput, concurrency, and resource consumption. Although nothing contributes more to poor performance than faulty data base and application design, these options (handled by someone well versed in the workings of the network and data base system) can provide significant performance benefits.

The model should be architected specifically with the principles of data base access and use in mind. The relational model must be refined and reviewed throughout the application design process. In addition, the data model must be normalized and synchronized to eliminate data redundancy to ensure the efficiency as a distributed model.

There is always an issue of data base server performance versus application performance because the two are so tightly intertwined. Server performance is affected by both the number of simultaneous users the server can accommodate and the request response time the engine can provide. Thus, one of the most important factors is per-user overhead. Other performance factors include the amount of memory available to the server, server use, and the data base's ability to manage each client request distinctly. How well or poorly the relational data base handles these issues has a direct correlation with how the application performs.

RELATIONAL DBMS AND SQL

Only one standard must be considered at the relational DBMS product level: SQL. All applications are designed to use ANSI standard SQL as the common means of accessing information. All relational DBMSs support the full complement of ANSI SQL, ensuring a common approach to information retrieval.

Differences among SQL data bases exist, as mentioned earlier, that affect compatibility among relational DBMS products. These differences, however, should not affect the applications' use of SQL to access data. Differences include data type support, operators and functions, proprietary extensions, utilities, system limits, messages and return codes, and operating system support. Potential problems arise only when distributed data is required to satisfy a specific request and the data is stored in multiple vendor data bases.

Multivendor Data Access

Accessing multiple vendor data bases by a single or multiple service request is a key issue. Several competing standards, blueprints, or protocols are being promoted by a variety of vendor and open standards organizations. These standards attempt to define a common mechanism for accessing distributed, possibly multivendor, data across the enterprise.

IBM has defined the Distributed Relational Database Architecture (DRDA), which defines a common method of accessing data across distributed IBM environments. DRDA should be viewed as a data gateway. Several vendors (e.g., Informix) have announced support for DRDA and have designed their products to access IBM relational data by SQL.

Open Data Base Connectivity (ODBC), is a Microsoft blueprint for distributed data management. ODBC should also be viewed as a data gateway. Most

Distributed Relational Database Architecture (DRDA)

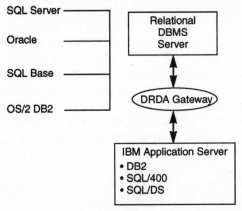

SQL Server

Oracle

SQL Base

OS/2 DB2

Relational DBMS Server

DRDA Gateway

IBM Application Server
• DB2
• SQL/400
• SQL/DS

ODBC Distributed Data Management

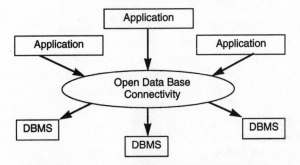

Application

Application

Application

Open Data Base Connectivity

DBMS

DBMS

DBMS

Software Access Group Remote Data Access

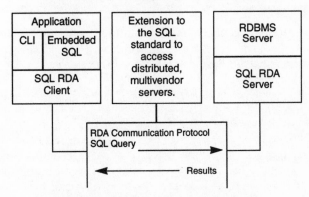

Application	Extension to the SQL standard to access distributed, multivendor servers.	RDBMS Server
CLI / Embedded SQL		
SQL RDA Client		SQL RDA Server

RDA Communication Protocol
SQL Query

Results

Exhibit VI-2-4. Distributed Data Management

data base vendors support the ODBC model. The diagram in Exhibit VI-2-4 illustrates how these proposals could be implemented.

CONCLUSION

This chapter has provided the framework for understanding the process of reengineering a company's host-based applications to take advantage of the efficiencies provided by distributed client/server architectures. The framework model must carefully reflect all aspects of the use of distributed, multivendor data base services. All features and functions of relational DBMSs must be identified and catalogued to ensure the most efficient performance of the client/server applications. Support for standards, interoperability, and distributed services must also be incorporated to make the promise of client/server systems a reality.

Both major and subtle differences exist among relational DBMS products and these varied approaches must be taken into account by the selected client/server architecture. Each of the products and their facilities, as well as the distributed data base-related design concerns, must be carefully evaluated. The model must successfully solve a variety of issues by isolating application features from the services required of the relational DBMS. In this way, each segment of the application—and associated relational data base service—can best perform its function with minimal impact on any other application segment.

Finally, the enterprise application model must be architected to conform with the standard design philosophies of interoperability, scalability, and open systems. The major architectural segments include data-related logic, presentation logic, application-specific logic, and control logic. Control logic includes communications, messaging, and distributed processing. Although this chapter concentrated on the data logic and related relational DBMS issues of the distributed model, the other segments of the application also need careful consideration, including:

- Presentation issues and implementing the application model across the common graphical user interfaces Windows, PM, and Motif.
- Application-specific business logic and the use of reusable, distributed object technology.
- Control logic that ties together the isolated segments of the application and the system services being used.
- Design and development tools that facilitate how the application will respond to changes in either the technology or the topology of the distributed network.

VI-3
DBMS Recovery Procedures

FREDERICK GALLEGOS • DANIEL MANSON

Many organizations, such as banks and airlines, have online computer systems that must function at all times. In most online applications, there are many application programs that access data bases concurrently. Therefore, the data bases must be correct and up-to-date at all times.

Yet technology is imperfect and computer systems are subject to many types of failure. When a system fails, recovery procedures must be in place to restore, validate, and return the system to normal.

Information is an essential tool used by all levels of management in planning and organizing, directing, and controlling an organization. Therefore, the security, availability, and integrity of information are of utmost importance. Technological advances have significantly influenced the way an organization's information is collected, processed, and distributed. Data base management systems (DBMSs) have evolved from some of these technological advances and are of primary concern to auditors and IS managers who are responsible for securing an organization's data while facilitating the efficient dissemination of information. Although DBMSs can organize, process, and generate information designed to meet user needs, the integrity and security of this information are also essential to protect users.

IMPORTANCE OF DBMS RECOVERY

Recovery—that is, the return to a fully operational environment after a hardware or software failure—is an important process. Moreover, the effects of a system failure on the organization must be curtailed to minimize any substantial financial loss. Actions must be taken to prevent DBMS failures or resolve them quickly if they occur.

It is not always cost-effective to implement all possible DBMS controls and use all known review techniques. The choice of whether or not to audit can have a direct impact on the financial consequences caused by these failures. A review of DBMS recovery ensures adherence to appropriate practices and procedures and minimizes business losses. A review further ensures that an organization can recover and return to full operational status following a disaster. For example, the January 1994 earthquake in the Los Angeles area caused sustained interruption of business in many organizations; those organizations that had established recovery procedures were able to more readily restore operations and minimize losses.

Developing, implementing, maintaining, and auditing the DBMS recovery controls and processes involve a considerable amount of money and company resources. Costs and benefits must be considered to ensure that company resources are expended efficiently. Systems managers who are either developing or maintaining a DBMS must understand data base structures and participate in the recovery process. This chapter explains the process and techniques for reviewing DBMS recovery.

THE RECOVERY PROCESS

The DBMS recovery process is designed to restore data base operations to their prefailure status. Users and IS professionals play a critical role in restoring the DBMS to operation; that is, after the system has been successfully restored, the entire staff must participate to ensure the security, integrity, and validity of the information and its transaction properties.

Transaction Properties

The transaction is the fundamental activity of a DBMS and an area of concern for the reviewer. Transactions maintain consistency constraints or controls determined for an application. This consistency must be maintained at all times, even during a transaction failure. Concurrent processing must also be protected against adverse effects during a transaction failure.

A transaction is a command, message stream, or input display that explicitly or implicitly calls for a processing action (e.g., updating a file). Transaction processing is a sequential process that does not overlap or parallel a single application. It is started with a **BEGIN TRANSACTION** and ended with an **END TRANSACTION** identifier. The following typical transaction properties must be reviewed in assessing recovery controls:

- *Atomicity.* During a transaction, either all or none of its operations are performed on the data base; that is, atomicity ensures the preclusion of partially completed transactions.
- *Permanence.* If a transaction completes the **END TRANSACTION** function, the results of its operation will never subsequently be lost.
- *Serialization of transactions.* If more than one transaction is executed concurrently, the transactions affect the data base as if they were executed in serial order; this ensures that concurrently executing jobs do not use inconsistent data from partially completed transactions.
- *Prevention of cascading aborts.* An incomplete transaction cannot reveal results to other transactions, thereby limiting the effect of a transaction error throughout the entire system.
- *Consistency.* A transaction that reaches its usual end commits its results to memory, thereby preserving the consistency of the data base contents.

Transactions are more effective when written in Sybase, Oracle, Access, or SQL than in COBOL, FORTRAN, or BASIC. They are well suited to structured programming and can help make systems development a routine process by modularizing the actions being performed in code and simplifying the treatment of failures and concurrency. These transaction properties have specific control functions (which, from a review standpoint, should be organized and verified for DBMS operational validity and reliability).

Causes of DBMS Failure

There are many causes of DBMS failure. When a DBMS fails, it falls into an incorrect state and will likely contain erroneous data. Typical causes of DBMS failures include errors in the application program, an error by the terminal user, an operator error, loss of data validity and consistency, a hardware error, media failures, an error introduced by the environment, and errors caused by mischief or catastrophe.

Typically, the three major types of failure that result from a major hardware or software malfunction are transaction, system, and media. These failures may be caused by a natural disaster, computer crime, or user, designer, developer, or operator error. Each type of failure is described in the following paragraphs.

Transaction Failure. Transaction failures occur when the transaction is not processed and the processing steps are rolled back to a specific point in the processing cycle. In a distributed data base environment, a single logical data base may be spread across several physical data bases. Transaction failure can occur when some, but not all, physical data bases are updated at the same time.

System Failure. System failures can be caused by bugs in the data base, operating system, or hardware. In each case, the transaction processing is terminated without control of the application. Data in the memory is lost; however, disk storage remains stable. The system must recover in the amount of time it takes to complete all interrupted transactions. At one transaction per second, the system should recover in a few seconds. System failures may occur as often as several times a week.

Media Failure. Disk crashes or controller failures can occur because of disk-write bugs in the operating system release, hardware errors in the channel or controller, head crashes, or media degradation. These failures are rare but costly.

By identifying the type of DBMS failure, an organization can define the state of activity to return to after recovery. To design the data base recovery procedures, the potential failures must be identified and the reliability of the hardware and software must be determined. The following is a summary of four such recovery actions:

- **TRANSACTION UNDO.** A transaction that aborts itself or must be aborted by the system during routine execution.
- **GLOBAL REDO.** When recovering from a system failure, the effects of all incomplete transactions must be rolled back.
- **PARTIAL UNDO.** While a system is recovering from failure, the results of completed transactions may not yet be reflected in the data base because execution has been terminated in an uncontrolled manner. Therefore, they must be repeated, if necessary, by the recovery component.
- **GLOBAL UNDO.** If the data base is totally destroyed, a copy of the entire data base must be reloaded from a backup source. A supplemental copy of the transaction is necessary to roll up the state of the data base to the present.

These definitions imply that the transaction is the sole unit of recovery in the data base, which reduces the programmer's required recovery processing inclusions.

Disaster Recovery Tools

There are numerous disaster recovery tools and techniques available that can assist an organization in DBMS recovery. For example, several software programs can scan the network and data bases and record the configuration of the systems. Novell's Netware Management System provides a logical view of the system and network. Other products such as LT Auditor, LAN Automatic Inventory, Palindrome, and LAN Directory are software support packages that can assist in DBMS documentation and recovery processes and functions.

Several companies use video camera techniques to document equipment, hardware, and software configurations. Others are using CD-ROMs as a technique for saving critical DBMS structures and data. Such applications of media or computer-assisted disaster recovery tools and techniques are providing organizations detailed documentation to aid troubleshooting DBMS problems, identifying weak points in the network or distributed DBMS, and reconstructing destroyed DBMSs.

TECHNIQUES FOR REVIEWING DBMS RECOVERY

The review of a DBMS recovery must ensure that employees with specific responsibilities perform their functions in accordance with operational policy and procedure. There are several useful DBMS recovery review techniques (see Exhibit VI-3-1).

There are two ways to make the system operate again. First, all transactions that have occurred since the last backup can be reapplied, which would bring the data base up-to-date. Second, the current contents of the data base can be taken and all transactions can be backed out until the integrity and validity of the data are restored. Whichever method is selected, it should be documented and a checklist of specific tasks and responsibilities identified.

The Review Plan

- Conduct data base survey:
  —Conduct background survey to determine organizational priorities for data bases.
  —Identify data base recovery procedure evidence.
  —Develop a data flow diagram of data base applications scoring high on the organizational priorities.
  —Identify data base recovery tools and techniques.
- Identify data base risks:
  —Conduct specific data base risk assessment.
  —Rank data base risks.
  —Develop measurable review objectives for recovery procedures.
  —Develop a review plan.
- Evaluate data base recovery controls:
  —Document data base segregation of authority.
  —Conduct a data base control review.
  —Develop data base control diagrams.
  —Identify and define data base recovery procedure vulnerabilities.
- Perform data base recovery procedure control tests:
  —Create a data base recovery control test plan.
  —Design a data base control test.
  —Conduct the data base recovery control test.
  —Evaluate data base recovery control effectiveness.
  —Evaluate the data base recovery tools and techniques.
- Analyze data base recovery procedure review results:
  —Document findings.
  —Analyze findings.
  —Develop recommendations.
  —Document recommendations.
- Review and report findings:
  —Create a review report.
  —Review report reasonableness (i.e., logic).
  —Prepare and disseminate report.

Review Procedures

- Equipment configuration:
  —List all the equipment under direct control of the department.
  —Note any special environmental requirements.
  —Determine the effective throughput.
  —Determine the transaction volume.
  —Estimate the extent of reliance on data base applications.
  —Estimate the extent of reliance on data base tools and techniques for recovery purposes.
- Systems maintenance:
  —List and evaluate all data base applications.
  —List and evaluate all data base utilities used for monitoring and recovery of data bases.
  —Note any backup procedures.
  —Note authority matrices or other authorization procedures.
- System operations:
  —Determine who is responsible for operations.
  —Evaluate effectiveness of existing recovery procedure documentation.
  —Evaluate backup procedures, including backup personnel training, backup schedule, and off-site storage of backup files.
  —Observe and comment on the level of physical security.
  —Observe and comment on the levels of physical security for hardware and data.
  —Determine whether the automated system bypasses any existing separation of duties.

Exhibit VI-3-1. Techniques for a DBMS Recovery

The DBMS typically provides exhaustive review trails so that the system can know its exact state at any time. These review trails should be complete enough to reconstruct transactions and aid in recovery procedures. A data base administrator should know how to use these review trails in recovery to fully understand the inner workings of the DBMS.

A data base that has been backed up regularly helps the system recover from a failure and begin operating again as soon as possible. Daily backups are sufficient in most organizations. Those organizations that must always have current data must sometimes perform hourly backups. Each backup should be well documented to provide further insight into the review process. A checklist is provided in Exhibit VI-3-2.

Review techniques should examine application design, security procedures, and personnel control to ensure that managers can meet emergencies and have effective contingencies in place. These three areas are extremely critical review points for the auditor, management, users, and IS personnel.

Application Design

It is important to build sound recovery procedures and processes into an application during the design phase. The design of an application should take

---

☐ Does each site maintain backup data in the same format?
☐ Are the retention periods for backup data sufficient to ensure the consistency of the data?
☐ Are there procedures to shut down the fully distributed data base system?
☐ Are there procedures to restart and recover one or all stations in the system?
☐ Are there procedures to test the restart and recovery procedures?
☐ Are all errors discovered by the DBMS logged for follow-up?
☐ Are failures in the DBMS documented for supervisory review?
☐ Are backup procedures for data base recovery periodically tested at a primary facility? At a backup data center?
☐ Are copies of critical files stored at a remote location restricted from unauthorized access?
☐ Are duplicate copies of critical documentation kept at a remote location and restricted from unauthorized access?
☐ Is at least one file generation kept at a location other than the file storage area?
☐ Are there provisions for periodic checkpoints of files (master data base and transactions) to ensure a basis for reconstruction of a damaged or destroyed file?
☐ Does management periodically review such instances for which recovery was necessary?
☐ Does management follow up preventive or corrective actions taken for data base recovery?

Exhibit VI-3-2. Backup and Recovery Facilities Checklist

into consideration the data base control issues that affect backup and recovery processes. Possible weaknesses in controls include:

- Inaccurate or incomplete data in the data base.
- An inadequate audit trail.
- An inadequate service level.
- Failure of the DBMS to function as specified.
- Inadequate documentation.
- Lack of processing continuity.
- Lack of management support.
- Fraud or embezzlement.

The data base administrator should be responsible for examining the backup and recovery controls being considered by the user and developer when reviewing application design. The user and the developer of the application must assess the risks of not having appropriate controls in place to aid in recovery. Some key controls that should be adopted are as follows:

- *Review trails.* A method of chronologically recording system activities that allows the reconstruction, review, and examination of each event in a transaction from inception to the final results.
- *Recovery procedures.* Automated or manual tools and techniques for recovering the integrity of a data base.
- *Application system failure procedures.* Procedures for users to follow in the event that their applications cannot operate.
- *Checkpoint data bases.* Copies of the data base and transaction files that are made at specific points in time for recovery purposes.

At a minimum, these controls should be tested during the module and integration testing phases of development. In terms of a new system review before implementation, these controls are most effective if thoroughly validated and approved by the user and developer before the system is placed into operation. One important issue to be considered in application design is data integrity.

Maintaining Data Integrity. Data integrity concerns the accuracy of the contents of the data base. The integrity of the data can be compromised because of failures (i.e., events at which the system fails to provide normal operation or correct data). Failures are caused primarily by errors, which may originate in programs, interactions between these programs, or the system.

A transaction is a sequence of actions. It should be designed and executed so that it either is successfully completed or has no effect on the data base. A transaction can fail to be completed for the following reasons:

- An action violates a security or integrity constraint.
- The user cancels the transaction.
- An unrecoverable I/O error occurs.
- The system backs out the transaction to resolve a deadlock.

- The application program fails.
- The system crashes.

Semantic Integrity. This term refers to the accuracy of the data base despite the fact that users or applications programs try to modify it incorrectly. Assuming that the data base security system prevents unauthorized access, and hence malicious attempts to corrupt data, most potential errors will be caused by incorrect input, incorrect programs, or lack of user understanding.

Traditionally, most integrity checking has been performed by the application programs and by periodic auditing of the data base. The following are some problems that occur when relying on application programs for integrity checking:

- Checking is likely to be incomplete because the applications programmer may not be aware of the semantics of the complete data base.
- Each application program relies on other programs that can modify the data base, and a problem in one program could corrupt the whole data base.
- Code that enforces the same integrity constraints occurs in several programs. This leads to unnecessary duplication of the programming effort and exposes the system to potential inconsistencies.
- The criteria for integrity are buried within procedures and are therefore difficult to understand and control.
- Maintenance operations performed by users of high-level query languages cannot be controlled.

Most of these errors could be detected through auditing, although the time lag in detecting errors by auditing can cause such problems as difficulty in tracing the source of an error and hence correcting it as well as incorrect data used in various ways, causing errors to propagate through the data base and into the environment.

The semantics, or meaning, of a data base is partly drawn from a shared understanding among the users, partly implied by the data structures used, and partly expressed as integrity constraints. These constraints are explicitly stated by the individuals responsible for data control. Data bases can also be classified as:

- A single record or set.
- Static or transitional.
- General or selective.
- Immediate or deferred.
- Unconditional or conditional.

A system of concurrent transactions must be correctly synchronized—that is, the processing of these transactions must reach the same final state and produce the same output. Three forms of inconsistency result from concurrence: lost updates, an incorrect read, and an unrepeatable read. Lost updates can also result from backing up or undoing a transaction.

Correcting Inconsistency Problems. The most commonly used approach to eliminate consistency problems is locking. The DBMS can use the locking facilities that the operating system provides so that multiple processes can synchronize their concurrent access of shared resources. A lock can be granted to multiple processes, but a given object cannot be locked in shared and exclusive mode at the same time. Shared and exclusive modes conflict because they are incompatible. The operating system usually provides lock and unlock commands for requesting and releasing locks. If a lock request cannot be granted, the process is suspended until the request can be granted. If transactions do not follow restrictive locking rules, deadlock can occur. Deadlock can cause the loss of an entire file: therefore, it is critical to have a recovery system in place to alleviate this problem.

The deadlock problem can be solved either by preventing deadlocks or by detecting them after they occur and taking steps to resolve them. Deadlocks can be prevented by placing restrictions on the way locks are requested. They can be detected by examining the status of locks. After they are detected, the deadlock can be resolved by aborting a transaction and rescheduling it. Methods for selecting the best transaction to abort have also been developed.

A synchronization problem can occur in a distributed data base environment, such as a client/server network. Data bases can become out of sync when data from one data base fails to be updated on other data bases. When updates fail to occur, users at some locations may use data that is not current with data at other locations. Distributed data bases provide different types of updating mechanisms. In a two-phase commit update process, network nodes must be online and receive data simultaneously before updates can occur. A newer update method, *data replication,* enables updates to be stored until nodes are online and ready to receive. Update methods must ensure data currency in all network data bases.

Security Procedures

A data base usually contains information that is vital to an organization's survival. A secure data base environment, with physical and logical security controls, is essential during recovery procedures.

Physical Security. In some distributed environments, many physical security controls, such as the use of security badges and cipher locks, are not feasible and the organization must rely more heavily on logical security measures. In these cases, many organizational members may have data processing needs that do not involve a data base but require the use of computer peripherals.

Logical Security. Logical security prevents unauthorized users from invoking DBMS functions. The primary means of implementing this type of security is the use of passwords to prevent access to files, records, data elements, and DBMS utilities. Passwords should be checked to ensure that they are designated in an intelligent, logical manner.

Security Logs. Each time an unauthorized user attempts to access the data base, it should be recorded in a security log. Entries in this log should consist of user ID, terminal or port number, time, date, and type of infraction. With this information, it is possible to investigate any serious breaches of security. From the data base administrator's standpoint, evidence that the DBMS is detecting security violations and that a consistent procedure is used to follow them up should be sufficient.

Personnel Control

Data base recovery involves ensuring that only authorized users are allowed access and that no subsequent misuse of information occurs. These controls are usually reestablished when a system becomes operational. When operations cease or problems occur, however, controls often become inoperative.

The three primary classes of data base users are data base administrators, applications and systems programmers, and end users—and each has a unique view of the data. The DBMS must be flexible enough to present data appropriately to each class of user and maintain the proper controls to inhibit abuse of the system, especially during recovery, when controls may not be fully operational.

Data Base Administrator. The data base administrator is responsible for ensuring that the data base retains its integrity and is accountable if the data base becomes compromised, no matter what circumstances arise. This individual has ultimate power over the schema that the organization has implemented. Any modifications or additions to this schema must be approved by the data base administrator. Permission to use subschemas (i.e., logical views) is given to end users and programmers only after their intentions are fully known and are consistent with organizational goals.

Because the data base administrator has immediate and unrestricted access to almost every piece of valuable organizational information, an incompetent employee in this position can expose the organization to enormous risk, especially during DBMS recovery. Therefore, an organization should have controls in place to ensure the appointment of a qualified data base administrator.

The data base administrator must ensure that appropriate procedures are followed during DBMS recovery. The data base administrator should also validate and verify the system once it has been recovered before allowing user access so that if controls are not functioning or accessing problems continue, users will not be affected.

Applications and Systems Programmers. After recovery, programmers must access the data base to manipulate and report on data according to some predetermined specification or to assess whether data loss has occurred. Each application should have a unique subschema with which to work.

After recovery, the data base administrator validates the subschema organization to ensure that it is operating properly and allowing the application to receive only the data necessary to perform its tasks.

Systems programmers must be controlled in a slightly different manner than applications programmers. They must have the freedom to perform their tasks but be constrained from altering production programs or system utility programs in a fraudulent manner.

End Users. End users are defined as all organizational members not included in the previous categories who need to interact with the data base through DBMS utilities or application programs. Data elements of the data base generally originate from end users.

Each data element should be assigned to an end user. The end user is then responsible for defining the element's access and security rules. Every other user who wishes to use this data element must confer with the responsible end user. If access is granted, the data base administrator must implement any restrictions placed on the request through the DBMS.

Assigning ownership of specific data elements to end users discourages the corruption of data elements, thereby enhancing data base integrity. Reviewers should ensure that this process exists and is appropriately reinstituted after the recovery process has been completed and operational approval has been provided by the data base administrator.

After recovery, the data base administrator should ensure that all forms of security practices and procedures are reinstated. These processes are a part of data base security.

CONCLUSION

Review of DBMS recovery is crucial to ensuring the integrity of a corporate information system. To adequately assess this complex issue, a review plan should be developed and procedures should be established for conducting the review. The procedures may involve the use of checklists or automated tools and techniques. The sample review plan and review procedures in Exhibit VI-3-1 and the backup and recovery facilities checklist in Exhibit VI-3-2 are designed to give guidance in developing these key documents and tailoring them to the organization.

VI-4

Geographic Information Systems as a Business Tool: A Case Study

ROBERT D. WILSON

The focus of this chapter is on the application of a geographic information system (GIS) as a decision support tool for a school district. A school district case study was chosen because the problems represented are transferable to other sectors of the economy.

A school district as a business confronts many of the same decisions and problems as do public and private companies. A school district must provide facilities, transportation, and staff for its students. Furthermore, it must acquire such goods and services from other businesses as gas, water, sewerage, paper, furniture, equipment, and food. Considering the capital outlay requirements that accrue to a school district as a result of significant residential or commercial development within its boundary (a new elementary school for 650 students costs $5 million), it is clear that reliable, accurate, and timely information is essential to aid in decision making. This case study demonstrates how a GIS can meet or exceed these definitional requirements of a standard decision support system (DSS), solving problems that have at least some structure that lends itself to computerized analysis.

A HISTORY OF GIS

Since the 1970s, there has been growing interest in representing data spatially to assist in resource allocation, sales territory definition, and business locations by type of industry. Yet the cost of the technology, in terms of computer hardware and software, kept this decision support tool out of the reach of most practitioners and researchers. In addition, firms are reluctant to adopt geographic information systems because the term itself implies a single use.

Not surprisingly, IBM was an early developer with its Geodata Analysis and Display System. Coming out of the IBM research laboratory in San Jose CA, it was considered experimental and costly for users. Nonetheless, IBM personnel conducted a number of case studies to test the use of the system. The results showed that this specific type of DSS was a valuable tool.

The GIS has not been recognized as a DSS for a number of reasons. Perhaps the most basic impediment continues to be the lack of knowledge about how this tool can be used. Another is that many organizations see the use of GIS as being in the domain of city planners or geographers as opposed to general business managers. Then, too, many managers think of the GIS as a technical person's tool that requires skills not typically possessed by middle- and upper-level managers when, in fact, any manager who can create spread-sheet models could operate most of the current PC-based GISs.

Hardware and Software Costs

Costs have also impeded wide recognition of the GIS. Hardware and software costs for implementation on a minicomputer, let alone a mainframe, can exceed the budget for many businesses. Add to that the costs for data acquisition, plus, in many instances, conversion for input. In short, a GIS requires a consequential capital expenditure. Staff requirements also add substantially to the funding of such a venture.

Recent developments in mapping software have, however, hurdled most of the obstacles related to cost. It is possible to install a full-featured GIS on a microcomputer. In a PC environment, hardware and software acquisition costs can run less than $10,000, depending on the selections made by the implementer. This estimate is based on a minimum hardware configuration using a 486 PC with 4M of memory, 200M of disk storage, a desk-size plotter, printer, and a digitizing tablet. Such a configuration places GIS technology in the hands of nearly any business user concerned with spatial data.

PRE-PC GIS PROCEDURES

Most public facilities, including school districts, that built DSSs in the early 1980s used existing spreadsheet, data base, and word processing programs that operated in a DOS environment. The model builder used them to form the basis of a single-purpose DSS. Data could be collected, analyzed, and presented in bound documents that narratively delineated the timing and location of a district's new "clients" (i.e., students).

This information created significant expenditure decisions for the district's management team. An added component was the creation of wall-size base maps that in turn were reduced for incorporation into the final copy of the study. The base map showed major physical features and the street network within the boundaries of the school district. Mylar overlays were generally drafted to depict such elements as land use, zoning, student distributions (current and future), attendance areas, and other features that the district might require. In nearly every instance, it was found that the map was the most useful decision support tool for the decision maker, making it easier to identify and interpret larger amounts of data.

Before the advent of GIS packages for the PC, an agency's only recourse for obtaining geographically related data was to enter a mainframe environment. This way, the district could have geographically specific data available. This was accomplished by using various government agencies that had the capability, with the existence of their geographic base file/dual independent map encoding files, to perform address matching. These agencies included the Southern California Association of Governments and regional city/county planning departments. Address matching allowed users to have a file of client addresses matched to a geographic base file. That process permitted appending data, such as the number of the census tract, block group and block, and ZIP code, to each individual student record. The files were then converted from tape to diskette for use in the PC environment. The information was imported into either a data base or spreadsheet program for further manipulation and analysis.

Forecasting Information

Studies dealing with forecasting future enrollment and the definition of attendance-area boundaries have always partitioned the district into small geographic areas for easier and more detailed analyses. When these boundaries conformed to the boundaries described by the Census Bureau's block groups, it was possible to assign a unique area for each student. It also allowed for relating the socioeconomic variables and housing and population data provided by the census to specific areas within the school district.

This information in turn was provided to the company drafting the maps so that an overlay could be created that showed distribution ranges of students in the district. Frequency distribution charts were also prepared. What was mssing, of course, was the ability to economically produce a map that displayed the actual location of each student. Many of the districts, recognizing the utility and value of such a map, had placed pins on a large map representing the exact location of students.

These studies also took a long time to complete. Depending on the size of the district and the number of staff assigned to such a project, a study could run three to six months. Outside assistance was usually sought to reduce the time involved, but with a corresponding increase in cost. Districts using consultants faced fees of $15,000 to $50,000.

EVOLUTION OF THE PC-BASED GIS

GIS technology has matured enough to create spatially correct (i.e., latitude/ longitude) maps on the PC. In general terms, these capabilities include data base management, statistical and arithmetic analyses, report generation, and graphical display of geographic features that are tied to the data base.

Furthermore, the systems have the capability of address matching the user's data file to specific geographic locations (geocoding). This permits the creation of pin maps with the PC. Also important is the ability to query the geographic data base and establish specific conditions that the data must meet.

The ability to produce maps on the monitor, printers, and plotters is also an obvious benefit. In short, the PC-based GIS has the ability to display spatial occurrences and the relationship between and among geographically specific variables. Furthermore, it is accessible to practitioners and other end users, not only to geographers.

APPLICATION IN A BUSINESS SETTING

The school district project used a PC-based GIS to prepare a study to determine, first, future facility requirements and, second, the proper ethnic balance for each of the schools in the district. The district's enrollment of about 5,000 students was distributed among four elementary schools, one middle school, and one high school. The district recognized that existing facilities were at or above capacity and residential development was continuing. Answering the questions of where and when new students would arrive in the district would be a major component of the study.

The ethnic balance issue did not affect the middle or high school because there was only one campus serving those grade-level groups. The elementary sites were, at the time of the study, under a grade-level organizational plan that assigned all kindergartners and first graders to one school, all second and third graders to another, and all fourth through sixth graders to another site. The remaining elementary campus had just been opened and served all grade levels, kindergarten through sixth. Assignment in this instance was based on the student's location to the new campus.

Because the school year was almost over, administrators did not believe that the reassignment on the basis of ethnicity, to take effect the next year, would be any more disruptive to the educational program than any other school start problem. It was hoped that the summer recess would give the district's administration time to formulate a plan for making the appropriate assignments. At that point a consultant was contracted to develop a strategy that would address and accomplish the objectives of the district.

Enrollment Forecasting

Enrollment forecasts were made as a separate but related component of the study. The enrollment projections, based on the timing, number, and location of new housing units within the district, were prepared outside the GIS. Using historical data to identify trends, the consultant forecast the racial composition of the future student bodies. This data was later imported to the GIS and plotted. Knowing the capacity of existing schools permitted the identification of future classroom requirements. Knowing the number of additional schools provided the ability to determine the acreage requirements. Predicting the location of the forecasted students narrowed the areas to search for available acreage. As a result, it was expected that an additional three elementary sites, one junior high site, and one high school site would be required during the defined planning horizon (seven years). With the cost of an acre of land running in excess of $100,000, site selection and acquisition, combined with the costs of the physical plant, constituted a significant decision point for school administrators.

Assigning Students to Schools

At the same time, the district was to formulate a plan to assign individual students to one of four existing elementary schools. The assignment was to meet the criterion of maintaining the ethnic profile of the district as a whole at each campus. Such a task is accomplished by defining boundaries that indicate which students go to which school. Boundaries typically follow the center line of streets, natural geographic features (e.g., streams, lakes, or mountains), or other manufactured features. The definition of such boundaries is usually a political and emotional issue in most districts. The display of data would potentially help mitigate negative reactions from students and parents and in turn be used to prepare transportation schedules and routes.

The need to adequately house existing and future students depends on accomplishment of the following:

- The identification of potential school sites and, concomitantly, acquiring sites for the construction of new schools.
- Establishing attendance-area boundaries for existing and new school sites that ensure racial balance.

Site Location Analysis

It was expected that a GIS would prove valuable in the area of site location analyses. The value would be realized in terms of reduced staff time needed for the preliminary identification of potential sites.

Parcel data from the tax assessor was loaded into the geographic data base and address-matched. This gave the staff such information as owner of record, land use designation, current zoning, assessed value, and acreage, among other data elements. Using specific criteria established by the district (e.g., 10 acres net for an elementary school site, not within two miles of an airport, not within specific distances of an active fault line or within a 100-year flood plain) made it possible to restrict the field of potential sites immediately. This was accomplished through queries of the data base to locate vacant land parcels meeting those specific criteria. It should be noted that these criteria are part of the geographic file and are displayed on screen during the decision analyses. With the use of a GIS, it meant that information on zoning, new developments, vacant parcels, student distributions, flood plains, or geoseismic hazards could be obtained textually and graphically. Plots of the location of parcels meeting these criteria were then evaluated for their proximity to the location of projected future student populations that had been determined previously.

Importing Student Records

The final activity was importing the student records. These records contained address information, grade-level standing, ethnicity, sex, and school of attendance. Using the address matching utility of the program, geographic coordinates (specific latitudes and longitudes) and census tract data were appended to each of the student records. Capacity data for each of the district's existing schools was also placed in an attribute file. This file was tied to the geographic layer of existing sites.

Much of the analysis took place in real time with district representatives seeing the results of their direction displayed on the computer screen. The district map was displayed on the screen and a simulated attendance area boundary was described by the drawing of a polygon representing a possible attendance area. One of the strengths of a GIS is that it permits many different layers of map features to be displayed at one time. Files are created (often referred to as attribute files) so that information about each of the features for each of the defined layers can be obtained directly from the map on the screen.

Drawing the polygons on the screen was facilitated because the street network was displayed along with the location of each student in the district. Each ethnic group, or even individual students, could be highlighted on the screen. When the polygons achieved the desired ethnic balance and met the other agreed-upon criteria, hard-copy plots were made for further study. By following this procedure, it was possible to present a number of options to the district staff in advance of a presentation to the board of education and parents.

The maps of the final options to be presented were of sufficient detail (at the street level) so that residents were easily able to locate the general area of their residence and thereby determine where their children would be going to school. Reasons for the changes, both the legal requirements and such pragmatic considerations as transportation costs and facility capacity, were explained in a narrative account of the results of the study.

Results of the School District Case

Four attendance-area boundaries were defined that assigned children to various schools. These boundary definitions met the ethnic balance requirements as determined by state guidelines. Five additional school sites were located meeting both state and district criteria. Narrative, tabular, and graphical information explained the findings. Six wall-size maps displaying the relevant geographic and student location data were prepared from the GIS. These maps showed alternative boundary configurations. Use of the GIS as a single-purpose DSS made it possible to accomplish the stated objectives in 10 working days.

The project itself lasted two months, largely owing to the scheduling of public hearings on the adoption of the proposed attendance-area boundaries. Costs were a fraction of those initially contemplated.

Unresolved Issues

Despite the logic of the proposed boundaries, the reduced time to prepare alternative boundaries and the lower net cost to the district, the GIS did not, nor was it expected to, allow the district's decision makers to escape emotionally based criticism by members of the community concerned by the adopted changes. There was the perception by the community that such analyses viewed children more as dots on a map to be moved randomly without taking into account issues of importance to the parent. The maps were perceived as impersonal tools used to achieve the objectives of the district administration.

Significantly, however, there were no challenges to the accuracy or reliability of the data. This may be due to the fact that the techniques employed were explained during presentation of the findings. Criticism focused on the boundary lines themselves. The most often heard comment was related to why the line could not be located somewhere else. It had been expected that the issue of privacy would be raised, but this never occurred.

CONCLUSION

It is possible to substitute any data base of clients, assets, or location-specific occurrences for students—for example, bank customers, registered voters, pet owners, vacant office space, daytime burglaries, retail outlets—together with their attendant attribute data, all of which can be related to geographic layers. Thus, many businesses can begin to appreciate the applicability of a PC-based GIS as an integral part of any DSS. Its strength lies in its ability to create new information based on the spatial relationship of the data sets associated with the features that have been mapped. If business users were to begin thinking that the *G* in GIS stood for graphical rather than geographic, and to think of it as an information system that displays data differently from a more traditional DSS, its adoption might proceed more quickly.

Generalized Uses in Planning and Demographics

One simple example is the creation of direct mail zones based on ZIP codes. Attributes such as income or age can be aggregated for these newly created areas. Another example is the creation of new features by overlaying one layer with another, where the intersection of the different layers forms the new records and features. A user might, for example, produce land parcels overlaid by zoning boundaries. Some data (e.g., land use and parcel type) would be copied to new records while the user could disaggregate tax revenue based on the proportionate share of the newly created areas. A user could create a buffer around some feature—for example, a proposed road extension—and determine the number of people affected along with the type of land and its value.

Residential and commercial development had to be assessed in the school district study; the implications here are equally relevant in planning studies for various types of enterprises—including architectural firms, land developers, bond and tax counsels, financial consultants, and cities. For example, when new homes are being constructed within specific areas, the locality's fire and police departments need to assess whether additional equipment and personnel are needed to accommodate the new residents and their property. The same issues relate to other providers of services or utilities, including distribution warehouses, retail outlets, and fast-food restaurants. Regardless of the type of business, the need for certain types of information, presented in helpful ways, is always of paramount concern.

Section VII
Object Orientation and Other Next Steps

Data sharing is made possible by distributed systems. This section explores some of the tools being used in what some people call next-generation distributed systems. The successful implementation of object technology is considered by many as essential to an organization's distributed systems strategy. Chapter VII-1 reviews "Object Technology Essentials," with descriptions of the different object-oriented programming languages, methodologies, and design approaches from which IS professionals can choose.

Locked within corporate data bases are hundreds of gigabytes of data waiting to be shared. All that data is fool's gold, however, if users cannot glean beneficial knowledge from it. Chapter VII-2 reviews some of the current software choices in "Data Base Mining Tools" for analyzing raw data and turning it into the real thing—unique business information and knowledge that can be shared and actually used to generate new opportunities for the business.

VII-1
Object Technology Essentials

RICHARD T. DUÉ

Object orientation is a fundamentally new way of thinking about information technology. It offers a new approach to reusing information systems plans, requirements, designs, and code. It is ideally suited to the implementation of client/server computing.

Object-oriented techniques promise to improve communication among all of the parties involved in the planning, analysis, design, use, and auditing of information systems. The implementation of this new approach involves new languages, new methodologies, new software, and, many times, new people. As with any new approach, there are risks as well as rewards along the way.

This chapter provides an overview of object-oriented programming languages (OOPL), object-oriented analysis, object-oriented design, and object-oriented enterprise modeling—all of which together are essential for the successful implementation of object technology as part of an IS organization's distributed systems strategy.

SIMULATION METAPHOR

For 25 years, many people from diverse backgrounds have been developing object-oriented approaches, methodologies, techniques, tools, and notations. No one single approach, language, or methodology is accepted by the majority of practitioners. There are many points of view and many different and sometimes conflicting definitions. The most important step in trying to understand this new technology is to clarify which approach and sets of definitions are being used in a particular situation.

The goals of object technology are reuse of system components and improved communications among everyone involved in developing, using, and managing information systems. These goals are pursued by shifting from traditional systems development practices to the assembly of systems from simulation models of real-world objects. These simulations provide formally contracted services that can be reused in a variety of information systems. The assembly of these collaborating sets of simulations depends on the developers:

- Following proven patterns.
- Using hierarchical libraries of models.
- Employing software brokers.

How Object Technology Differs from Traditional Programming

Object orientation, or what is increasingly referred to as object technology, had its origins with the Simula programming language in 1967. Simula was originally developed as a programming language that would develop and use simulation models of things that existed in the real world. These simulation models could be used to help the user understand and control the real-world environment.

The simulation approach is a radical departure from the typical data processing approach of analyzing, design, and programming the algorithms and data of an information system. Exhibit VII-1-1 lists ways in which the object paradigm differs from the traditional information approach.

Traditional data processing is actually carried on at an abstract level from reality. Such events as business transactions occur in the real world. Data processing systems, like accounting and management reporting systems, are used to generate, manipulate, and report on data that represent these real-world events. Object technology, by contrast, attempts to create and maintain models of how things behave in the real world and of how real-world events influence this behavior.

The major benefit of the object-oriented paradigm is that it can facilitate the development and reuse of components in the assembly of new systems. For example, the simulation model of a person can be assembled into systems that describe employees or customers or managers. In each case, the person would still have the same name, the same parents and the same spouse and children and would continue to live at the same location and to grow older.

This object-oriented view of the world as tangible objects with behaviors is much easier for most people than trying to cope with a variety of traditional data processing abstractions like files, tuples, and algorithms.

Mistakenly, people consider object orientation to be merely a set of techniques, tools, or notations that are used to develop traditional applications

Procedural Thinking	Object-Oriented Thinking
What does the system do?	What objects does the system comprise?
What is the system's purpose?	How can the developer model the system dynamically using objects, their behavior, and other objects they use?
How does the developer design and code to achieve this functional behavior?	
Focus on algorithms	Algorithmic functions deferred

Exhibit VII-1-1. A Shift of Mind-set

programs. By some estimates, more than 80% of programs written in so-called object-oriented programming languages fail to take advantage of the object technology approach that includes object-oriented enterprise modeling and development methodologies as well as applications programming.

ESSENTIAL DEFINITIONS

The lack of generally agreed-upon definitions of object technology terms can be a source of problems. With more than 50 different published methodologies and the lack of any one acknowledged technology leader, even the selection of the basic terms that need to be defined is difficult. The essential terminology includes, at least, the following terms: *object, class, contract, encapsulation, identity, inheritance (delegation), messages,* and *polymorphism.*

What Is an Object?

The common dictionary definition of an object is something that is perceptible by one or more of the senses, especially vision or touch, or that is intelligible to the mind. The *IBM Dictionary of Computing,* however, has 13 different definitions of object including "a passive entity that contains or receives data (e.g., bytes, blocks, clocks, fields, files, directories)," and "in SQL, anything that can be created or manipulated with SQL statements, such as data bases, tables, views, or indexes." The IBM dictionary defines data objects as: "a collection of data referred to by a single name." There is nothing in the IBM definitions that obviously refers to things perceivable to the senses or to simulation models.

These two sets of definitions represent major differences in the interpretation and understanding of the concept of objects. People with a traditional data processing background, especially in relational data base, frequently use the world *object* in the sense of the IBM dictionary definition, referring to objects as collections of data or as icons that represent collections of data, or programs. In general, the traditional data processing community sees object orientation as an extension to software engineering, with objects replacing modules of code. The traditional data processing approach uses such techniques as data flow diagrams, entity-relationship models, and state transition diagrams to separately model the data, the functions, and the behavior of objects.

Most often those with business or engineering backgrounds define the word *object* in terms of things in the real world and building models of reality. These people see object orientation as a completely new approach that combines data, process, and behavior into a single, encapsulated entity.

Donald Firesmith, in his review of 16 object-oriented methodologies, found seven basic categories of object definitions:

- An abstraction of a thing.
- A thing.

- An encapsulation of data (or state) and operations on that data.
- An instance (of a class).
- Something with an identity (and an address).
- An abstraction of real-world entities.
- A general term for all object-oriented things.

SELECTING A DEFINITION

It is important that everyone involved in an object-oriented project is using the same philosophical approach and a similar set of definitions.

The criteria for making a selection include:

- Whether the philosophical approach is simpler than any other.
- Whether it promotes communication and understanding of the system among all interested parties.
- Whether it promotes reuse of requirements, analysis, design, components, documentation, and testing plans.

The following working definition is recommended:

> An object is something that can be perceived by the mind or the senses. An object can be represented by a uniquely identifiable dynamic simulation model. These simulation models report on the outwardly observable behavior of the object. This behavior can be interpreted simultaneously from a number of different points of view.

Dynamic simulation models of real-world objects can be understood by people with many different backgrounds. Dynamic simulations conform to the original intent of the Simula language. They can be compared to reality. They can easily be shared and reused. Because they provide a single focal point for normalized (i.e., standardized) data and normalized process, they are much simpler to construct and understand than approaches that require multiple models for data, process, and state transitions.

The definitions used in the rest of this chapter are derived from the two major standards groups in the area of object technology: the Object Management Group (OMG), an international software consortium that promotes the practical application of object technology, the ANSI accredited X3H7 Object Management Standards Committee, and the majority consensus of the major object technology methodologists. The rest of the essential definitions are surprisingly in accord.

Class. A class is a template, a "factory" or a "cookie-cutter" that can be used to create new objects that share common meaning, structure, or behavior. Every object is a unique instance of a class. Classes contain the definitions of the data structures, methods, and interfaces of software objects. Some classes are only used for conceptual purposes. For example, the class of mammals can be used to group all subclasses of mammals (e.g., tigers and whales). The conceptual class *mammal*, however, cannot directly create objects. Instead, the conceptual subclass contains general attributes (e.g., warm-blooded) that are reused or inherited by all of its subclasses.

Encapsulation. Encapsulation is the packaging or hiding of a set of data and procedures into a single structure. Encapsulation provides a clear separation between the external behavior of an object and how that behavior is implemented. For example, one external behavior of a person object is that it grows older. The data and procedures used to implement growing older are hidden from the user.

Identity. Identity means that objects can be uniquely identified. This is a key requirement for the sharing and reuse of objects. Some methodologists are now suggesting that identity may be the key concept of object technology.

Identity requires that something can have recognizable boundaries. By contrast, in the traditional data processing paradigm the data and the processes that acted on data are stored separately in data bases and application programs. The various programs used to process data could contain different definitions of the data elements, and different (possibly conflicting) business rules. The object technology concept of identity means that the same data will always be processed by the same set of procedures.

Inheritance. Inheritance is a relationship among classes that allows classes of objects to have access to the resources of other classes. Inheritance is used to reuse common resources. Inheritance is expressed in terms of a hierarchy where classes are arranged in terms of "kind of" or "part of" relationships. Another approach to inheritance is *delegation*. Delegation is used to break complex systems into simple, cooperating classes that can be called on to provide services.

Messages. Messages are the primary means by which objects communicate and interact. A message may be an event or it may be a request for a service, or it may be a service provided by an object in response to a request. Objects do not exchange data or processes (which are hidden from view by encapsulation). Instead they exchange services (i.e., processed data).

Polymorphism. Polymorphism means that different classes of objects may respond to the same message in different ways—that is, although the service requested in a message stays the same (e.g., **Pay the employees**), the data and methods used to provide this service could be changed or updated. Polymorphism allows the underlying classes of objects in a system to be continually improved or updated in a manner that is hidden from the users.

OBJECT-ORIENTED PROGRAMMING

An OOPL is a language capable of implementing the features of object technology.

Selection of an OOPL

Once an organization has decided on its philosophic approach to object technology and has selected a methodology to implement this approach, it can proceed with the selection of an appropriate OOPL. Exhibit VII-1-2 shows the time-line development of languages that can be used for object-oriented programming.

Procedural languages that have been provided with object extensions (e.g., C++, Object-Oriented COBOL) still allow programmers to write code in the traditional, procedure-oriented manner. Organizations should instead investigate those OOPLs that were designed to support the object paradigm (e.g., Smalltalk, Eiffel, Objective C). Exhibit VII-1-3 lists representative OOPLs.

Object-Oriented CASE Tools

The real advantages of object technology cannot be accessed by writing still more code that has to be debugged and maintained. Ideally, objects should be assembled from existing code.

Visual programming techniques may be employed to assemble existing libraries of classes and objects by manipulating graphical icons instead of writing lines of code. Typical visual programming tools include WindowBuilder (Objectshare, Inc.), PARTS (Digitalk), and VisualAge (IBM). Object-oriented CASE tools offer a different, though possibly complementary, approach. These tools (some of which are listed in Exhibit VII-1-4) can be used to translate diagrams developed by the various systems development methodologies into object-oriented code, or even to reengineer existing code into object diagrams.

Time Frame	Language
1960s	LISP and ALGOL (while not object-oriented, LISP and ALGOL both influenced subsequent object-oriented language development)
	Simula 67
	LOGO 69
1970s	Smalltalk 72
	Mainsail
	Flavors
	C (while not object-oriented, C influenced subsequent object-oriented language development)
1980s	Smalltalk-80
	Softnet 83
	Objective C
	Classical
	C++
	Object Pascal
	Eiffel
1990s	Self
	Emerald/Jade

Exhibit VII-1-2. Development of Object-Oriented Programming Languages

Language	Vendor	Operating System
C++ language systems	AT&T (Greensboro NC)	UNIX
C_Talk	CNS Inc. (Eden Prairie MN)	MS-DOS
C++ and Common View	Computer Associates (Islandia NY)	MS-DOS
Classic-ADA with Persistence	Software Productivity Solutions (Melbourne FL)	VMS, UNIX, Aviion
Eiffel	Interactive Software Engineering (Goleta CA)	VMS, UNIX, Macintosh
ENFIN	Easel Corp. (Burlington MA)	MS-DOS, OS/2, Windows
Object Works/Smalltalk	ParcPlace Systems (Sunnyvale CA)	MS-DOS, OS/2, UNIX, VMS, Macintosh
Objective-C	Stepstone Corp. (Sandy Hook CT)	MS-DOS, OS/2, AIX, UX, SunOS, Macintosh
Smalltalk/V	Digitalk, Inc. (Los Angeles CA)	MS-DOS, OS/2, Macintosh
Smalltalk-80	Xerox Corp. (Rochester NY)	Macintosh, Xerox

Exhibit VII-1-3. Representative Object-Oriented Programming Languages

OBJECT-ORIENTED ANALYSIS AND DESIGN

There are numerous descriptions and comparisons of the nearly 50 published object-oriented analysis and design methodologies. One of the most interesting was prepared by the Object Management Group which developed a standard questionnaire that was filled out by the methodologists themselves. Exhibit VII-1-5 names some of the chief methodologies that IS organizations have to choose from.

Selection of an Object Methodology

Object methodologies can be generally placed into two categories: evolutionary and revolutionary.

Evolutionary Methodologies. Evolutionary object methodologies are derived from software engineering and information modeling. Evolutionary methodologies (Martin/Odell, Rumbaugh, Yourdon/Coad) break down the analysis of objects into the separate consideration of an object's data and processes (or methods) and the dynamic modeling of an object's behavior over time. Each perspective is modeled using software engineering and information modeling

Product	Vendor	Methodology
Object Maker	Mark V Systems (Encino CA)	More than 20 object-oriented and software engineering methodologies
Object Modeler	Iconix Software Engineering (Santa Monica CA)	Rumbaugh, Yourdon/Coad
OMW & Prokappa	Intellicorp (Mountain View CA)	Martin-Odell, Rumbaugh
Ptech	Associate Design Technologies (Westborough MA)	Martin-Odell
Rational Rose	Rational (Santa Clara CA)	Booch
Teamwork/OOA	Cadre Technologies (Providence RI)	Shlaer-Mellor
The Object Engineering Workbench	Innovative Software (Frankfurt am Main, Germany)	Martin-Odell

Exhibit VII-1-4. Representative Object-Oriented CASE Tools

techniques. Data is modeled with entity-relationship diagrams, process is modeled with data flow diagrams, and behavior is modeled with state transition diagrams.

Revolutionary Methodologies. This approach (favored by Booch, Jacobson, and Wirfs-Brock) models the behaviors of objects (i.e., responsibilities) and the messages (or contracts) that are passed among groups of collaborating objects. Revolutionary methodologies require the user to "think like an object." The CRC (class, responsibilities, and collaborations) technique, developed by Ward Cunningham and Kent Beck, is used to record the classes of objects and their behaviors (responsibilities) and to indicate which objects need to interact (collaborators).

Most of the major methodologists are starting to consolidate the features they have found most useful into their own approaches. Over the next few years, emphasis on the revolutionary methodologies will include some form of Use Case scenarios, CRC modeling, and formal specification and contracting, as well as the use of brokers, layered class libraries, and information system patterns and frameworks consisting of proven collections of objects (these features are described later in this chapter).

ENTERPRISE MODELING

Object-oriented enterprise modeling is the extension of the object approach to building dynamic models of the organization in much the same way that information engineering extended the concepts of software engineering to

- Ada Box Structures Method (Comer 1989)
- ASTS Development Method (Firesmith 1992)
- The Booch Method (Booch 1991)
- Extended Buhr Design Method (Vidale/Hayden 1986)
- Frame-Design Methodology (Andleigh/Gretzinger 1992)
- FUSION (Coleman and Arnold 1992)
- General Object-Oriented Development (Seidewitz/Strak 1986)
- Hierarchical Object-Oriented Design (HOOD Technical Group 1991)
- Layered Virtual Machines/O-O Design (Nielsen/Schumate 1988)
- Method for the O-O Software Engineering of Systems (Henderson-Sellers/Edwards 1993)
- Model-Based O-O Design (Bulman 1987)
- Model-Driven O-O Systems Analysis (Embley et al 1992)
- Multiple-View O-O Design (Kerth 1989)
- Object Behavior Analysis (Gibson 1990)
- Object Behavior Analysis (Rubin/Goldberg)
- Object Modeling Technique (Rumbaugh et al 1991)
- O-O Analysis (Coad/Yourdon 1991)
- O-O Analysis (Martin/Odell 1993)
- O-O Analysis (Stoecklin et al 1988)
- O-O Design (Berard 1993)
- O-O Design (Coad/Yourdon 1991)
- O-O Design (Martin/Odell 1993)
- O-O Domain Analysis (Berard 1993)
- O-O Requirements Analysis and Design (Anderson et al 1989)
- O-O Requirements Analysis (Bailin 1989)
- O-O Requirement Analysis (Berard 1993)
- O-O Role Analysis, Synthesis and Structuring (Reenskaug et al)
- O-O Software Development (Colbert 1989)
- O-O Software Development (Lorenz 1993)
- O-O Software Engineering (Jacobson et al 1991)
- O-O Structured Design (Wasserman et al 1989, 1990)
- O-O Systems Analysis (Seidewitz 1989)
- O-O Systems Analysis (Shlaer/Mellor 1988)
- O-O Systems Development (Henderson-Sellers 1991)
- ObjectOry (Jacobson 1991)
- Responsibility Driven Design (Wirfs-Brock et al 1990)
- Software Construction through O-O Pictures (Cherry 1988)
- Synthesis (Page-Jones, Weiss, and Buhr 1989, 1991)

Exhibit VII-1-5. Object-Oriented Analysis and Design Methodologies

Software/Information Engineering	Object Technology
Structured Programming	*Object-Oriented Programming*
1960s to 1970s	1990s
Dijkstra, Parnas	Coad, Gamma et al, Beck and Cunningham
Four basic programming structures (Sequence, Do While, Case, If-Then-Else)	Some preliminary work with patterns, idioms
Structured Design	*Object-Oriented Design*
1970s	1980s to 1990s
Yourdon, Constintine, et al	Booch, Wirfs-Brock, et al
HIPO, Structure Charts	Use Case, CRC
Structured Analysis	*Object-Oriented Analysis*
1980s	1990s
Demarco	Numerous notations, but no generally accepted approach
Information Engineering	*Object-Oriented Enterprise Modeling*
1980s	1990s
Martin, Finkelstein	Jacobson, Henderson-Sellers
Enterprise modeling	Preliminary work

Exhibit VII-1-6. Comparison of Software/Information Engineering and Object Technology Development

building static models of the organization. Exhibit VII-1-6 compares the development of software engineering over the past 25 years with the work of object practitioners.

The development and implementation of object technology seem to be following the same bottom-up path as the development and implementation of software and information engineering. It has taken 25 years for software engineers to learn that developing quality structured code requires effective structured design methods, including structured analysis that depends on a strategic plan linked to the goals of the organization. If object practitioners apply the lessons of the software and information engineering learning curves, the time-consuming, resource-intensive, top-down, static enterprise models developed by information engineers can be replaced by dynamic, iterative models of the object that make up the enterprise.

OBJECT-ORIENTED DATA BASE MANAGEMENT SYSTEMS

An object-oriented data base management system provides persistent storage that supports the object-oriented approach. Certain data base transitions become necessary as organizations migrate from the static data models of relational and other traditional data base technologies to the dynamic, multimedia models of object technology. For example:

- Computer words, fields, files, and records are replaced by objects and episodic memory.
- Hard data is replaced by soft data (e.g., projections, extrapolations, forecasts, and hypotheses).
- Data is replaced by multimedia information (e.g., text, documents, image, voice, and graphics).
- Preestablished queries are replaced by ad hoc queries.
- Crisp queries are replaced by fuzzy queries.
- Simple retrieval is replaced by complex retrieval from distributed data bases.
- Keywords are replaced by memory-based reasoning.
- "As is" presentation is replaced by analytical evaluation.

Two approaches to the development of object-oriented data bases are under way. The first approach is to extend the features of existing relational data base management systems to include object capabilities. Typical products, mostly from large established vendors, include the extensions to Oracle Version 8 (Oracle Corp) and O-OODB (Hewlett-Packard Co).

The second approach is to develop a new data base management system based on the object approach. Typical products, mostly from small start-up companies, include Gemstone (Servio), Ontos (Ontologic), Versant (Versant), and ObjectStore (Object Design).

NEW APPROACHES REQUIRED FOR OBJECT-ORIENTED SYSTEMS DEVELOPMENT

A new way of thinking requires new methods and techniques of systems development. Among these new approaches are design by contract, hierarchical class libraries, brokers, and agents.

Design by Contract

The design by contract approach requires the development and assignment of multipart contracts to the services provided by each class of objects. These contracts are formal specifications that describe the behavior of each class of objects. Contracts are composed of the following clauses:

- *Precondition.* The precondition clause specifies all the conditions that must be true before the services of this class of objects can be used. For example, before a **Paymaster** object can pay the employees, there must be money in the bank, there must be employees, there must be an authorization, and it must be payday.
- *Postconditions.* The postcondition clause specifies all the conditions that will be true after the class of objects provides its services. For example, the **paymaster** object will pay the employees according to the existing

payroll agreements and in conformity with the current taxation requirements.

- *Invariants.* Invariants are those conditions that the class of objects agrees to abide by during its activities. For example, the paymaster object agrees not to overdraw the payroll account without authorization.

Contracts may have other clauses that detail the actions to be taken during error conditions, the methods that the class of objects will actually use to provide its services, and testing procedures. The CRC technique can be used to develop the service contracts. In this case, the class responsibilities are described in terms of the preconditions, postconditions, and invariants of each class of objects involved in the system.

Once the service contracts are developed and tested against predetermined scenarios, the next step is to locate the classes that will supply the required contracted services. Classes may be found directly in class libraries or may be located through the use of software brokers.

Class Libraries

Class libraries are collections of related classes of objects. These collections may be specifically designed for a particular industry (i.e., banking or transportation) or they may be more general collections (i.e., Smalltalk or C + + language libraries). Class libraries may be arranged into layers.

The layered approach (shown in Exhibit VII-1-7 and discussed next) offers the opportunity to leverage and reuse the work undertaken at the lower levels of the class library. People working at different layers of the class library need not understand the internal workings of the other layers.

Atomic Classes. The layered approach views classes from four levels of abstraction. The first level consists of basic, or atomic, classes. This is the level of object-oriented programmers who develop the lowest-level systems building blocks. This level may be subdivided into further layers or clusters of classes that provide basic services for string handling, graphical user interfaces, mathematical functions, data base functions, and communications. This atomic level probably contains 5,000 or more members (an estimate based on the size of existing Eiffel, C + +, and Smalltalk libraries) that should be developed by object-oriented language or class library vendors. This level provides the essential infrastructure of the object technology approach.

Business Processes. The second layer consists of business process classes, which are the fundamental, stable building blocks of all applications. Data is not necessarily the stable component of the enterprise, especially as enterprises continually reinvent themselves, merge, downsize, and divest. The stable parts of the enterprise are the basic business processes of purchasing, reporting, control, and security. These business process classes will be specified by business systems analysts by combining the basic atomic classes. Little or no code development should be performed at this level.

Layer	Who	What
Layer 1: Atomic or base classes	Class constructors (software engineers)	Libraries, software integrated circuits, standard components, reusable functionality, common business objects, standard packaging are available from multiple vendors.
Layer 2: Business process models	Model builders (business systems analysts, object modelers)	Comparable to PC boards, these models handle standard business functions (purchasing cycle, customer interactions) and maximize reuse of every atomic class.
Layer 3: Management or applications	**Prototypers (users)**	Solve a business problem by mixing and matching models; independent of model details; produce very little new code; software by assembly, built through rapid prototyping.
Layer 4: Enterprise engine	Enterprise modelers, **business process** engineers	A distributed expert system (inference engine, rule base, data base) for gradual merging of models and applications. Collaborative effort throughout organizations that depends on standard classes and structures, not just a model—an active engine that evolves along with the company.

Exhibit VII-1-7. Layered Class Libraries

According to preliminary estimates, this layer should probably contain only 20 to 30 business process models. These fundamental models include such processes as:

- Mediation (one object requesting a service from another object through a third object).
- Transaction (one object requesting a service directly from another object).
- Transformation (conversion of a service into another form).
- Edit (verification of a service against a standard).

If there is a need for additional atomic classes to specify a business process, the business systems analysts must negotiate with the atomic class developers to provide the new atomic classes. Business systems analysts should not be allowed to program new atomic classes.

Management or Application Classes. The third layer consists of management or application classes. Developed by users, these application classes are assemblies of business processes. Only minimal coding (just that necessary to tie together existing classes) should be undertaken at this level. If the business process classes do not exist in the business process layer for the application modeler to use, the user must negotiate with the business process modeler to provide the required class.

Enterprise Engine. The fourth layer of the model is the enterprise engine level. At this layer, enterprise modelers and business process engineers model the interaction of the application classes to provide a dynamic simulation of the enterprise. These dynamic, real-world simulations will eventually evolve into the accounting, communications, and IS reporting systems of the organization. The model of how the objects that make up the enterprise interact actually becomes the information system.

Design Patterns

Important new work has begun on the identification and development of design patterns. Generative patterns are patterns that have embedded design principles. The user merely follows the guidelines. So far this work is only preliminary, but considerable resources are now being applied to identify these patterns.

Brokers

Brokers are used to assist in the location of classes or services. Requests for contracted services are sent to the broker (a piece of software in a network). The necessary classes are located. Eventually, networks of brokers will receive "advertisements" from class libraries that will detail available services and their costs.

The OMG originally issued the specifications for a Common Object Request Broker. Products have been developed by Hewlett-Packard (ORB Plus), Hyper-Desk (HD-DOMS), IBM Corp (SOM), and Iona Technologies (Orbix).

Agents

An agent is an object that is created to do some work on the behalf of another object or person. Agents can be used to help locate design patterns or class libraries across a network. Agents could also be used to interpret object models from various perspectives. For example, an agent viewing the enterprise model from the perspective of the marketing department might interpret the behavior (or the role) of a particular person quite differently than from the perspective of the accounting department (e.g., an employee).

CONCLUSION

Object technology is a new way of approaching information technology. The key to understanding this new approach is to understand the particular philosophy of object technology being proposed in a given situation.

Implementation of object technology requires investment in new programming languages and new tools to assemble code. It requires new systems development methods and techniques. New tools, including class libraries, object-oriented data base management systems, brokers, and agents need to be installed. The biggest challenge, however, may be getting existing personnel to start to think in terms of the object paradigm.

Because of all the changes that must be made to move to object technology, many traditionally trained personnel may have difficulty in making this transition; evolutionary methodologies may not enforce the movement to the object paradigm. Instead, organizations following the evolutionary approach may only end up with poorly written and inefficient process-driven code that will not yield any of the benefits of the object-oriented approach. Revolutionary methodologies are therefore recommended in many situations.

VII-2
Data Base Mining Tools

FRITZ H. GRUPE • M. MEHDI OWRANG

D ata bases in large organizations contain vast amounts of data on clients, investors, consumers and their buying habits, products, and services. These large data bases contain hundreds of gigabytes of data that are essential for an organization's operation. Although corporate data bases grow by a gigabyte or more of data each day, the expansion often results from the accumulation of data of limited scope. A credit card company, for example, captures transactional data that ensures the accuracy of payments, credit requests, and mailing lists and that provides a basis for approving new cardholders. Management information systems must then summarize this type of data in management reports that executives can use in their decision making.

To a large extent, transaction-oriented data bases lie fallow, even though buried within them is information that is useful for generating facts and relationships that are valuable in creating new business. The question is how to mine raw data for information that can provide a company with significant competitive benefits available only to that company as sole owner of the data.

THE GOALS OF DATA BASE MINING

Data base mining aims to use existing data to invent new facts and to uncover new relationships previously unknown even to experts and analysts thoroughly familiar with the raw data. Humans are especially adept at these tasks, but the brain makes such advances slowly and sporadically. Computer data bases pose additional, unique problems of their own. For example:

- Data base structures are highly complex and distributed. They contain numerous tables connected through abstract linkages that the mind finds difficult to trace.
- Digitized data bases are hidden from sight so the details in the records are unseen and unanalyzed.
- The size and distributed nature of data bases make it impossible to detect hidden patterns and ill-formed relationships.

The term *data base mining* has a variety of meanings. It includes, for instance, the derivation of useful information from a data base through the use of creative queries, such as "Which airline passengers flew to Germany last year and might be asked to respond to special pricing on tickets for this year?" Data base mining also includes the identification of relationships that would have gone undetected without the application of specialized approaches.

For example, one application determined that certain bank customers with occasional overdrafts and characteristic deposit histories were especially good candidates for home equity loan advertising. Another, a fraud detection system, identified a fraudulent mortgage unit that changed names frequently and defrauded many different banks, duplicating in minutes the findings of a team of investigators who worked with the same data for two years.

Underlying Technologies

The improvement in the value of a data base's holdings in large measure is the result of rapid progress in hardware and software technologies. These developments include:

- *Faster processors.* Significantly greater computational power is brought to bear on procedures that involve extensive data base processing and pattern-recognition processing.
- *Parallel processing system and current processing languages.* These systems introduce the potential for analyzing data in ways previously beyond realistic computer capabilities.
- *New software technologies.* Products emerging from artificial intelligence, as well as innovative mental constructs about how to carry out intelligent data base mining, present new opportunities to reduce processing time and efficiently narrow search paths.
- *Reduced data storage costs and larger secondary devices.* With decreased processing times, data can be made available online in amounts that were impossible earlier.

QUALIFYING A PROBLEM
Knowing When to Mine

As is true of all computer applications, selecting the correct tool for a problem greatly affects how quickly a solution is found. Data base mining is appropriate when the following problem scenarios exist:

- Large data bases prevent efficient examination of records to detect relationships and select important facts.
- Data base structures are complex and involve substantial numbers of variables that may or may not be related to one another.
- Existing querying techniques, decision models, and statistical techniques are insufficient for discovering new knowledge, or an organization lacks expertise in these areas.
- Better predictive models are needed.

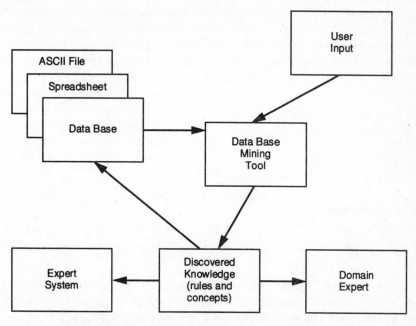

Exhibit VII-2-1. Data Base Mining and Discovery Environment

Exhibit VII-2-1 depicts some of the elements that are part of a data base mining and discovery environment. Several key steps in commencing with a data base mining project include:

- Identifying an extensive data base that is to be analyzed.
- Deciding whether the tool is to be used to test hypotheses on what knowledge may be contained in the data base or whether the tool should generate hypotheses.
- Selecting an appropriate tool.
- Generating and testing hypotheses.
- Validating the discovered knowledge.
- Using the discovered knowledge by integrating it into corporate expert systems and into expert practice, or by refining the data base for more effective future action.

CURRENT SOFTWARE CHOICES

The costs of data base mining vary depending on the size and type of data base as well as the computer platform. Specialized workstations can run upwards of $40,000, and massively parallel computers can cost more than $1 million. More sophisticated projects may involve staff for more than a year in data formatting and in training. Many other projects, however, are less expensive and simpler.

Several approaches are available for extracting knowledge from existing data bases. Because each approach addresses specific problems and varies in its utility, direct comparisons and rankings among products can be misleading. Among the approaches are:

- Purchased software.
- Neural networks.
- Expert systems.
- Case-based reasoning systems.
- Data base software extensions.

Data Base Mining Software

Recently, tools specifically designed for data base mining have been released. The tools differ substantially in the types of problems they are designed to address and in the ways in which they work.

DataLogic/R (Reduct Systems). DataLogic/R is a PC-based package that uses rough sets, an offshoot of fuzzy logic, to help users ferret out rules that characterize the data in the data base. It then suggests how to make decisions on categorizing the data for optimum analysis.

Users discover the new knowledge in the form of rules through DataLogic/R's pattern-recognition, modeling, and data analysis techniques. In general, the software is able to deal with uncertainty in data, analyze hidden facts in data, represent new knowledge in a rule format, and create models for prediction and classification. DataLogic/R has been successfully used in applications such as consumer survey analysis, process control measurement, substance toxicity identification, insurance analysis, and fault detection.

IDIS:2—The Information Discovery System (IntelligenceWare). IDIS:2 also examines data bases with the intent of hypothesizing possible rules for explaining relationships among variables. It can uncover information based on questions no one thought to ask by positing a hypothesis and then testing it for accuracy and relevancy. It concludes with a list of rules in two- and three-dimensional, hypermedia graphs.

IDIS uses induction, guided by the user, to assign weights to attributes used in the rules. It finds suspicious entries and unusual patterns automatically, including data items that violate correlations, extreme boundary items, and items that exceed normal standard deviations. IDIS has been used to discover knowledge in areas as diverse as financial analysis, marketing, scientific and medical research, quality control, and manufacturing.

Recon (Lockheed). Recon permits users to engage in two forms of data mining. Users can forward hypotheses that are tested by Recon, or they can allow Recon to extract relationships from the data independently.

Recon interconnects with mainframe, commercial data base management systems, and with other knowledge sources, such as spreadsheets and ASCII files.

Nicel (Nicesoft). Nicel allows users to apply easy-to-use, fuzzy-rule-based logic for querying purposes. Fuzzy logic lets the user classify entity records by soft attributes such as "good," "bad," "tall," and "short." This capability enables the extraction of information with queries based on concepts that are not directly found in the information contained in the records.

KnowledgeSeeker (Angoss). KnowledgeSeeker permits a user to select an entity's attribute and to determine the degree to which other attributes affect that attribute's value. Built-in statistical routines automatically generate the analyses in easy-to-understand decision trees. The software also produces rules that can be used by experts and expert systems.

Neural Networks

Data base mining can also be performed with neural networks, systems that attempt to replicate the interaction of neurons in the brain. Neural networks can be used to create knowledge in a way that humans may not have or may not be able to articulate.

A neural network parallels a human's learn-through-repetition technique. Given a series of examples, the neural network is expected to learn in a manner that is analogous to memorization. The neural network attempts to induce patterns that distinguish examples from one another. Then, given a new example, the neural network uses its past learning to categorize the current situation.

Use of a neural network follows a top-down development process in which the analyst posits the effect a group of variables might have on an outcome or outcomes, and then runs the network to determine whether a relationship can be unearthed. For example, an analyst can provide a neural network with accounting ratio information for a variety of companies along with the knowledge of which companies failed and which succeeded. The neural network examines and reexamines this data hundreds, perhaps thousands of times, attempting to organize underlying patterns. Eventually, it learns the pattern, and when given comparable ratios for a new set of companies, it can predict with a high level of accuracy which companies will succeed and which will fail.

Neural networks have been used to forecast electronic network and component failures, identify loan applicants who are likely to default, carry out image recognition, spot health problems, and perceive stock and bond market fluctuations. Surprisingly accurate predictions and identifications have been made by neural networks in areas in which human experts have had difficulty defining and programming traditional systems to do these tasks.

Neural network software packages are readily available for personal computers and mainframes at commodity prices.

Expert Systems

Expert systems are a recognized and accepted form of artificial intelligence. Generally, expert systems employ fairly specific rules, such as "If SAT-score is greater than 1200 then honors-English is true."

Whereas many expert systems applications are limited to diagnostic and prescriptive tasks, some can be used to locate relationships and examples of relationships that may be suspected but unverified. For example, a health organization might have a data base of persons who had contracted a variety of diseases and another data base that contained genealogical relationships among people whose disease histories are found in the other data base. Some pattern-matching expert systems are capable of determining which diseases might be genetic because they exhibit characteristics found predominantly in males or commonly found both in parents and in children.

In business applications, these pattern-matching systems can be used to identify airline passengers who travel particular routes or potentially fraudulent credit requests that differ from an individual's normal buying habits, and to scan electronic network statistics for patterns that usually precede component failures and shutdowns.

Another class of expert systems induces new knowledge from cases. A spreadsheet-like screen is used to represent the cases so that most of the columns contain the variable information available about the cases and a final column contains the outcome or the decision made by an expert who handled the cases. Each row represents the complete information about one case. The software induces an optimized set of rules to handle the cases and to create a dialog and analysis system.

Case-Based Reasoning Systems

Some organizations have created large numbers of cases that store information about the solutions to a variety of situations. Case-based reasoning systems model the behavior of experts who reach conclusions by drawing on good and bad experiences they have encountered through the years. Experts see a problem, recognize it as being similar to one they have seen before, answer a few questions that seem important to confirming its applicability or need for adaptation, and reach a conclusion. They assess the effect of their decision and file the case away in the back of their minds. Later, when a new problem occurs, experts recall from memory the cases most similar to those at hand and adapt the previous solution to the current problem as necessary. When the revised solution is tried, the new, completed case is recalled for future use.

Problems arise because even experts can forget their experiences. If these people leave a company, their experience is also lost as a corporate resource. Case-based reasoning software is somewhat like data base management software. It facilitates the recording of information about cases—a problem description, pertinent questions used to focus the problem, a proposed solution, and the consequences. The software provides a robust means of indexing and retrieving known cases that suggest solutions to the current problem. The content of the cases may consist of only loosely organized text. Case-based reasoning has no particular mining strategy; a user of such a system simply stores cases on the assumption that it is more efficient to store all of them than to attempt to decide which ones will be most useful in the future.

Case-based reasoning softwarre has been used to support help desk operations, provide sales support, catalog and locate in-house expertise, conduct situation analyses, and locate appropriate documentation.

Data Base Software Extensions

The integration of expert systems and data bases is becoming increasingly important to a large class of users. When data mining—capable, rule-based expert systems are combined with relational data base systems, users have a tool that allows them to build smarter, more powerful applications.

A tight coupling of the two technologies is most favored by integrating rules with structured query language (SQL). Intelligent SQL extensions can take advantage of object-oriented features as well as of predicates for querying and retrieving multimedia objects. This capability is appearing in newer products with intelligent data base capabilities, including:

- Comprehensive integrity constraints expressed easily in pattern-matching rules.
- Support for flexible query systems for handling inexact, imprecise queries.
- Support for intelligent, less esoteric, more forgiving (i.e., more flexible) user interfaces and for associative structuring information with hypertext.

These types of capabilities are already found in Ingres Corp.'s Ingres RDBMS v6.3 and AI Corp.'s Knowledge Base Management System (KBMS).

DATA BASE MINING IN ACTION
Using Discovered Knowledge

The knowledge gleaned from data base mining can be used in many ways. For example, the Army and Air Force Exchange Services (AAFES), the primary retailer for military installations around the world, has information on 2.5 million customers in 17,000 businesses. A data base mining tool was used to assist AAFES in determining the expected purchasing behavior for many classes of individuals and to predict their future buying behavior. The data was used for inventory control and product distribution. Such data can also be used in the form of if-then rules and studied by:

- Experts to make better decisions.
- Knowledge engineers to create an expert system or knowledge base, and

to expand, modify, and improve existing expert systems and knowledge bases.

- Data base system managers to tune existing data bases by improving the logical data base design. New knowledge about attributes and their relationships may suggest the absence of attributes and entities or their misrepresentation in the data base.

Other data base mining applications that have realized a high return for their users include the following examples:

- A cruise line filled empty berths on expensive tours by identifying high-potential sales to customers.
- A credit bureau increased control over losses in its loan portfolio by selecting out likely defaulters.
- An insurance company searched its data for patterns indicating fraud.
- A medical supplies company increased its return on advertising by targeting doctors who were most likely to make second purchases.
- A collection agency improved its ability to determine which delinquent accounts were most likely to be collectable.
- A bank initiated an auto loan campaign by predicting which customers were likely to be buying a new car.
- A telephone company predicted which of its newest customers were likely to turn over in a short period of time, limited its advertising to them, and increased its evaluation of their payment patterns.
- A health insurance company discovered that understaffed medical units were sending patients for tests as a means of warehousing them until staff could deal with them.
- A life insurance company discovered the patterns that led to early cancellation of insurance policies.
- A researcher discovered the conditions under which it was most likely that companies would take corporate write-downs.

LIMITATIONS OF DATA BASE MINING

Current data base mining technologies vary greatly, and potential users should be aware of their limitations.

Limited Explanation Mechanisms. A given tool may indicate that it has discovered some new knowledge in the form of relationships, rules, and concepts, but the rationale behind the discovery may be hidden from the user. The better the mechanism provided by a tool for explaining its discovery, the better able the user is to assess the finding and to distinguish between real knowledge and an anomaly of little significance.

Limited Data Formats for Input. Not all tools are able to handle different methods of representing data. While all can handle numeric data, they are not equally able to conduct mining operations with text, graphs, mathematical formulas, or graphic images. Even unformatted data files present a problem, so most data base files must be properly formatted.

Limited Validation Techniques. When a tool presents discovered knowledge, it does so through the application of a specific form of analysis and logic, such as abduction, induction, and deduction. It may not have the ability to cross-validate the discovered knowledge.

Another problem is that some of the data provided to the tool may be incorrect. A tool must be robust enough to decide that a conclusion is applicable with some degree of certainty even though exceptions exist. Similarly, the tool should be able to discern why some exceptional cases do not conform to an otherwise more broadly applicable rule.

Computational Expense. Undirected searches for knowledge are expensive. Tools that are asked to determine whether variables A through Z have some bearing on outcomes can generally do so efficiently. When a blind search is being made of a data base, many possible input patterns must be compared with many potential outcome patterns. An exhaustive search is time-consuming and, potentially, very expensive.

Limited Support. Not all platforms, data base file formats, or data base file sizes are supported. Some products are PC-based, some are mainframe-oriented, and some can function in client/server, cross-platform environments. There may be limits in the number of fields or records a data base being analyzed can contain. Data files may be required to be of fixed sizes and formatted for specific data base management systems. Reformatting data for a platform other than the one on which it is housed may be expensive. Although neural networks can handle image files, most data base mining tools cannot.

CONCLUSION

Data base mining applications are enabling IS and business managers to discover new knowledge that was previously locked in their data bases. This knowledge takes the form of new relationships induced by the data base mining system, the confirmation or rejection of relationships assumed by the users and tested by the system, and new facts added to the knowledge base.

The rapid accumulation of data mandates that companies take full advantage of the knowledge contained in their data base systems. Data mining is a process by which the data can be analyzed so as to generate new knowledge in a form that answers questions that managers may not even have thought to ask. Companies that capitalize on their data bases can become the sole proprietors of a substantive, unique competitive advantage.

Index

D

Object-oriented systems development
    (*cont*)
  operations concept *S-80–S-81*
  preexisting implementation objects
    S-81–S-82
  reasonable risk versus team approach
    S-75–S-77
OMT, *see* Object Modeling Technique
Open Data Base Connectivity *S-298*
Operating Systems Computing
    Architecture *23–24*
Operations
  data models *409–410*
  users' view of object-oriented systems
    S-80–S-81
Organizational issues
  business process reengineering
    S-39–S-47, S-89–S-98
  change management *92–95,*
    S-93–S-95
  downsizing, business and IT factors
    S-99–S-108
  horizontal corporations *S-142–S-144*
  object-oriented technology, transition
    to *S-73–S-87*
Organizational structure
  data administration *164*
OSCA, *see* Operating Systems
    Computing Architecture
OS/2
  data base design *653–667*

P

Pacific Bell
  case study *23–24*
  communications fabric *26–28*
  repositories *42–43*
Performance measurement
  measurement tools *79–81*
  measuring quality *82–87*
  measuring service *81–82*
  stages of growth *77–79*
Performance monitoring
  Sybase DBMSs *724–726*
Physical data base design
  entity identifiers *482–499*
Planning
  distributed DBMSs *S-277–S-278*
  enterprisewide information
    management *273–282*
  object-oriented systems *782–785*
  strategic concerns *51–53*

Policies
  data administration *161*
Process administration
  repository administration *173–174*
Process models
  entity-life histories *S-174*
  integrated with data models
    S-141–S-153
Process-oriented methodologies
  compared with data-driven
    methodologies *S-125–S-139*
  enhanced structured analysis
    S-125–S-139
Production data
  domain study technique *S-155–S-170*
Programming
  object-oriented languages *S-328–*
    S-329
Project management
  data model, repository *206–207*
  using Excelerator *359–372*

Q

Quality
  data model repository *204–205*
  effective strategy elements *181–185*
  financial impact of poor-quality data
    S-52
  information integrity, problems and
    solutions *S-49–S-60*
  IS approaches *180–181*
  IS group organization *185–188*
  Malcolm Baldrige National Quality
    Award *109–111, 121–122*
  manufacturing data example
    S-113–S-115
  performance measurement *82–97*
Query optimizer *711–713*

R

Rapid applications development
  client/server environments *585*
Rating
  Malcolm Baldrige National Quality
    Award *111–113*
Reengineering, *see* Business process
    reengineering
Referential integrity
  defining business rules *691–692*
  defining foreign keys *691*